DURING MY TIME

Florence Edenshaw Davidson

A HAIDA WOMAN

Florence Davidson, 1980

DURING MY TIME

Florence Edenshaw Davidson

A HAIDA WOMAN

Revised and Enlarged Edition

Margaret B. Blackman

University of Washington Press
Seattle and London

Douglas & McIntyre
Vancouver/Toronto

*This book was published with the assistance of a grant
from the National Endowment for the Humanities.*

University of Washington Press
PO Box 50096
Seattle, WA 98145-5096
www.washington.edu/uwpress

Douglas & McIntyre
2323 Quebec Street, Suite 201
Vancouver, BC Canada V5T 4S7 ISBN: 978-0-295-97179-7
www.douglas-mcintyre.com

Cataloging-in-Publication Data is found at the end of this book.

The paper used in this publication is acid-free and 90 percent recycled from at least 50
percent post-consumer and at least 50 percent pre-consumer waste. It meets the minimum
requirements of American National Standard for Information Sciences—Permanence of
Paper for Printed Library Materials, ANSI Z39.48-1984. ⊖ ♻

Cover photograph by Ulli Steltzer.
Frontispiece photograph of Florence Davidson by Margaret Blackman.

For her children, their spouses,
and all who know her as "Nani"

Chapters 4 through 9 constitute Florence Davidson's first-person account of her long and rich life. The ornament that introduces her narrative is a dogfish shark by her grandson Robert Davidson.

CONTENTS

viii   *Contents*

10. Discussion   139

ILLUSTRATIONS

Preface to the Revised Edition

Squeezed between hardcover is the text of a life, its beginnings, its turning points, its closure at the time of the telling. It represents in some ways a final statement, an authoritative text on a life lived and recalled, but in reality a life story is never finished with publication. The book presents but one version of the life as told, and the story and the text are further subject to alterations over time as the narrator ages, rethinks, revises, and retells, and as the editor reconsiders the representation of life history material. Such re-examination, in both its affirmation and revision of the original, enriches our understanding of the life history process. At a time when reflexivity, the questioning of textual authority, and close examination of narrative structures direct many anthropological endeavors, new readings of old texts is a critical enterprise. But few anthropological life histories have undergone re-examination to the extent of being issued in second editions.[1]

Within this context, I was motivated to re-examine *During My Time.* In the summer of 1990, ten years following completion of the manuscript, I sat first with Florence Davidson to record her reflections on her published life story and then with several members of her family to record theirs. My narrative of that research

1. See, for example, Keesing (1983), Underhill (1978). Marjorie Shostak is in the process of writing a second edition of *Nisa.* Other accounts ask new questions of old texts: e.g., Krupat (1985), Brumble (1988), Bataille and Sands (1984).

and of the magnificent 95th birthday party fête held for Florence the preceding year comprises the epilogue, "One More Time."

An issue central to the writing of that epilogue is the nature of Native American biography and life history today and our unique role as authors/editors of those works. Questions of audience, the politics of cultural representation, and the changing narrative of Native American history are all raised in the re-examination of Florence's story and my attempt to update it.

The collaborative nature of life histories from inception to print, especially those from Native North America, is emblematic of the times in which we write and of the larger relationships between the scholarly community and the communities of people we research. Much has been written recently in anthropology of the dispersal of ethnographic authority, the democratization of anthropological research, the blurring of lines between the researcher and the researched.[2] Canadian native people have asserted their current status as "First Nations People" at the same time that the anthropological community has elevated its native "informants" to "native teachers," "research consultants," and "native experts." Edward Bruner (1986) and, following him, James Clifton (1989) document the changing anthropological and historical view of Native American cultures, from a narrative of forced acculturation and social disorganization leading to assimilation, to one of self-determination, resistance, and nationhood. The change in the narrative of Native American history follows sweeping political and economic changes in the years following World War II, during which time Native Americans gained greater control over their own destinies. Under today's conditions, anthropologists have difficulty doing research without formal tribal approval and "deliver their manuscripts to tribal governments for commentary, criticism, and correction before publication" (Clifton 1989:4). Obviously such circumstances make portrayal of conflict and other sensitive issues both more difficult and more challenging in life histories. At the same time they also make the life history a welcome genre in native communities. The anthropologist is led to exemplary lives, not just because the published life stories are to be offered to the larger world, but because the narratives return home to become community history as well as models for the fashioning of lives and life stories. Florence is a good model. She did what was expected of

2. See, for example, Marcus and Fischer (1986), Clifford and Marcus (1986), and Clifford (1988).

a woman of her time and did it well: she is community-spirited and has tirelessly served her community through her various leadership roles within the Anglican church. She was and continues to be a devout Christian. She raised her children to be prominent and active citizens; she shows, in the Haida way, "respect for herself." Florence and her family fulfill their social-ceremonial obligations. And they manage their money well, with the result that very few of their large extended family are on welfare. Florence's is the exemplary life, its value enhanced because of her age and the period of history to which her experience reaches.

In a community such as Masset, a life history is never simply the product of two individuals' collaboration. Florence's account was subject to a number of cultural constraints. Issues of cultural representation and presentation of self are crucial in Northwest Coast societies, with no exception in Masset. One's prominence and social standing should be apparent, but not through public self-proclamation. It is acceptable to describe the hard work you've always done, but you shouldn't "brag" about being from a chief's family, extol your own or your children's good behavior or accomplishments, or publicly berate someone else, even though in certain circles you may do all these things. Gossip, accusations, commentary on other people's social misbehavior and stinginess in comparison with one's own exemplariness fill the spaces about the kitchen tables in Masset, but are not fare for public speechmaking, nor for life histories, particularly if the author wishes to maintain good ties in a village where inevitably one's book is "read."

Florence's own editorial hand in her life history was apparent from the very beginning. "I don't tell everything—what's no good" she cautioned, as I noted in the first edition. On more than one occasion, she would instruct me to "shut that thing off" while she relayed something important that was not to be included in the book. Interviews with her and her family in the summer of 1990 included similar instructions and/or material proffered on tape but "off the record." Some reviewers of the first edition of the life history complained about these omissions: "The untold stories lie beneath the facts. The main element missing in this life story is conflict" (Jackson 1983:56). If we are interested in how people construct their identities and how they tell their stories, we must read the omissions, with the understanding that they, in their own way, also tell the story. On a more operational level, the very kinds of things that lead to lawsuits when biographers transgress agreements with their subjects make the anthropologist at the least an unwelcome

guest in the native community and increasingly lead to formal
resolutions banning anthropologists, as happened with one
ethnographer in Masset in 1983.[3]

Every life history interviewee obviously edits the telling of his or
her story, and consequently every life history is a partial story. But
some life stories contain more conflict or seem more candid, less
guarded, than others. In some cases the explanations may lie in
culturally specific traditions of self-revelation and public discourse,
but the reasons may be more blatantly political. In Marjorie
Shostak's (1981) popular life history of a !Kung San woman, *Nisa*,
the interviewee speaks freely about her sexuality, her husbands, her
extramarital affairs. Had members of the interviewee's own
community had access to the book's contents, her story might have
been less freely told, the author concludes.[4] But Nisa's people are
not literate and do not speak English, and she knows little of the
world that her story has reached. By contrast, Florence's book is not
only marketed in her own community but nonlocal purchasers come
to meet her, locals read the book, and she and members of her
family have given the book as presents. Her narrative conveys her
public self; "the world's Nani," as she sometimes jokingly refers to
herself, offers the world her story.

The individuality of the life history endeavor can be misleading.
Florence worked with me always on an individual basis and, very
much her own person, decided what to include in her story.
Nonetheless, that she is also the senior member of a large,
prominent, and very protective family was not lost on the final
document. Family members offered retrospective views on the book
in 1990, and even though they were not interviewed when I did my
initial research between 1977–79, a copy of the manuscript was
circulated among Florence's children in Masset. Both directly and
obliquely their comments reached me. They expressed more concern
about my parts of the manuscript than about their mother's
narrative, though one comment was made about my grammatical
editing (or lack thereof) of one of Florence's statements. There was
some distress at my reliance on "books" rather than people as
authoritative sources on Haida ethnography, as well as concern
about my choice of words in certain passages. In particular, they
focused on my use of the term "ordinary" in describing their
mother's life. "Ordinary" held connotations of "common," and
Florence, of course, was anything but "common" in the Haida social

3. See Ames (1986:43–44).
4. Marjorie Shostak, personal communication.

hierarchy. Clarification was easy enough to make, as I did by noting that the reference was to Florence's self-perceptions of the uneventfulness of her life. More important, this was a lesson both in the care with which appropriate words are selected in the Haida world and in the power of words to affect a person's social standing.[5] Family were equally concerned lest Florence be identified with comments about the Haida ranking system; especially bothersome was quoted material on this ranking system (p. 24) attributed to Florence. Social position is everything in Masset, but when it comes to mention of the aboriginal social system of chiefs, commoners, and slaves, people are quick to publicly assert, "but we're all equal now." Noting that so-and-so's great-grandfather was a slave or perhaps even mentioning the qualities that identified those who did and did not belong to chiefly families is kitchen-table talk, but not acceptable public discourse, permissible for the ethnographer's edification, but not for attribution in print to the human source. To talk about such things publicly is not "high class." The information was left in; the reference to its source was deleted.

Despite their pre-publication concerns, the family appear generally happy with the book. It has brought Florence both some income and some positive attention from the outside world. She is, after all, now "the world's Nani." The book is testimony to who she is, not only through her own words but also through those of an outside speaker, the anthropologist. It is, so far, the only life history of a living Haida.[6] Its uniqueness is not lost on Florence. One morning in 1983 as we lingered over tea at her kitchen table, she told me of another Haida woman and the ethnographer who attempted to do her life history; "They tried to *copy* us," she sniffed. As the only one, Florence's life history is a model of sorts. An elderly Haida woman in the summer of 1989 approached an ethnographer working for the Masset Band and asked if she would be willing to write her life history, "just like Florence Davidson's." The unspoken caveat was, "only better." Of course, *During My Time* is also not without its detractors in the local Haida community; Florence's long-time rivals predictably pronounced it a pack of lies the minute it was published.

5. Proper and skilled speechmaking is a valued Haida attribute, so it is not surprising that such concerns would extend to the biographer of a Haida. See Boelscher (1988) for a discussion of contemporary Haida speechmaking.

6. Biographical accounts of the artistic careers and works of Haida artists Robert Davidson and Bill Reid have appeared (Stewart 1979; Shadbolt 1986), and there are biographical accounts of past Haida as well (Robinson 1978; Morley 1967). However, all these differ considerably from the life history.

Though it is not known exactly how the book is "read" in Masset (save that my parts, as one family member confessed, could be deleted without harming the integrity of Florence's life story), that it *is* read and even marketed locally speaks volumes on the anthropologist/Native American community relationship.

I talked with family members about the book. Not all had read it from cover to cover despite the pre-publication scrutiny given the manuscript. There was interest in what I had to say in respect to the issue of cultural representation, but that aside, it became apparent that life histories intended for local use do not need introductions, analyses, summaries, and afterwords. Some outsiders concur that the narrative is best left to stand on its own. Complained one reviewer of the book, "*During My Time* threatens to overwhelm Nani's delicate, rather shy reminiscences with an overly academic context. . . . Blackman is formal and scrupulous in providing ethnographic background, bracketing Nani with forewords and afterwords, footnotes and bibliographies" (Jackson 1983:56).

But how was Florence's narrative itself perceived by her family? Everyone agreed that there were no surprises nor any glaring omissions in Nani's story, even though in our interviews each contributed new dimensions to Florence's story. One comment, offered by daughter Virginia Hunter, was particularly revealing regarding ownership of the story and the role of the collaborator in its creation. Racking her brain to recall the book she had read so long ago, she suddenly remembered a portion of it that struck her as strange. "I just wondered," she questioned me, "why Mom kept talking about having her period. A woman has her period. They're so superstitious about things like that. I couldn't understand why she would talk about something like that in her book, because they weren't even allowed to talk about what they went through." I remembered well the interview Florence and I had about her seclusion at menarche and our subsequent discussion of menstrual customs, a subject she would not consider broaching until the male linguist residing with her at the time had vacated the house for the day. That important life-cycle material was included in the manuscript at my urging (see chapter 7), yet obviously it was seen neither as normal Haida discourse nor as *Florence's* discourse on *her* life.

In every life history, the final shape of the narrative, both consciously and not, is determined by the editor/author and the narrator. Asymmetries in this collaboration, however, give the advantage to the editor. The narrator, less familiar with the world of books and publishing, may defer to the editor, as Florence did sometimes in our interviews when she instructed me: "Just ask me questions." Or as she told me during our most recent interview: "Just write it down the way you think it's best." The life story is also manifestly a product of the times in which it is told and written. As I confessed in the first edition, my inquiry was driven towards more traditional Haida customs that continued to be practiced by Florence and others of her time; thus my focus on her seclusion at menarche and her arranged marriage and my interest in feasting and potlatching. Given the notable Haida ceremonial efflorescence in recent years which has paralleled the political evolution of the Haida Nation, if Florence's story were told today, it might well focus more on recent ceremonial events than it did between 1977–79.[7] Similarly, my own inquiry would attend more to domains short shrifted in the original, such as the role of the church and Christianity in Florence's life.

In the intervening years since *During My Time* was published, public interest in the life history has continued to intensify. In a survey taken in 1985, the Library of Congress reported that more people had read a biography in the previous six months than any other form of literature, and since the 1960s the number of biographical titles has virtually doubled each year (Oates 1986:ix). There is a universal appeal to the life history, for it is testimony that each of us has a life worth relating, a story to tell. It is an inclusive, as opposed to an exclusive, form. The life stories of the Florence Davidsons take their places among the ghost-authored autobiographies of the Nancy Reagans and the Donald Trumps. The life story is also seen—for a price—as anyone's route to immortality or at least to a place, however modest, in history. The February 1989 issue of the popular high-tech catalogue *The Sharper Image* made the following limited offer to its more up-scale customers: "Hold the story of your life in your hands in a custom-written, leather-bound biography." Touted as a personalized treasure that would only appreciate in value with each reading, it was available for a mere $27,000. Appealing to a much wider audience, the U. S. Postal Service in 1988 offered free genealogical charts as part of a program encouraging children, through oral history interviews, to learn from their grandparents their family history. Works such as William Zimmerman's *How to Tape Instant Oral Biographies* and the *Foxfire*

---

7. Just within Florence's family since 1987, in addition to her birthday feast, there have been three memorial potlatches, two totem-pole raisings, and the taking up of a chieftainship; planned for the fall of 1991 is another headstone-moving and a totem-pole raising.

series also make the point that the life history is not confined to the rarefied realm of the academy but is a form of endeavor open to all.

The life history is enjoying a renewed popularity in Anthropology as well. The sharing of ethnographic authority, the growing recognition of multivocality, heterogeneity, and cultural diversity within cultures once oversimplified as homogeneous have bestowed increased credibility and value on personal experience and individual narratives. No longer justified primarily in terms of what they reveal about culture or how they amplify other ethnographic data, life histories are increasingly being read and understood as texts that reveal the multiple ways in which people conceptualize, integrate, and present their lives to others.

More difficult to calculate is the personal value of the life history. For both the subject and the interviewer, the life history endeavor holds a gift. For the narrator, it offers an unparalleled opportunity for life review to an attentive audience; for the interviewer, it offers the receipt of a well-told story with all its insights, reflections, and shared experience. As one anthropologist confessed, the life history endeavor is "a constant meditation on life."[8] For Florence and me, the process is ongoing; I return each year not only to renew our close personal relationship and to have my daughter know the woman she calls her great Nani, but to continue to touch and learn from the life Florence has shared with me.

MARGARET B. BLACKMAN
January 1992

---

8. Gelya Frank, personal communication.

Preface to the
Original Edition

Poets and photographers refer to them as the Misty Isles—the Queen Charlottes, nestled in the sometimes turbulent waters off the northern mainland coast of British Columbia. These islands hold for me, as for the many others who live or visit here, a special enchantment. I have marked my life's most weighty problems in measured footsteps along the sandy miles of spruce-rimmed North Beach, watched the moon rise in full splendor above the yawning tranquil mouth of the Yakoun River where the Masset Haida go to fish each spring for salmon. And, at times, my mind has glimpsed fleeting shadows from the islands' past: Haida hunters in search of seals at the land's edge, women and children roasting the lupine roots they called "black bear's tail" in stone-lined pits on the meadowland of Rose Spit. For me, there stand before the mile-long row of modern houses in the Haida village of Masset fading images of cedar-plank community houses, oversize animals entwined in their skyward climb up cedar totem poles, and long, graceful canoes beached above the high-tide mark, images known now only in photographs taken by adventurous visitors from the last century. As late as 1970, when I first came to know the Queen Charlottes, these images were recalled in the memories of a few elderly Haida who had been born in the old-style houses, but today, eleven years later, they and their remembrances have gone to their ancestors.

I have made the journey from the urban East to the Queen Charlottes several times. In 1970 I came with my former husband, Jim Blackman, to spend the year studying Haida culture history gleaned from the memories of Haida elders and from the volumes of museum and archival photographs I had amassed. Two years passed before I returned to the islands in the summer of 1973 to research changing Haida kinship organization. The following summer I came again, to study the traditional and changing relationship of the Haida people to their natural environment. In August of 1975 I flew to the Charlottes with my colleague and friend, now husband, Ed Hall to introduce him to "my" Misty Isles.

In 1977 I made the journey twice, ostensibly for study purposes but as much for sentimental as academic reasons. I had come to fulfill a promise made to Florence Edenshaw Davidson of Masset in 1973: we would, one of these days, sit together and record her life history, which would eventually be published as a book. I had never seriously questioned why I would do it, save when justification had to be made to secure funding for the project. Justification for me lay in my personal relationship to Florence Davidson. She had served as my main female teacher in my previous Haida studies and we had developed a close working relationship; she had taken me into her home and I lived with her during most of my field research; but, most importantly, she accepted me, as she has others, as a grandchild. To live once again in her home, to learn from her, to be a recipient of her sparkling humor and grandmotherly love—these were the main reasons I found myself on a plane from Vancouver bound for the Queen Charlotte Islands in January and again in June of 1977.

Then as I flew northward, and now as I write, my visual images of Florence Davidson are vivid. A short, sturdy woman whose once black hair has grayed in front, she has a dignity and bearing which make her seem taller than she really is. In 1977 she was eighty-one, but her physical strength and energy, her involvement in Masset ceremonial life, and her mental spirit belie her years. I see her now, dressed in an elegant long black dress, Haida carved gold bracelets encircling both arms, standing to make a speech in Haida at a feast, most likely a feast she herself has hosted. In the early mornings I often awoke to find her in a housedress or bathrobe pummelling down the mound of bread dough rising in an enormous enamel washbasin on the kitchen table. I remember her from 1973 in slacks, headscarf, and gumboots, expertly slicing salmon at her Yakoun River fish camp where I had joined her for the several days she spent putting up her annual stock of sockeye. I recall a photograph I took of her in 1971, dressed in hat and gloves about to depart for an Anglican Church Women's conference at a Nass River Indian village. Her gloved hands clutched two large tins of seaweed which she had dried to trade with the Nass natives for eulachon grease. Most often, though, I see her laughing, talking in Haida to a visitor over a cup of tea as they sit at the old oak table in her ample kitchen.

I have seen her, too, through the eyes of others. Weaving a hat, she smiles from the pages of Ulli Steltzer's *Indian Artists at Work* (1976). She appears in two National Film Board of Canada films ("Haida Carver" and "This was the Time"), which feature her artist grandson Robert Davison; and not long ago in a CBC television advertisement for Canadian Indian art, she was sewing a button blanket at her dining room table. Her charm infects even those who do not know her as I do. The two work-study students at the college where I teach became fascinated with the personality on the tapes they were laboriously transcribing. "Such a neat lady. What a sense of humor," they exclaimed. And, at their request, I brought out slides and photographs so they might better visualize the woman whose voice they had come to know.

Florence Davidson has served as a willing informant for several researchers besides myself, on projects ranging from ethnobotany to linguistics to native education. Though a meticulous chronicler of her own culture, it is neither the intellectual challenge nor the documentary significance of her role that motivates her; rather, she dwells on the people behind the projects. "I think of them just like my own," she says of most of them. Virtually all younger people who pass through her large home as boarders and / or researchers are soon instructed to call her "Nani" (Haida for "grandmother"). She once laughingly remarked, "Everybody calls me Nani. I must be the world's nani." The universal grandmother: indulgent but teasing, somewhat aghast at the strange doings of the modern generation yet still eager to try new things, knowledgeable in the old ways, retrospective. That is how I have come to know her as Nani; that is how I hope readers of this work will see her.

Many people have contributed in various ways to this manuscript, and to them I extend my heartfelt thanks.

Marjorie Mitchell gave me a summer home in Victoria where most of the writing of this manuscript took place. She and Anna Franklin offered invaluable support and advice during the writing, provided photographs, and shared in Nani's world with me. Barbara Efrat of Victoria provided housing during my archival research in the summer of 1978 and supplied me with cassette tapes through the Linguistics Division of the British Columbia Provincial Museum.

Susan Kenyon critically read the manuscript and offered extensive commentary. I have also benefited from the comments and suggestions of Betty Berlin, Barbara Hall, Edwin S. Hall, Jr., Robert

Davidson, Dorothy Grant, Miles Richardson, and Ulli Steltzer, who read the manuscript or portions of it. Julie Kokis, Tina Howe, and Elizabeth Quinlan transcribed the forty-five hours of life-history tapes. Mary Beth Johnson and Debora Lang typed the manuscript. Norm Frisch prepared the map and genealogy. Robert Levine and Barbara Efrat offered assistance with the orthography.

Research was funded by an Urgent Ethnology contract from the National Museums of Canada, a National Endowment for the Humanities Summer Research Fellowship, and a grant from the Phillips Fund of the American Philosophical Society.

Many people from the Queen Charlottes have contributed to my research. Lola Dixon first introduced me to Florence Davidson in 1970; Howard Phillips lent photographs for inclusion in the manuscript; Dixie and Howard Post provided hospitality and friendship during the seasons of my field research. Nani's nine children and their spouses (Alfred and Rose Davidson, Virginia and Dave Hunter, Claude and Vivian Davidson, Sarah Davidson, Primrose and Victor Adams, Emily and Dave Goertzen, Myrtle and Sid Kerrigan, Aggie and Sam Davis, Merle and Knud Andersen, Clara and Brian Hugo) have provided many kindnesses during the years of my comings and goings to the Queen Charlottes. Others from Haida Masset, some now deceased, have shaped my image of the islands, and I acknowledge in particular the assistance of William and Flora Russ, June and Reno Russ, Percy Brown, Amanda Edgars, William and Emma Matthews, and Peter Hill. I am grateful to Nani's grandson Robert for the use of his dogfish design in chapters 4–9.

More than anyone else, Florence Davidson has given substance to my image of the Queen Charlotte Islands and their people. As teacher, friend, and grandmother she has enriched my life, and I thank her for sharing her life history with me and with readers of this book.

Royalties accruing to the author from publication of this book will go to Florence Davidson.

MARGARET B. BLACKMAN
July 1981

ORTHOGRAPHY

Haida words are spelled phonetically throughout the text. Although there are several works on the Haida language (see Levine 1973 and Lawrence 1977 for works written for a general audience), there is no standard orthography for Haida. Vowels and consonants not listed are pronounced the same as their English equivalents. Haida place names are Anglicized to conform to current map usage.

a	as in f<u>a</u>ther
ae	as in <u>a</u>t
E	as in l<u>e</u>t
e	as in l<u>a</u>te
i	as in b<u>ee</u>t
ɨ	as in <u>i</u>t
ə	as in <u>a</u>ccompany
ay	as in l<u>i</u>ght
u	as in t<u>u</u>ne
ʊ	as in p<u>u</u>t
o	as in <u>o</u>at
ł	unvoiced l, made by placing the tongue in the l position and blowing air out laterally
z	as in dog<u>s</u>
c	as in <u>ch</u>urch
x	as in the German *ich* ("I")
q	made like k only farther back in the throat
ʔ	glottal stop; the sound or "pause" that occurs in "oh oh"
'	all sounds followed by an apostrophe are made with a constricted glottis
ʕ	a sound produced by constriction of the pharyngeal cavity; similar to the sound one makes when blowing on eyeglasses prior to cleaning them

DURING MY TIME

Florence Edenshaw Davidson

A HAIDA WOMAN

CHAPTER 1

The Life-History Project

. . . the life history is still the most cognitively rich and humanly understandable way of getting at an inner view of culture. [No other type of study] can equal the life history in demonstrating what the native himself considers to be important in his own experience and how he thinks and feels about that experience. [Phillips 1973:201]

The Life History in Anthropology

The writing of native life histories has long been regarded by anthropologists as a legitimate as well as popular approach to understanding and describing other cultures.[1] In 1922, for example, anthropologist Elsie Clews Parsons wrote in the preface to her biography of a Zuni woman: "In our own complex culture biography may be a clarifying form of description. Might it not avail at Zuni?" (Parsons 1922:158). Alfred Kroeber, who wrote the introduction to *American Indian Life*, in which Parsons' article appears, believed that the unique contribution of this collection of biographical sketches was their insight into the social psychology of the American Indian. Unfortunately, most of the contributors to this volume found it necessary to fictionalize the life histories, inventing characters for the ethnographic data on the individual life cycle.

1. *Lives: An Anthropological Approach to Biography*, which appeared just as this book was going to press, provides an introduction "to the full historical and conceptual development of the life-history method in anthropology . . . and discusses the relevance of this method to a wider audience" (Langness and Frank 1981:5).

While it is fortunate that fictionalized life histories have been the exception in anthropological research, their very existence points to the significance of the medium for presenting the cultural record. The utility and success of the life-history approach in anthropology can be attributed to a number of factors. In the first place, the basic fabric of ethnology is woven from the scraps of individuals' lives, from the experiences and knowledge of individual informants. Many ethnographic accounts of subsistence activities, marriage, and ritual observances, for example, are derived directly from the personal experiences of members of a culture, and as anthropologists work closely with selected informants, the presentation of ethnographic data from the longitudinal perspective of the individual life is not surprising. "Culture" as lived by the individual represents the ultimate inside view, and the life history thus serves as a useful complement to the standard ethnography.

The life history also complements the ethnographic account by adding to the descriptive an affective or experiential dimension. We know, for example, from early ethnographic accounts of Haida culture the form and function of the girl's puberty ritual and the structure of Haida marriage, and from more recent ethnohistoric studies we know the changes wrought in Haida culture following contact. But these sources do not really address the question of meaning: What was the puberty seclusion really like? What did it mean to the individual to have his or her marriage arranged at an early age? How did individuals respond to various cultural changes? The life history is uniquely suited to addressing this kind of question.

The life history is also an appropriate medium for the study of acculturation. In many cultures the lives of natives span periods of critical and rapid culture change; the life history affords a personalized, longitudinal view of these changes.

Kluckhohn (1945), in a now classic article on the use of personal documents in anthropology, adds that life histories can be avenues to understanding status and role, individual variation within cultural patterns of behavior, personality structure, deviance, and idiosyncratic variation.

Native Americans have been by far the most popular subject material for life histories. Interest in the lives of American Indians began in the nineteenth century as famous and notorious Indian leaders commanded the attention of the public and sparked the writing of romantic and sentimental biographies. Langness (1965), for example, lists thirty-six American Indian life histories published between 1825 and 1900. A more recent and comprehensive accounting of Native American life histories (Brumble 1981), which brings the list up to the 1980s, contains over five hundred entries. Were one to include the numerous non-first-person accounts of Native American lives, which Brumble does not, this total would be considerably larger. The earliest anthropological life histories were also of American Indians (Kroeber 1908; Radin 1913). The recently published biographical sketches in *American Indian Intellectuals* (Liberty 1978) point to a still-current interest in the "great men"[2] of native society, though simultaneously there has been a growing interest in recording the lives of ordinary Native Americans.

Inspired in part by Franz Boas' early interest in the individual and his field research on the Northwest Coast, a number of life histories of Northwest Coast natives have been published over the years.[3] Edward Sapir included a fictionalized life history of a Nootka trader in *American Indian Life* (Parsons 1922); Diamond Jenness (1955) relied upon the personal reminiscences of "Old Pierre" to compile his treatise on Katzie supernatural beliefs; and Marius Barbeau's discussion of Haida argillite carvings (1957) included data on the artistic careers of the major Haida slate carvers. Further recognition of the importance of genealogical and life-history data to the study of native Indian art in British Columbia led the Vancouver Centennial Museum in 1977 to initiate a comprehensive collection of biographical data on British Columbia's Indian artists.

Two Northwest Coast life-history documents span successive generations of recent Southern Kwakiutl culture history and are particularly valuable for their documentation of continuity and change in that culture. In 1940 Kwakiutl Chief Charlie Nowell dictated his life story to Clellan Ford (1941), and in the 1960s James Sewid related his personal history, with the editorial assistance of anthropologist James Spradley (1969). Aside from Barbeau's brief biographical sketches in *Haida Carvers in Argillite* (1957) and the account of Chief Gəniyá ("Cunneah") in Robinson's *Sea Otter Chiefs* (1978), the only Haida life history is that of Peter Kelly of Skidegate (Morley 1967). To date, no life histories of native Northwest Coast women have been published, though as early as 1930 several short life histories of Kwakiutl women were collected by Julia Averkieva, a student of Boas (Rohner 1966:198).

2. Two of the biographies included there are of women: Sarah Winnemucca (Northern Paiute) by Catherine Fowler and Flora Zuni (Zuni) by Triloki Nath Panday.

3. Boas (1943) later eschewed the life history as a legitimate approach to the study of culture.

In fact, for native North America as a whole there are more than three times the number of male life histories as female life histories. At least in the case of the life histories authored or collected by anthropologists, this imbalance is in large part due to the fact that male ethnographers, who until recently have greatly outnumbered female ethnographers, understandably came to know and work more closely with the male members of the cultures they studied. Then, too, as Rosaldo (1974) has noted, men live much of their lives in the public arena, as policy makers, warriors, intellectuals, and philosophers in native societies. Given such roles it is not surprising that anthropologists should have found the lives of men more visible, interesting, absorbing, and significant than the lives of women. This viewpoint has often affected even those who do write about native women's lives. Ruth Underhill, for example, justifies Papago Maria Chona's narrative by demonstrating her affiliation with important men: "As a woman she could take no active part in the ceremonial life. But her father was a governor and a warrior; her brother and husband were shamans; her second husband was a song leader and composer" (Underhill 1936:4). She does add, however, that a Papago woman's life is interesting in and of itself "because in this culture, there persists strongly the fear of woman's impurity with all its consequent social adjustments."

I suspect that anthropologists are more influenced by their own cultural background than they would like to acknowledge. Perhaps the relative neglect of women's lives in other cultures stems also from the fact that autobiography in the Western tradition has been primarily a male form. As Pomerleau notes:

> The traditional view of women is antithetical to the crucial motive of autobiography—a desire to synthesize, to see one's life as an organic whole, to look back for a pattern. Women's lives are fragmented.
> . . . the process is not one of growth, of evolution; rather . . . earlier and more decisively than for a man, the curve of a woman's life is seen by herself and society to be one of deterioration and degeneration. Men may mature, but women age. [1980:37]

In the same volume Jelinek summarizes, "Insignificance, indeed, expresses the predominant attitude of most [literary] critics towards women's lives" (Jelinek 1980:4).

Only recently have anthropologists taken the view that, even in the absence of criteria such as a belief in woman's impurity or relationships to powerful men, women's lives are inherently worthy of consideration. If we are to understand women and their roles in cross-cultural perspective, it is axiomatic that we know the breadth and depth of their life experiences, the ordinary as well as the extraordinary. Margaret Mead has provided us with the latter type of document in her autobiography *Blackberry Winter* (1972), and in the wake of the women's movement a number of anthropological monographs that focus on the lives of ordinary women have been published (e.g., Strathern 1972; Jones and Jones 1976; Weiner 1976; Dougherty 1978; Kelley 1978). Accounts of native women's lives written for a more general audience have also appeared in recent years. In the native North American literature are an overview of the female life cycle in many different tribes (Neithammer 1977), a biography of a well-known Ojibwa woman (Vanderburgh 1977), and autobiographies written by a part-Cree woman (Willis 1973) and a métis woman (Campbell 1973).

Florence Davidson's life history is the account of one who faithfully fulfilled the expected role of women in her society. For most of her life she has remained outside the public domain; above all else she has participated in her culture as mother and wife, and today she would undoubtedly sum up her identity in the word "Nani." Despite the social position she has enjoyed as the daughter of high-ranking parents and the esteem that she has earned, Florence Davidson views her life as "ordinary," in the sense of being uneventful. Once during our taping she sighed and then laughed, "If only I lied, it could be so interesting!" Aside from recounting the life experiences of an octogenarian Haida woman, her narrative presents a picture of an individual operating in a culture neither traditionally Haida nor fully Canadian, a culture undergoing tremendous change, yet intelligible and meaningful to one living in it.

The Haida had been exposed to Christianity for only about twenty years when Florence Davidson was born in 1896, and just fifteen years prior to her birth the Masset Haida had become reserve Indians. A few Haida were still living in cedar-plank houses when she was born. The female puberty seclusion was still practiced during her adolescence, and marriages were, as a rule, arranged. Her life spans the beginning and end of a resident Indian Agency in Masset, the development of schooling from the one-room mission school through the residential boarding schools to the modern public educational system, and the evolution of transportation from the dugout canoe to daily jet service on the Queen Charlotte Islands.

Florence remembers a time when the ceremonial button blankets, devised probably in the 1850s by native people, were disdained and her grandmother cut the small buttons from hers to give to her granddaughters for their babies' clothes. Today Florence Davidson has become perhaps the foremost Haida button blanket maker, sewing exquisite appliquéd blankets from her grandson Robert's patterns. She recalls the time in 1932 when William Matthews took his uncle's place as town chief of Masset without a semblance of a traditional installation ceremony. Forty-four years later when Oliver Adams succeeded his uncle, William Matthews, he hired Florence Davidson to cook for the feast; she sang a Haida song in his honor and was recognized for her efforts at the potlatch marking his chieftaincy.

There were no totem poles carved during Florence's childhood, save the few commissioned of the last of the old carvers at five dollars per foot by museum collectors. In 1969 Florence and Robert Davidson gave a potlatch honoring the erection of the pole their grandson Robert had carved for the Masset people. In short, Florence Davidson's life weaves through a significant period of Haida culture history, a time that saw the disappearance of many traditional practices (the puberty ceremony, arranged marriages, most forms of potlatching) and the rebirth of others (such as the visual and performing arts).

RECORDING THE LIFE HISTORY

My only special preparations for the journey to Masset in January of 1977 included packing a wool shirt and rain slicker, a tape recorder and forty hours of tape, a journal, a copy of Murdock's *Our Primitive Contemporaries*, which contains a chapter on the Haida, and Clellan Ford's life history of Charlie Nowell to show to Florence Davidson as an example. I had not given extensive thought as to how we would proceed, confident that the problem would resolve itself once I arrived in Masset. My only worry was that I might have the same experience as anthropologist Nancy Lurie, who secured in her first brief session with Mountain Wolf Woman, the Winnebago woman's entire life history (Lurie 1961:XIV). Luckily I need not have worried: "I'm full of stories yet," Nani pronounced about halfway through the project.

The quickest method of getting to Masset is to take a jet from Vancouver to Prince Rupert and from there a float or amphibious plane to New Masset on the islands. No matter how rough the weather, I never fail to enjoy the forty-five minutes from Prince Rupert to Masset. Ten minutes in the air, from a point not far out to sea, one can see in the distance the long dark tongue of Rose Spit licking the waters of Dixon Entrance. Minutes pass; the sand bluffs

Button blankets worn by Florence Davidson (*left*) and other Masset Haida (photograph by Ulli Steltzer)

of the east coast of Graham Island make their appearance and the familiar landmark of Tow Hill rises several hundred feet into the air from the sands of North Beach. Geologists call Tow a volcanic intrusion; the Haida say he has a brother up Masset Inlet with whom he quarreled and that is why he stands alone now at the eastern extremity of the islands.

The plane flies over the ancient beach ridges ancestral to the present sands of North Beach and along Tow's backside. Yakin Point, where Tow paused in his westward migration, intrudes into the cold waters of Dixon Entrance, and beyond I recognize Kliki Creek where Nani, my anthropologist friend Marjorie Mitchell, and I went to collect spruce roots in the summer of 1974. We cross the mouth of Chowan Brook where Nani and her mother used to pick crabapples.

Ten miles from Masset is the "elephant pen," the local name for a Canadian Forces communications installation whose circular wires and fences look incongruous against the spruce and sand. The plane crosses the village of New Masset giving a glimpse of the Forces base and housing, the new hotel with the only beer parlor for miles around, the high school, the government wharf, the Co-op store. Water splashes the belly of the plane as it descends into the waters of Masset Inlet. Grudgingly, it struggles up on land coming to rest beside the tiny air terminal.

Haida Masset is three miles from New Masset and every taxi driver knows how to find Florence Davidson's house, or just about any other local house for that matter. Each time I return to the village, I mentally tick off the changes in its facade. Since I have been coming to the islands, the village has expanded as far southward toward New Masset as available reserve land will allow. It now moves westward, into the piled-up stumps of once timbered land. In January of 1977 traces of bright blue paint that adorned the exterior of Peter Hill's little house in 1970 had been washed away by the frequent rains, Alfred Davidson's fine large home had burned to the ground, Joe Weir's house had been razed to make way for a more modern one, the Yeltatzies had added a large picture window to the side of their home, and a rental duplex had been built catty-corner to Nani's house.

The taxi turns down an unpaved side street and comes to rest just short of the Anglican Church and Robert Davidson's magnificent totem pole. Despite the external changes in the village, Nani appears little different to me than she did in 1975 or in the years I knew her previous to that. She waits in the open door and enfolds me in a warm hug as I set down my suitcase.

Nani lives alone now in a sprawling one-story house, originally designed and built with the comforts of a large family in mind. Her front door opens into the spacious "front room," constructed as in other older Masset homes large enough to hold the entire adult population of the village. The front room has seen numerous feasts and potlatches, but normally it contains couches and overstuffed chairs pushed against its perimeter. The Sunday dining table sits in the room's center; plants fill the front window, and Robert Davidson's Haida designs, family photos, and religious mementos adorn the walls. Five bedrooms open off the large central room at its far end; at the opposite end, a leaded-glass door leads into the parlor—remodelled between January and June of 1977—panelled and carpeted in thick red plush. Many of our summer taping sessions were held in the quiet softness of this sitting room.

My favorite spot in the house and the room where I have spent the most time is Nani's expansive kitchen. I mark the passage of my Masset visits by the additions to her kitchen: new appliances, a new shelf, new flooring, a different color scheme. When I first came to Masset in 1970, the wash was done on the back porch in a wringer washer and Nani used to lug the heavy baskets of wet clothes across the yard to hang on the long clothesline, but by 1975 the old machine had been replaced by a new spin washer and dryer (gifts from a daughter and son-in-law), which occupy a prominent position in the kitchen. The village has had electricity since 1964 (and before, if one counts the portable generator that lighted the church and vicarage). Freezers and refrigerators followed in its wake, dramatically altering old patterns of food preservation and storage. Nani's kitchen contains both of these appliances, and a second freezer, filled to the top with venison, herring roe, berries, and fish, sits on the back porch pantry.

The most eye-catching feature of Nani's kitchen is the long bank of open shelves along one wall, which display some two hundred bone china cups and saucers, plus everyday dishes and the mugs from which we drink our breakfast coffee and afternoon tea. An oaken table, one of the few pieces salvaged from a house fire in 1952, faces the large kitchen window. In many ways this table is the focal point of the household. At it most meals are taken, visitors are received and served tea, and here Nani sits to rest from her baking or to weave a cedar bark hat. I have spent much of my fieldwork time here, too: interviewing Nani, writing in my journal at night, drinking coffee and gazing at the ever-moving waters of Masset Inlet, talking with Nani and others over tea.

By the summer of 1977, however, the view from the table had

Florence in her kitchen (photograph by Margaret Blackman)

changed. I recorded the change, somewhat petulantly, in my
journal.

> I always liked sitting here and writing, looking up now and then to see
> Hannah (who lives next door) going in or out and collecting my
> thoughts as I watched the changing configurations of the western skies.
> But now a plank ledge runs the length of the window and the foliage of
> some fifty African violets sitting on it obscures much of the view. A
> fuchsia hangs from the ceiling and its embrace with a leggy geranium
> blots out Emma Matthews' house . . . ."

Even the long plank could not contain all the products of Nani's
amazing green thumb; I discovered yet more African violets atop the
washing machine, their leaves aflutter when the machine entered its
spin cycle.

Nani's house is seldom inactive, and then only for a relatively
short period, as she typically retires at 11:30 and arises as early as 5
A.M. Usually there are other boarders; various children, children-in-
law, and grandchildren drop by during the day, and the health aide
stops in on her rounds of the village. Hannah Parnell and Dora
Brooks, Robert Davidson's lineage nieces, and Carrie Weir, a sister's
daughter, appear every day or so to visit and have tea; and, not
infrequently, someone from New Masset comes by to introduce a
visiting friend to Nani.

Nani's tremendous energy is evident in the wonderful creative
confusion that pervades her home. On a typical day loaves and
loaves of bread rise in the kitchen under the protective covers of
fresh linen towels; the combined vapors from a pot of stew and the
kettle of "Indian medicine" beside it on the stove mingle and steam
the kitchen window; an unfinished cedar bark hat stands spiderlike
on the front room dining table; a small cat darts under a chair
rustling the wide dry strips of cedar bark draped over it; Nani's
crocheting lies where she left it on one of the front room
chesterfields; the kitchen radio blaring messages to people in
remote mainland communities competes with "The Edge of Night"
emanating from the television in the front room; in the smokehouse
adjacent to the house, Nani hangs halibut fillets on racks above the
smoldering alder fire. Such was the setting in which Nani related
her life story to me. Why she agreed to relate it is the result of
several factors, among them her familiarity with anthropological
inquiry, the compatibility of the life history mode with Haida values,
and, not insignificantly, her relationship to me.

From the time she was very young Florence Davidson was aware
of the interest of outsiders in Haida culture and artifacts. Her father
worked for C. F. Newcombe of the Provincial Museum in Victoria as

an informant and artist, and Florence recalls Newcombe's many visits to her father's home. She is too young to have had personal memories of John Swanton, who relied upon both her father and her uncle as informants and resided with the latter during his fieldwork in 1900–1901, but she may have heard them speak of him. In the later years of her marriage the Davidson home was frequented by the occasional anthropologist. Wilson Duff, for example, interviewed Florence more than once about her father and his forebears, and Mary Lee Stearns visited the Davidson home several times in 1965–66 to interview Robert Davidson during the course of her study of contemporary Masset culture (Stearns 1975, 1981).

Following the death of her husband in 1969, Florence emerged as a knowledgeable elder in her own right. In addition to her work with me, which began in 1970, she served as an informant on Haida ethnobotany for Nancy Turner in 1970 and 1971 (Turner 1974). In 1974 Florence was one of several Haida elders who contributed data to Marjorie Mitchell for a multi-media curriculum project on the Haida. In the early 1970s Florence worked briefly with linguists Barbara Efrat and Robert Levine of the British Columbia Provincial Museum, and since 1975 she has served as a linguistic informant for John Enrico, now a permanent boarder in her home. Moreover, she has appeared at museum openings as an elder ambassador of her culture, publicly demonstrated her skills at basket and button blanket making, and welcomed into her Masset home countless friends of white friends interested in Haida culture and eager to learn something of it from this grandmotherly representative.

In a brief life history of Flora Zuni, Panday cautions that the life history is not a natural or universal narrative mode among American Indians, noting that "Pueblo traditions do not provide any model of such confessional introspection" (1978:217). I am not certain if the life history is a Haida narrative form, but certainly as an anthropological form it is compatible with Haida traditions. The phrase used repeatedly by Florence Davidson during the course of her narration and selected by her as the title of this work—"during my time"—is a free translation of an often used Haida time referent, *di ɡeneng ge gut ən di unsiding*, "I see it [or, I know it] all of my lifetime." Such personalization of events goes hand-in-hand with the well-known emphasis in Northwest Coast culture upon the individual. The importance of rank, the feasting and potlatching that encouraged competition and individual expression, the custom of acquiring newly invented names at potlatches, and the mortuary potlatch as a vehicle for formally remembering a person long after his or her death (see Blackman 1973), all exemplify the significance of the individual in traditional Haida culture. Though Florence lamented the ordinariness of her life, the question "Why would anyone be interested in my life story?" understandably never arose.

Finally, although some anthropologists, such as Kluckhohn (1945:97), have regretted the intrusion of the anthropologist into the native life-history document, it goes without saying that the relationship between anthropologist and life-history subject is critical to the telling of the story in the first place and ultimately to the understanding of the final record. I agree with Brumble, who notes that "much of the fascination [with life histories is] a result of, rather than in spite of, their being so often collaborative" (1981:2).

Florence Davidson and I come from different worlds and different generations. Her children, the welfare of her family, and the church have been the focus of her long life; I have no children and at the center of my life is my academic career. She has lived the life of a housewife and mother, and I have not. How strange I must sometimes seem to her, spending long periods of time far from home, traveling freely, childless at an age when I should have a large family of my own. "How's your big family," she often teases me when we talk long distance. I once asked her what I might do to show I had "respect for myself," an important Haida virtue. "Dress up and stay home," she retorted, with laughter in her eyes. Yet our cultural, social, and age differences are softened by the mutual respect and affection we have developed over the years of our collaboration and friendship. My own grandmothers, strong, creative women and important figures in my childhood, did not survive into my adulthood. In many important ways, Nani has filled that gap in my life. Her life history was given to me, I think, as an anthropologist dedicated to learning the "old-fashioned ways," as a granddaughter curious about a grandmother's past, and as a woman interested in the events and people that shape women's lives. I doubt that Florence Davidson could have comfortably related her life history to me before I had established my commitment to learning about her culture, and I am certain that she could not have told her story to a man.

Although I had written Nani regarding arrangements for the project, we did not discuss it in any detail until my arrival in Masset. That first night I indicated to Nani that it would be nice to include what she knew about her ancestors. She thought for a moment and began relating how her father and grandfather had seen lucky signs in the woods, how her mother and her mother's mother's sister had been rescued from the smallpox epidemic, and how her grandfather had been called to take the chieftainship at Kiusta. When I protested that I had not yet unpacked my tape recorder, she replied, smiling, "It's OK, I was just practicing for tomorrow."

The following day she deliberated for some time about where to begin her narrative and settled on the drowning of her brother Robert, which occurred one month before her birth. From that point on, however, there was little chronological order to the narrative. Often she would select a topic to initiate the day's recording: "Let's talk about when my mother and I used to go for spruce roots"; or, "Did I tell you about the time when we built this house?" On other occasions she would leave the decision up to me, asking, "What shall we talk about?" or commanding, "You ask me questions." I would then pick a topic from the growing list I had compiled since my first day into the project.

When Nani was bereft of life-history memories we would explore kinship, reincarnation, Haida names, and numerous other ethnographic topics that I felt I had not sufficiently covered in my previous research. To a large extent my own interests biased the life-history data I obtained. For example, my concern with Haida ceremonial life, modern Masset's primary link with the past, led me to inquire repeatedly about feasts and potlatches given by ancestors and relatives. My interest in pollution taboos resulted in a lengthy digression into puberty and pregnancy proscriptions and male/female separation, topics that were not of as much interest to Nani. Because missionaries long ago had discouraged the custom and imposed European standards of decorum upon the Haida, Nani was somewhat embarrassed to discuss her puberty seclusion knowing that the account might be published. I, on the other hand, felt the subject significant enough to pursue until she had exhausted her memory. In addition, my view of life history as retrospective led me at certain times to ask questions that might elicit reflective responses. Typical examples include: What makes you happiest? When are the saddest times? What are the biggest changes you have seen? What would you most like to be remembered for? How would you describe yourself? Accordingly, Florence's "Reflections" (pp. 136–38) consist primarily of answers to questions that I posed.

Understandably, Nani sometimes dwelt on topics that were of great importance in her own life but not of as much interest to me as an anthropologist, in particular the impact of the church on her life, her role in it, and the meaning of Christianity to her. I do not know what form the life history might have taken had I avoided any intrusion, but given our relationship that would have been impossible. The final narrative is a measure both of our collaboration and of our sometimes divergent interests.

The schedule of our work was dictated by Nani's daily routine and the time constraints of my short field visits. We worked in the morning, the afternoon, sometimes after dinner, and occasionally just before bedtime. Most of the time we were alone, and when visitors called, our work was put aside. Often after a long day Nani lay on a chesterfield in the front room and I sat on the floor holding the microphone toward her. Sometimes, to avoid the noise and activity of the kitchen, we retired to her bedroom; she sat on her bed and leaned back against the wall, crocheting as she talked, except on Sundays when she put her handiwork aside. At times she wove on one of her cedar bark hats at the dining table. Once I taped her as she whittled cedar splits to be threaded through the black cod she was preparing to smoke. A song she sang on that occasion is punctuated by the sound of metal cutting red cedar. I sometimes joined her in activity. In January 1977, she gave a memorial feast in honor of her sister's daughter from Seattle who had died the preceding November, and we tried to tape in the kitchen amidst the preparations. Nani filled tarts with raspberry jam and I punched a plastic pattern into fourteen dozen doughy buns while we discussed earlier feasts. The quietest, most comfortable place to talk, though, proved to be the front parlor, where we worked during most of the June 1977 session.

Place or context played a considerable role in triggering Nani's memory. As we sat at the kitchen table one January day, the rain pelting the kitchen window reminded her of q'ən dleł ("everything's scarce"), the traditional Haida term for this time of year; a discussion of the seasons followed. Baking bread one Monday morning Nani recalled the days when she used to bake in the summertime at North Island for the fishermen. A juvenile eagle that scavenged a piece of drying halibut in June reminded Nani of her first attempt at slicing halibut and the chiding she received from her step-grandfather for the jagged-edged fillets she had hung to dry. Sometimes discussions of the project with other villagers brought to mind events from the past. Emma Matthews once reminded Nani of a play wedding they had staged as children. Some topics were easier for Nani to discuss than others. She recounted deaths in the family and the events leading to them in great detail, but when I asked her to describe the village and certain villagers as she remembered them from childhood, the details were sparse. I once asked her to describe her aunt, Martha Edenshaw; puzzling a moment over my request, she pointed to a photograph on the wall and answered, "She looks

Margaret Blackman and Florence Davidson, 1979 (photograph by Anna Franklin)

just like her picture." "But how do *you* think of her?" I continued. "I think of her just like the picture," Nani responded unhesitatingly.

Nani was aware of numerous gaps in her narrative. When I talked to her on the phone between my infrequent visits to Masset, she would often say, "after you left I remembered lots of things. I wish I could write them down because I forget them." Subsequent visits in 1978, 1979, 1980, and 1981 brought more reminiscences, but undoubtedly there are events and thoughts that she might wish to include which have eluded her memory. Occasionally, too, Nani was unable to remember something in the detail that I would have liked, reminding me quite appropriately, "It wasn't important to me then; how was I supposed to know that white people might be interested in it years later?"

From time to time, Nani's mischievous sense of humor crept into our work. Discussing her father's house where she had spent her childhood, I asked what it was like inside. She retorted that it was five stories, had "spring beds," and was covered in thick, thick carpeting. "I'm getting crazier than ever—what if you write that down," she said, dissolving in laughter. I recorded the contexts of all our taping sessions in the daily journal I kept, a practice I have always followed in fieldwork. Later, the journal became invaluable as I tried to remember what the house looked like that June, why Nani recalled this or that on a particular day, or why a certain subject had been sparingly discussed.

Florence Davidson's narrative is a circumspect one. Though she related to me both off and on tape things she did not wish to appear in print, her recollections by and large are devoid of the petty jealousies and rivalries that are part of the fabric of Masset life. There is little mention of the misdoings of self and others: illicit sexual liaisons (which figure prominently in some native male life histories[4]), witchcraft, or feuds between families. "I don't tell everything—what's no good," she said. Throughout our work Florence was conscious that the final product was to be a public document, though I imagine she was more concerned about its public status within her own community than in the larger world. This consciousness clearly guided not only what she related but how it was related. This bias may be characteristic of autobiography, regardless of culture. Jelinik, for example, speaking of autobiography in the Western tradition, notes:

> Irrespective of their professions or of their differing emphases in subject matter, neither women nor men are likely to explore or reveal painful and intimate memories in their autobiographies. . . . The admission of intense feelings of hate, love and fear, the disclosure of explicit sexual encounters, or the details of painful psychological experiences are matters on which autobiographers are generally silent. [1980:10, 12]

The division of the narrative into chapters is an artifact of my own thinking, not that of Florence Davidson's, although I did discuss its organization with her in the summer of 1978, and the chronology closely parallels the traditional life stages distinguished among the Haida. Nani requested that I edit the narrative to "fix it up" and "make it look right." I rearranged the narrative in chronological order, made certain grammatical and tense changes, and deleted redundancies, but those who know Nani will recognize her style of speaking. A section of the original narrative is presented in the appendix so readers may see its unedited form. Unfortunately, neither the original transcription nor the final edited version can adequately capture Florence Davidson's personality—the inflection

---

4. Charlie Nowell, for example, discusses his premarital and extramarital affairs (which he estimates at more than two hundred) quite openly and in some detail (Ford 1941). To what extent this revelation is a product of Clellan Ford's well-known anthropological interest in human sexual behavior is not known.

of her words, her accompanying gestures, her sometimes subtle, always gentle humor, which was often turned upon herself. Nani related her life history in English, interspersed with Haida words that I knew, and now and then she repeated an English sentence with its Haida equivalent.

Following my two trips in 1977, I returned twice to visit and work with Nani as the manuscript progressed through stages of completion. In August of 1978 I took with me the completed introductory chapters and rough version of her narrative. As I typed the narrative portions in July I was astounded at the growing list of questions I was amassing. The project had supposedly been completed the preceding summer, but I found I had neglected some basic life-cycle topics: how long mothers typically nursed their children, the significance of menopause for Haida women, the learning of sexual behavior, and others. In addition, I had enumerated questions dealing specifically with Nani's life history, such as whether the first children of Isabella and Charles Edenshaw had been born in a traditional house and where Isabella and Charles had lived after they were first married. Fortunately, I secured answers to most of my stock of questions during a week's return to Masset in August of 1978.

With the manuscript complete except for the Discussion and the Afterword, I returned in the summer of 1979 for another week. This time my main purposes were to check the large genealogy I had constructed and to read Nani's narrative to her. In addition, I sought her reflections on friendship, growing old, the changes she had witnessed, and the people she has admired. In July of 1980 I returned again, this time to work specifically with Nani on Haida kinship, but our tape recordings included some life-history data that have been incorporated into this narrative. My last visit with Nani before the book went to press, in July 1981, resulted in a few corrections and minor additions to the narrative.

Archival Research

A considerable amount of ethnohistorical research both preceded and followed my fieldwork. In earlier trips to the Provincial Archives of British Columbia in Victoria I had surveyed most of the material relating to the nineteenth-century Haida, but had not explored extant twentieth-century materials. During July and August of 1977 and 1978 I researched these materials. Especially significant were two newspapers from the Queen Charlottes, the *Queen Charlotte Islander* and the *Masset Leader*, which were published during the

second decade of the twentieth century. In addition to presenting
local news, the *Islander* also ran a series of lengthy articles on the
Haida during 1911, 1912, and 1913, written by Charles Harrison, a
former missionary. Perusal of materials relating to Thomas Deasy,
Indian agent at Masset from 1910 to 1924, revealed documents
written by a Haida. Alfred Adams, Florence Davidson's uncle,
carried on a regular correspondence with Deasy from 1924, when
the latter left the Queen Charlottes, until the time of Deasy's death
in 1936. Deasy's reports to the Minister of Indian Affairs, published
in the annual reports from 1911 to 1920, present a detailed and
generally sympathetic portrait of the Masset community.

From research conducted at the Church Missionary Society
archives in 1972, I had compiled all the pertinent correspondence
written by Masset missionaries from 1876 to 1913; some of this
material has contributed to the present volume. The early marriage
and baptismal records for St. John's Anglican Church at Masset,
housed in the diocese headquarters in Prince Rupert, provided
marriage dates for several of Florence Davidson's relatives and
ancestors, documented Isabella Edenshaw's births prior to Florence,
and pinpointed the baptismal dates for Florence and her sisters.

Ethnohistorical and ethnographic data have been drawn together
to form the traditional and historic picture of Haida women in
chapter 2. Additional data from more recent historical documents
and from my own field journals are interspersed with Florence's
narrative, both to lend a broader perspective to her account and to
present a contemporary non-native view of the Haida.

CHAPTER 2

The Haida Woman

The women also to a great extent share the good qualities of the men. . . . They are exceedingly strong and can cut firewood, sail and paddle canoes, and work equally as hard as the men. They are all handsome and possess agreeable features when classed with the other coast Indians. [Harrison, April 29, 1912]

A Sketch of the Traditional People

They called themselves *Haada*, "people," and their world was divided into two islands, Haida Island (the Queen Charlottes) and the larger seaward country (the mainland). Both places were supported by a supernatural being, "Sacred One Standing and Moving," who in turn rested upon a copper box (Swanton 1909:12). The Haida population of some nine thousand was distributed among winter settlements located along the more protected shores and inlets of the Queen Charlotte Islands and, by the mid-eighteenth century, in southeastern Alaska. The large cedar-plank houses comprising these villages were built close together, nestled against the treeline and facing the beach in one or two long even rows. Above the storm-tide mark along the beachfront were erected the forest of totem poles so frequently remarked upon by nineteenth-century visitors to these remote shores. Advertising the greatness of their owners or owners' kin, some rested against the houses, some stood freely before the houses, and still others, shorter than the preceding types, contained the remains of the dead.

A maritime fishing, gathering, and hunting people, the Haida
dispersed from March to November to resource areas where they
fished, hunted sea and land mammals, gathered seaweed and other
wild plants, and collected shellfish. The winter months, spent in the
villages, were punctuated by the giving of potlatches and feasts, a
prerogative of the wealthy.

Traditional Haida society was stratified into three categories: the
y'aʔɛEyt (nobles), the *ʔisʔaniya* (commoners), and the *hǝldǝnga*
(slaves). This stratification was underpinned and reinforced by the
ceremonial distribution of wealth and food in potlatching and
feasting, respectively. The *y'aʔɛEyt* were the "chiefs," the holders of

high-ranking hereditary titles, the house owners, the wealthy, the ambitious, the clever, and the lucky. They were kind, generous, polite, and well-spoken; they fulfilled kinship obligations and had "respect for themselves." They gave potlatches and feasts to make good their names and to assure that their children would be y'a?ʕEyt, for the route to high status was through the potlatching efforts of one's parents. Ideally, this upper stratum of society exemplified all the desired and valued Haida qualities.

The ?is?aniya, on the other hand, were traditionally regarded as "kind of poor"; they did not show proper etiquette, did not exemplify "respect for self," talked "any old way," and were lazy. They were outnumbered by the y'a?ʕEyt. The haldənga were slaves or the descendants of slaves, captives taken in warfare or persons purchased as slaves from other tribes. They were without status, regarded as chattels, used as labor, and valued by their y'a?ʕEyt owners for the prestige their possession conveyed.

The Haida class division crosscut the descent organization of society. Descent was traced matrilineally, and named matrilineages, each headed by a chief, were the important resource-holding corporations. Lineages owned, among other properties, fishing streams, stretches of shoreline, stands of cedar trees, a corpus of hereditary names or titles, and "crests." The last, largely zoomorphic symbols, comprised the subject matter of most Haida art. Carved and painted on totem poles, feast dishes, chief's seats, frontlet headdresses, screens, housefronts, and canoe prows and paddles, among other items, crests symbolized the lineage affiliations of their owners.

The more than forty Haida lineages were grouped into two matrimoieties—Eagle and Raven—which, like the lineages, were exogamous, but unlike them, were not corporate. In addition to their marriage function, the moieties were ritually significant; one feasted and potlatched members of the opposite moiety and called upon them to perform mortuary functions. The larger significance of the Haida moiety division is exemplified in their classification of mythical beings and deities into this same dual schema.

Sources and Lacunae

There are several well-known ethnographic accounts of Haida culture, beginning with geologist George M. Dawson's 1878 study appended to the report of his geological survey of the Queen Charlotte Islands (Dawson 1880). Some thirty years later, John R. Swanton, a member of the Jesup Expedition of the American Museum of Natural History, conducted what still stands as the most thorough investigation of traditional Haida culture. His extensive *Contributions to the Ethnology of the Haida* (1909) was augmented a few years later by the ethnography that Edward S. Curtis prepared in 1916 as part of his twenty-volume study of North American Indians. Brief field research conducted in the summer of 1932 by G. P. Murdock resulted in important additions to our understanding of Haida social and ceremonial organization (Murdock 1934a, 1936). Additionally, Murdock provided a summary of Haida culture in *Our Primitive Contemporaries* (1934b). Ethnographic as well as ethnohistorical data on Haida culture are also found in the numerous accounts of eighteenth-century trading voyages to the Queen Charlotte Islands (e.g., Bartlett 1925; Dixon 1789; Ingraham 1971; Marchand 1801), in the published and unpublished writings of missionaries (e.g., Collison 1915; Harrison 1912–13; Harrison 1925), government agents (e.g., Deasy 1911–20), and museum collectors (e.g., Swan 1883).

Although the Haida have been well recorded in the ethnographic literature, there are certain lacunae in this material. Perhaps most importantly, ethnographic as well as historic sources on the Haida chronicle a male world seen through the eyes of male writers, a bias present in most earlier ethnographic literature from all areas of the world. The lives of women are described primarily as they impinge upon or complement the lives of men. Menstruation, pregnancy, and childbirth, for example, had wide ramifying effects upon the Haida community and consequently these aspects of the female life cycle have been of sufficient interest to be reported in some ethnographic detail. But what of girlhood, the learning of female roles, the availability of power and authority to Haida women, achievement in female terms; what of the experiences of aging, menopause, and widowhood? We know little or nothing of these cultural domains from the literature.

In short, the culture of Haida women has not been described. Yet, in order for a life-history narrative to have meaning, one must understand the traditions from which it derives. In this chapter I draw together scattered data from ethnographic and historic sources and from Florence Davidson's remarks upon Haida women in "the olden days" to form a picture of the cultural position of traditional Haida women. In particular I have dwelt upon the life cycle, the division of labor, ceremonialism, and the value system. By the time Florence Davidson was born, the Haida had been exposed to Euro-American culture for over one hundred years and were considerably acculturated in many respects. More changes followed during the long years of Florence's marriage. These changes are also briefly reviewed in this chapter, in terms of their effect upon the lives of Haida women.

The Life Cycle

Traditionally, the Haida preferred female to male children (Murdock 1934b:248). Female children signified future expansion of the matrilineage, and their marriages brought males into the household to assist their fathers-in-law in "making canoes, fishing and hunting" (Harrison, November 25, 1912). On the other hand, it was important that a woman also have male children so that her brothers would have nephews to assist them and to succeed to their positions when they died.

Males and females were treated differently from the moment of birth. The umbilical cord of a baby girl was cut with a knife belonging to her mother; that of a boy was cut with the father's knife (Murdock 1934b:248–49). Personal names (as opposed to honorific names) were bestowed in infancy and were sex linked. According to Murdock (1934:249), the mother, after consultation with the child's father and grandparents, named a male infant after his real or classificatory paternal grandfather, while a female was named after one of her "grandmothers," a second-generation woman of the infant's own or the father's father's lineage. Harrison (November 25, 1912) notes that a shaman was often called in to determine which matrilineal ancestor had been reincarnated in the newborn and to name the infant accordingly.

While still infants, both males and females had their ears pierced, and, if of high rank, children of both sexes were tattooed on the arms, hands, and legs, and occasionally on the chest and back. It was customary, Harrison reports (December 16, 1912), for the parents to give small potlatches when their child was named, when its nose and ears were pierced, and again when it was tattooed.

The item of adornment that marked the Haida female, the labret or lip plug, was acquired during girlhood. An early maritime explorer (La Pérouse 1798:165) remarks that all Haida women wore the labret, while most other ethnographers have claimed that the lip plug was a distinguishing mark of high-status women. Former missionary Charles Harrison described the procedure of insertion and the significance of the implement:

> . . . a hole is cut through the lower lip and an ivory or bone plug is inserted until the wound had healed. After healing the hole is stretched from time to time until it reached about half an inch in diameter and

about an inch in length. . . . These labrets are increased in size according to the rank of the person wearing them, and according to the number of children she had become the mother of. [Harrison, May 20, 1912]

A visible marker of both female status and high rank, the labret was evidently also symbolic of the emphasis the Haida placed upon female fecundity.

No formal restrictions seem to have been placed on the association of the sexes during childhood. Swanton (1909:60) mentions two games that were played together by boys and girls, but otherwise there are no ethnographic data on childhood play activities. Children's activities seemed to be generally sex segregated by Florence's time, as she noted that "boys played together and girls played together." Work activities during childhood were definitely sex differentiated and became more marked when a boy at age ten or eleven left his mother's household to reside with one of his mother's brothers. Under the tutelage of his mother's brother a boy received formal instruction in ceremonial roles and assisted his uncle in various economic activities. He was toughened by harsh discipline and rigorous physical activity.

Rigid and ritually maintained differences between the sexes began with a girl's puberty ceremony. The *təgwəná*, or first menstruation seclusion, marked a very real change of life for a girl because, upon her emergence from this ritual seclusion, she was acknowledged to be a woman and was now marriageable. Charles Harrison described the ritual as follows:

> In the olden days when a girl reached maturity she had to pay strict attention to the order of the medicine man and pass through certain trying ordeals and ceremonies. A small tent was generally erected for her accommodation at the back of her father's house and in this tent she had to exist for fourteen days and sometimes longer.[1] Her face was generally painted and she had very little food given her. Should she during this period be compelled to go outside of her tent and accidentally meet a man, her face had to immediately be covered with her blanket. During this trying time she also wore a peculiar cloak made out of the inner bark of a cedar tree which covered her head and reached down to her knees, leaving only a small aperture for her eyes so that she could see where she was going. This cloak was only worn on this peculiar occasion so that when seen wearing this garb all the people looked upon her as about to pass from girlhood to womanhood.

1. Swanton (1909:48) and Curtis (1916:126) note that the period of seclusion was twenty days.

During the time she lived alone in the tent she was supposed to wear the robe both day and night. . . . When her time had expired and the doctor had given his consent the parents of the girl were accustomed to make a great feast and all the people in the village were invited to attend. When all were assembled the screen or the door of the tent was raised and the girl was seen sitting with her back to the guests dressed in the garb above referred to. This was removed by a woman authorized by the doctor to do this work and as soon as this sign of her degradation had disappeared the girl commenced to sing and dance before all the people present the songs and dances that she had been previously taught for this occasion. . . . After the feasting and congratulatory speeches were ended the rest of the night was spent in dancing. This custom has completely died away with the death of the last *Sa-ag-ga* [shaman].[2] [Charles Harrison, November 25, 1912]

During her seclusion a girl was visited exclusively by her female relatives—older sisters, mother, grandmother, and, perhaps most important, father's sisters (*sqaʔanləng*). From the latter she received formal instruction in womanly behavior: how to behave toward one's husband, how to rear children properly, standards of etiquette. Appropriate female behavior included submission, contentment, and industry (Dawson 1880:130B), endurance, modesty, a retiring disposition, and moderation in eating and drinking (Curtis 1916:126). Instruction and the various taboos enjoined upon the girl were designed to elicit these qualities.[3]

Childhood was both actually and symbolically terminated by the

2. Dawson (1880:131B) notes that the "coming out," described here by Harrison as involving a ceremony to which the entire village was invited, was a Tsimshian custom. He adds, "Similar customs probably exist among the Haidas, though I did not learn any details concerning them." Harrison, in his writings on the Haida, occasionally summarizes, or takes directly, passages from Dawson. I believe Dawson to be the source of Harrison's comment on the coming-out celebration, particularly as such a ceremony is not reported elsewhere in the Haida literature or mentioned by modern informants. I do not, however, believe that this ethnographic laxity on Harrison's part should be taken as a general indictment of Harrison's Haida material. Charles Harrison spent some twenty years among the Masset Haida, spoke the language fluently, and observed and recorded many aspects of traditional Haida culture.

3. Taboos and prescriptions included the following: no talking or laughing; no use of the regular house entrance; no looking at the house fire or the sea; no eating of fresh fish, seaweed, or shellfish; no contact with the hunting/fishing/gambling equipment of male household members; fasting and abstaining from drinking water (see Swanton 1909:49–50).

surrender of childhood toys and trinkets to the father's sisters during the period of seclusion (Murdock 1934b:250). At the end of her seclusion the girl's transition to womanhood was given public acknowledgment, as noted by Harrison above. Florence Davidson reported only that a small potlatch was given by the young woman's mother to women of the opposite moiety, particularly, and sometimes exclusively, to the young woman's father's sisters.

With menarche, the Haida female acquired a significant, if negative, power. Menstrual blood was considered extremely polluting. It could detrimentally affect shamanic powers, hunting and fishing equipment, the abundance of certain food resources, and a man's economic powers or his luck at gambling. Hunting, fishing, and gambling paraphernalia were kept outside a house in which a menstruating woman dwelled, and during her periods a woman was forbidden to walk in front of a man or step over salmon spawning creeks. Florence Davidson summed up Haida conceptions of this female power by remarking, "Once women change their life, they [men] are scared of them." She added, however, that a woman would not consider purposefully using this power against a man, though such uses of polluting power have been reported from a few other cultures (for example, see Strathern 1972: 255 for New Guinea).

Marriage usually followed shortly after the *təgwəná* seclusion. Murdock (1934a:359), Swanton (1909:50), and Harrison (November 25, 1912) credited a girl's mother with playing a decisive role in her marriage; according to Murdock, she arranged the marriage. Harrison contends that a young man took the initiative in selecting a prospective bride, but adds that the girl's mother had to approve. Though Murdock (1934b:251) notes that the wishes of the young couple received consideration in marriage arrangements, Florence Davidson's personal experience suggests that a young girl could not override the wishes of her elders. Also in Florence Davidson's case, somewhat contrary to the ethnographic accounts, marriage negotiations were between her husband-to-be (and his group) on the one hand, and her father and, ultimately, her maternal uncle, on the other.[4] According to Florence, traditionally as well as more recently, "the girl's uncle decided who she married. As long as your

4. In this case, Florence's maternal uncle was deferred to not only for traditional reasons but because, as an acculturated, enfranchised native knowledgeable in the ways of whites, it was hoped he could effect an accommodation of Haida tradition to white marriage practices.

uncle thinks it's all right, they all agree with him." The traditional marriage ritual that followed the negotiations is described in some detail by Swanton (1909:50–51).

Beyond the prescriptions of moiety and lineage exogamy, bilateral cross-cousin marriage was preferred: a girl would marry a real or classificatory father's sister's son or mother's brother's son.[5] Some pairs of Haida lineages reveal long histories of these preferred intermarriages. Several examples can be seen in Florence's genealogy. Residence after marriage was initially with the bride's parents because of the requirement of bride service; following that, residence was avunculocal, that is, with the husband's maternal uncle. In the event that the preferred pattern of cross-cousin marriage was followed, a girl would likely remain in her natal home for the duration of her marriage.

Polygyny was practiced but, according to all accounts, was not very common. Dawson, writing in 1878, noted that "[polygyny] was formerly more usual, but was always mainly or entirely confined to recognized chiefs. I could hear of but a single instance in which a man yet has two wives. . . . Three or four wives were not uncommon with a chief in former days . . ." (Dawson 1880:130B). There are no ethnographic data on the relationship between co-wives. Florence Davidson reports, however, that her "grandfather," Albert Edward Edenshaw, had two wives, the elder of whom was the mother's sister of the younger (see genealogy). His first wife encouraged him to take her sister's daughter as a second wife. The relationship between these two women was evidently quite harmonious.

According to Curtis (1916:121), most marriages were of relatively short duration. The separation of spouses (Curtis mentions only husband leaving wife) was common, and if a man simply left his wife, there was no redress. If a man mistreated his wife or abandoned her for another woman, however, he was held liable to her parents (in particular to her mother; see below). If a woman

5. Regular practice of bilateral cross-cousin marriage over the generations results in the genealogical merging of these two kin types; that is, father's sister's son is also mother's brother's son. In their description of Haida social structure, Rosman and Rubel distinguish between the marriages of chiefs and others, noting that the general preference was for marriage to father's sister's daughter and that the possibility of mother's brother's daughter marriage "appears to be restricted only to chiefs" (1971:39–40). My data do not suggest such strictly limited mother's brother's daughter marriage.

committed adultery, neither she nor her lover were accountable to her husband, though the latter might seek revenge. Rather, the lover was accountable to the woman's mother. Adultery was grounds for divorce among the Haida.

Large families were desired and it was expected that a woman would become pregnant within a few months following marriage. Florence Davidson noted that the inability to conceive was invariably blamed on the woman. When pregnant, a woman continued her routine daily activities, modified only by the observance of a number of taboos, almost all of which were designed to protect the developing fetus and assure an easy delivery. For the same reasons, the child's father and other household members were also subject to certain restrictions.[6] Parturition, according to Murdock (1934b:248), took place within the house, but according to Florence Davidson, women traditionally gave birth outside the house in a small hut specially constructed for the occasion. She noted, "They used to say they have the baby outside, not in the house because they have respect for their house keeping clean."[7] The afterbirth, soiled bedding, and clothing were later burned, and the mother remained in relative seclusion for ten days (Murdock 1934b:249).

Within the household, Murdock reports (1934b:252), a husband exerted but mild authority over his wife, which he was ashamed to show in the presence of others. Harrison, on the other hand, saw male authority as more decisive:

> The father was beyond any question master in his own house. To the mother belonged a peculiar domestic importance but both she and her children always obeyed the will of the actual lord of the household. The father was a master without being a tyrant; the mother was a subject without being a slave; and the children did not act in opposition to their parents' wishes. . . . [August 19, 1912]

6. Swanton gives examples of the "many things which a pregnant woman was not permitted to look at, and [the] many things which she must not eat" (1909:47). Taboos upon other household members included not playing with bows and arrows in the house (to avoid putting out the fetus' eyes). A pregnant woman's husband was enjoined from trifling talk with other women he was in love with, lest his wife should die. Florence Davidson adds that if the pregnant woman's husband slept with other women, the baby, out of jealousy, would refuse to be born.

7. That is, childbirth is polluting. The house is kept ritually clean by removing parturient women.

Harrison does not expound on a woman's "peculiar domestic importance," and the other ethnographic accounts offer no clues. Regarding the status of wives, Dawson, more in line with Murdock, notes that "the women appear to be well-treated on the whole, are by no means looked upon as mere servants, and have a voice in most matters in which the men engage" (1880:130B).

In her narrative, Florence Davidson remarks that a woman should have respect for her husband and look up to the men of the community as the leaders of the people. With age, however, appeared to come a measure of authority for a woman. A mother-in-law, for example, exerted some influence over her son-in-law who was expected not only to provide her and her husband with food but was required to pay her a considerable amount of property should he commit adultery. A woman could exact a similar property settlement from the suitor of her adulterous daughter (Swanton 1909:51). Following menopause, which apparently had none of the negative connotations it has in Euro-American society, a woman had access to cultural domains that were previously endangered by her menstrual periods (see sections, "Economics and the Division of Labor" and "Cultural Specialists," below). There was no Haida term specifically denoting the physiological experience of menopause; it was simply noted that when a woman reached a certain point in life, she ceased becoming pregnant. Florence observed that women who had had many children experienced no physical difficulties with menopause.

A married woman could hold property independently of her husband (Swanton 1909:54; Murdock 1934a:371) and a woman often received property from her parents as endowerment for her marriage. At her death her property was passed on to a daughter. Though a woman might continue to reside in her natal home following her marriage, the house itself and its name were con-sidered male property; this had a critical effect upon the status of those widows who did not remarry.

Both the levirate (marriage to deceased husband's brother) and the sororate (marriage to deceased wife's sister) were traditionally practiced by the Haida. A man, however, had considerably more freedom in remarrying than a woman. A widower was required to give the mortuary potlatch for his deceased wife, and until he did so, he was beholden to his wife's family. It was preferred that a deceased woman's sister "take her chair" (the sororate) and her family would try to hold onto a man who had married into their lineage. Once a widower had given the mortuary potlatch, however, he was technically free to do as he pleased. A widow, on the other hand, was expected to marry a man of her husband's lineage, either a younger brother or a nephew. Late nineteenth-century church records and the recollections of Masset Haida indicate that the spouse was often quite junior to the widow. Florence's "grandmother," widow of Albert Edenshaw, is a case in point: two years following Edenshaw's death in 1894, she was married to one of her husband's nephews (Phillip White), who at age twenty-four was some twenty years younger than she. Although an older widow exerted considerable influence over her young husband, who "was just like a slave to his uncle's wife," she had little or no voice in the selection of her new husband. Florence Davidson recounted one such levirate marriage which dates from the mid-nineteenth century:

> *Taianat* married an old, old lady, his uncle's wife. He was about ten or eleven and was out playing while they prepared for the wedding. His mother called him home, washed the mud off his feet, and put a shirt on him. "You're going to stay with that old lady, your uncle's wife." But he didn't understand. His mother took him inside to the top step [of the housepit] and sat him beside the old woman on a pillow. All the food—smoked dog salmon soaked in salt water—was served. "Eat, dear, eat," the old lady said to him, but he didn't want to eat. "I wonder why that old thing said that to me," he asked. "Look at all my granddaughters, those pretty girls. I'll die quick and you'll marry one of them." He looked at the girls and he hated them. The old lady was supposed to let her new husband sleep by her, but he didn't want it. Maybe when it started to get cold out he started sleeping by the old woman.

The levirate was really the only security a widowed woman had, for a widow who did not remarry was often left destitute. She was not allowed to stay in her former husband's home, and, if lucky, she escaped with a few personal belongings when her husband's heir took over the house and its property. Masset people cited several instances when widows hurriedly left their former husbands' houses and, with their children, sought sanctuary in the homes of matrilineal relatives. These women were pitied and high-ranking people were instructed to be kind to them and offer them food. Widowers, as noted above, did not suffer a symmetrical fate.

Mourning rituals were identical for widow or widower (Murdock 1934a:373). The grieving spouse remained isolated for a period of time and ate very little because, in Florence Davidson's words, "if they think nothing of it [death], there's no luck. You have to deny yourself." Mortuary potlatches were given for both men and women of high rank.

ECONOMICS AND THE DIVISION OF LABOR

Although some economic activities, such as collecting shellfish and cooking, were performed by both males and females, in general the Haida division of labor was marked. Men might beachcomb during the winter following onshore storms to collect clams and cockles that had washed ashore, but clam digging and the implement of procurement, the *gl*ɨ*gú* (digging stick), were considered part of a woman's domain. The sexual division of labor was summed up for me by one elderly Masset man who offered the following comment on the essential property of a newly married couple: "Every man's got to have his fishing line and devilfish stick and every woman her digging stick."

The gathering of plant resources was women's and girls' work; young boys did not normally accompany their mothers on such expeditions. What little gathering men did complemented that of the women. Both sexes, for example, collected spruce roots, but women dug the small delicate roots for hat and basket weaving, and men the large roots from which they made fish traps and snares. Similarly, both men and women collected cedar bark, but women sought the inner bark for weaving mats, and men the large sheets of outer bark for roofing.

Women's abstention from certain economic activities seems to have been rationalized and prohibited on the basis of pollution taboos associated with menstruation and reproduction (see, for example, Swanton 1909:219). Fishing lines and hooks, sea mammal clubs, bows, arrows, and any other items of subsistence technology used by males were kept outside the house, concealed from the view of female household members. Menstruating women were believed to have supernatural visual powers capable of causing considerable damage. Were a menstruating woman to see a man's fishing or hunting equipment, all of his economic endeavors would be doomed. If a woman were to attempt to hunt or fish herself, her efforts would go similarly unrewarded. For this reason, the Haida say, women never fished or hunted. Nor did women collect octopuses, comestible shellfish but more commonly used as halibut bait. Were a woman to catch an octopus near its rocky den, all octopuses would permanently abandon the site.

Male economic activities could be further influenced by domestic activities. Baby tending, for example, was fraught with potential ruination of male economic prowess. A man might play with his small children, but his handling of a soiled or wet baby would diminish his luck at hunting or fishing, perhaps spelling economic disaster for the entire household. To assure the ritual purity of male members of the household, men's clothing was washed separately from that of women and children. Ritual cleanliness brought economic rewards, for "those who were 'clean' were blessed with food and riches," according to Florence Davidson. Men could negatively affect their own economic endeavors by having extramarital affairs or by leaving their wives. A man who did so would lose his luck at hunting or fishing. Ritual purity and consequent economic "luck" were also acquired or enhanced by drinking medicine,[8] a male prerogative. Women, too, drank medicine, but only to cure sickness, not for "luck."

The sexual division of labor in trading is not clear. Swanton (1909) and Curtis (1916) make no mention of women in trading; Murdock (1934b:377), in his brief discussion of trading partnerships, implies that the parties are male but does not discuss trade more generally. Early maritime traders' accounts from the late eighteenth century, however, suggest that Haida women played a significant and authoritative role in trading activities at the time of first contact. In his journals of 1790–92, Joseph Ingraham, for example, offers the following comment:

> Here in direct opposition to most other parts of the world, the women maintain a precedency to the men in every point insomuch as a man dares not trade without the concurrence of his wife. Nay, I have often been witness to men being abused by their wives for parting with skins before their approbation was obtained. [Ingraham 1971:132]

The men of the ship *Columbia Rediviva* similarly remarked on the ascendant role of Haida women in trade:

> The women in trade, as well as in everything else which came within our knowledge, appeared to govern the men; as no one dared to conclude a bargain without first asking his wife's consent; if he did, the moment he went into his canoe he was sure to get a beating . . . and there is no mercy to be expected without the intercession of some kind female. [Howay 1941:208]

Howay adds in a footnote that "all witnesses agree on this" (1941:208). On the basis of the above and similar evidence from the late eighteenth century, it seems quite possible that women played a significant role in trading, particularly as they could hold property independently of their husbands. Given the acknowledged role of

8. Florence could not specify the type of "medicine" drunk.

men as traders, however, it may be that they represented their wives in exchange and that the dominant role of women reflects the latter's interest in their own property.

Dawson downplayed the general economic contribution of Haida women, noting that ". . . the women do not contribute materially to the support of the family, attending only to the accessory duties of curing and preserving the fish . . ." (1880:130B). Swanton suggests the symbolic importance of woman's freedom from economic activities in the following remark: "A young, unmarried woman was not allowed to do much work, and lay in bed a great deal of the time. This was so that she might marry a chief, and always have little work to do" (1909:50). From Florence Davidson's comments it seems unlikely that even a high-ranking woman would actually have little work to do. Though she might have slaves to gather firewood and assist in the processing of fish and other foods, the desire for prestige and the ambition characteristic of the Haida spurred all toward the accumulation of wealth and surplus resources. Florence's remark that "we try all our best for our children" applies equally to the aboriginal Haida whose paramount concern was securing a place for their children in the social order. Neither is Dawson's comment that women do not contribute materially to the support of the family an accurate assessment of the economic position of Haida women. The ability of a woman to process foods, particularly fish, was of considerable concern to all. A woman adept at slicing and drying fish was greatly admired for her skills. Furthermore, the limitations on the quantity of salmon a household could garner for winter stores was dependent not upon the number of fish that men could catch but on the number that women could practicably clean, slice, and dry. Thus female skills were critical to the ability of a household to provision itself and to lay aside a surplus for feasting and pot-latching.

Ceremonial Division of Labor

Men and women also filled complementary roles in ceremonialism. Both sexes hosted potlatches, though the house-building (*watəł*) and mortuary (*sik'*) potlatches were normally sponsored by males,[9] and the *təgwəná* (female puberty potlatch) was an exclusively female

9. Murdock (1936:12) argues that a woman (the wife of the new house owner) was the actual host of the *watəł* potlatch. Rosman and Rubel (1971:57–64), following Swanton (1909), present a convincing argument that the man was the potlatch host. I have suggested elsewhere that while

event. Either a man or a woman might give a vengeance (*gədáng*) or face-saving (*ʦənsəngáda*) potlatch, as these were precipitated by some impertinence shown the individual or some embarrassment suffered, regardless of sex.

Both men and women were recipients of potlatch wealth and, as children at their father's potlatches, received equal attention in the form of tattoos and honorific names. A woman might be selected to perform ceremonial labor at a potlatch, such as the preparation of new house timbers. Though her husband actually performed the work in her stead, she would receive the payment for the service (Murdock 1936:5).

Potlatches were the only occasions when high-ranking individuals were initiated into the dancing societies, which were attenuated versions of Northern Kwakiutl dances acquired from the Tsimshian in the eighteenth century (see Swanton 1909:156–76). Depending on the source consulted, the Haida had between six and eleven such dances. Curtis (1916:142) noted that "women were barred from the more important dances," and Swanton's catalogue of dances by the sex of the performers (1909:161) concurs with Curtis' generalization.

Murdock describes several other dances that punctuated potlatch celebrations but in these the sexual division was not so marked, though in one dance (*sα'adal*) only the men carried rattles (1936:4). Dawson adds, however, that "the women occupy a prominent place in this dance, being carefully dressed with the little marks [?] and *nax-in* [Chilkat blankets] . . . previously described" (1880:128B). Women could wear the chief's headdress, or *amalahait*, a frontlet bearing a carved crest figure, encircled with sea lion whiskers (containing eagle down), and trailing numerous ermine pelts. The *amalahait* and Chilkat blanket were worn in the dance performed by high-ranking men and women as a welcome to visitors. This dance was still being performed when Florence Davidson was a child.

Women's traditional roles in feasting are not clear. Murdock (1934a:364–65) cites evidence indicating that women not only attended but hosted feasts at which males were present. Swanton's description of the *sik'* potlatch implies that both males and females were guests at Haida feasts (1909:176–80), and Charles Harrison's accounts from 1911 to 1913 indicate the same. Florence Davidson, on

---

the male role may receive the most emphasis, the *waɬɬ* may be interpreted as hosted by a man and his wife (Blackman 1977:45). It is worth mentioning, however, that even Murdock (1936:19) notes that a woman could not hold a *waɬɬ* for her children by herself.

the other hand, stated that, prior to her time, only the men used to
attend and host feasts and that attendance at feasts by couples is a
relatively recent practice inaugurated during her early childhood.
The attendance of feasts by couples also points to the breakdown of
moiety organization, for traditionally one only feasted members of
the opposite moiety. Regardless of the discrepancy in these
accounts, it is clear that the participation of women in feasting
increased dramatically in the twentieth century.[10]

The most important ceremonial role a woman played was as a
sqaʔan, a father's sister (or, more generally, a female of father's
lineage). This role was not matched by any comparable male ritual
role. The *sqaʔan* was a focal person in the lives of her brother's
children from the moment of their birth to their placement in the
grave. She cut the umbilical cord, was the ritual if not actual tattooer
of the children, tended to her brother's daughters during their
puberty seclusion and witnessed their emergence into womanhood.
Regardless of whether her brother's son married her own daughter,
she was present at the marriage to usher the bride to her nephew's
side, and, according to Murdock (1934b:364), she gave the wedding
feast. Her own name might eventually be passed on to her brother's
son's daughter. A *sqaʔan* tended her brother's children when they
were ill and fulfilled her final ritual duty in the life cycle of a
brother's child by preparing the body at death and keeping a
mourning vigil for four days. Today the modern legacy of this final
ritual act is realized when the deceased's *sqaʔan* washes off the
headstone before it is placed on the grave.

Cultural Specialists

Positions of household and external authority—house, lineage, and
town chieftainships—were regarded as male positions, though
aboriginal examples of women chiefs are not unknown. Curtis, for
example, recounting a legendary war between the west coast and
southernmost Haida, notes that the chief of the Do-hade, or West
Coast, people was a "great fat woman" (1916:172). The assumption
of chieftainships by women became more common in late post-
contact times. Dawson, in this regard, notes that "only recently and
because of the depletion of the population have women succeeded
to the seats of nobility" (1880:118B). Florence Davidson concurred,
noting that women assumed chieftainships only when there were no

10. Susan Kenyon notes that the same has happened in the Westcoast
(Nootka) community of Kyuquot (personal communication).

male heirs. Masset people recalled one instance from the late nineteenth century when a woman assumed a lineage chieftainship only because there was no male to take the position; when her own son became an adult, the position was passed on to him. Harrison reports a potlatch given at the raising of the last totem pole in Masset, which stood before the house of a woman chief named Kitkune (see genealogy): "Thousands of dollars worth of blankets, crockery, guns, bracelets, coins and goods of all descriptions were given to testify to the fact that this woman was indeed a great, wealthy, and important chieftess" (September 9, 1912). Traditionally, not only would the position have been occupied by a man, but the potlatch would have been hosted by a male. Women did, however, regularly participate in lineage councils in aboriginal times (Murdock 1936:17), and accordingly had a voice in the selection of successors to lineage and town chieftainships. Unfortunately, these powers are not detailed in the ethnographic literature.

Harrison notes a special role filled only by old women who were paid mourners at funerals.

> These were generally the witches of the tribe that did this work and also assisted the devil doctor at births in his search to locate definitely what ancestor's soul had taken possession of the newly born child's body. These old women acted the part of *accouchers* [sic] at births and washed and dressed the corpses for burial and consequently were looked upon with great respect. [December 2, 1912]

Though Harrison mentions only old women as shamanic assistants in the above account, shamanism was a specialty open to both Haida males and females. Most ethnographic accounts, however, imply that practitioners were, as a rule, males, and one might suspect that unless past menopause a female shaman would be at a certain disadvantage. As Curtis remarks: "Females except old women and girls under the age of puberty were barred from the house in which a shaman was at work lest someone in her periods blight his power" (1916:137). The literature, however, does not indicate that female shamans must be past the climacteric, nor is there any reason to believe that female shamanic powers were in any way diminished from those of males. Florence Davidson, in fact, recalled a woman shaman from her childhood who commanded the respect of the village because she had predicted World War I long before its occurrence.

In aesthetic specialties there were marked male/female differences. What is normally regarded as Haida "art" was traditionally a masculine art. The painting or carving of mythological or crest figures were male prerogatives. This division of aesthetic labor serves to explain why women assigned the ritual task of tattooing a brother's child delegated the task to a male (see Murdock 1936:8; Curtis 1916:125): tattoos were crest art.

Women's art, by contrast, was geometric, confined to the decorative weaving of spruce roots and cedar bark. It derived from natural forms (the "snail's track," for example, was a common hat brim pattern), not from mythological or sociological sources. Zoomorphic and anthropomorphic crest designs were not a woman's domain, and this division of aesthetic labor has persisted well into the twentieth century. Button blankets, for instance, were and are designed by men, though cut and appliquéd by women. Under unusual circumstances a woman might paint crest and other male designs. Florence's mother, Isabella, for example, painted designs on the spruce root hats she wove after her artist husband's death, and Florence herself designed and painted the prow of a canoe built by her husband and his brother in the 1930s. As noted in her narrative (chap. 9), however, she felt uncomfortable in the role of artist: "I just painted once, on that big canoe. I never tried to carve; I thought it was meant to be for men. No women carved or painted during my time; they were all weaving."

CULTURAL VALUES

Haida women were valued as perpetuators of the lineage and it was anticipated that a woman would bear many children (ten, a ritually significant number, was mentioned as an ideal by Florence Davidson). The reproductive power a woman possessed was natural, not cultural (Rosaldo 1974:30). Women had life-giving (bearing children) or death-bringing (causing the death of a husband in warfare) powers because of their physiological functions; these powers developed as they matured but could not be actively sought. Men, on the other hand, had culturally bestowed powers, acquired through observing prescriptions (drinking medicine, following certain hunting rules) and proscriptions (avoiding female powers). Female power was serendipitous in effect, controlled and confined by observance of taboos, but not manipulated to effect results.

The marked pollution taboos that colored relationships between males and females may have been in part rationalized on the grounds that Haida women were believed to be the sexual aggressors. In this regard, James Deans emphatically states that "their women considered it their duty to encourage at all times sexual intercourse" (1891:23). Unfortunately, other early Haida ethnographers are silent on the details of sexual behavior.[11] Florence Davidson's account suggests only that young women may have been relatively ignorant of sex; if sexual aggressiveness was characteristic of traditional Haida women, it must have developed after some years of postmarital sexual experience. Assuming Deans is correct in his statement, the taboos enjoined upon women could have served to contain and confine potentially disruptive female sexual aggressiveness.[12]

In other respects, however, women were regarded as far from aggressive. As previously noted, among the desirable qualities inculcated in young females were modesty and a retiring disposition. Harrison's admiration for the physical strength of Haida women notwithstanding (see epigraph to chap. 2), women were regarded as the weaker sex both mentally and physically. "If women want to do anything, they [men] thought they can't do it," Florence Davidson explained in regard to the competence of women.

But there was room for individual variation from this norm. Coming from a family with a dearth of males, Florence was instructed by her father and her mother's brother: "Don't be hopeless, like a girl." Perhaps because she heeded their advice, Florence Davidson became the very strong and respected woman that she is today.

CULTURE CONTACT AND SEX ROLES

Contact with Euro-Canadian and American culture wrought both subtle and profound changes in traditional Haida sex roles. These changes were not necessarily uniform; the status of women was differentially affected by the various agents, events, and processes of culture change. The early maritime trade of the late eighteenth century and the subsequent Hudson's Bay Company-dominated trade, the contact culture experienced in Victoria, wage labor, the dramatic population decline of the 1860s and 1870s, missionization, and the Indian Act, all contributed in varying ways to reshaping the role of Haida women.

11. Murdock does discuss "semi-sanctioned" extra-marital sexual relationships and sanctioned premarital relationships (1934a:364, 375–76). The latter contrasts with Florence Davidson's discussion of the protection of adolescent females.

12. Wanton female sexuality is a rationalization in a number of cultures for the avoidance and control of females by males.

Maritime Trade, 1785–1825

Maritime trader accounts cited earlier stressed the preeminent role of Haida women in trading. Other features of this early trade with Euro-Americans, however, point to the clearcut dominance of native males in the trading economy of the late eighteenth and early nineteenth centuries. First, the trade was based on the exchange of sea otter furs. While the processing of these furs was a female task, the hunting of sea otter was a prestigious and ritually imbued activity of high-ranking males. So also were the formalities of trading. One has only to consider the intensity and magnitude of the trade to see how significantly it loomed in the lives of the Haida, particularly Haida males. Wike (1951:10) estimates that during about a twenty-five-year period, American traders (the most active in the trade) acquired 350,000 otter pelts from the natives along the coast, the bulk of which came from Haida and Westcoast (Nootka) territories. In return the natives received some seven million dollars worth of goods. As the foreign demand for otter pelts grew, the Haida diverted increasing amounts of energy from other activities into hunting, processing, and trading sea otter furs. This demand probably affected males more than females as the former were both the hunters and the primary traders.

The variety of goods introduced to the natives likewise suggests a male emphasis in the trading economy. Though flour, cloth, kettles and other utensils, and decorative items, such as Chinese coins, mirrors, and thimbles, could be counted as women's goods, the staple items of the trade—iron tools and guns—were male goods. In sum, the maritime trade might be viewed from an economic perspective as having stimulated male domains of Haida culture, though not necessarily at the expense of female domains.

In another respect, however, the maritime trade may have contributed to the degradation of Haida and other Northwest Coast women. Women were offered to white traders, perhaps as part of the ritual exchange between the trading parties. Spanish explorer Jacinto Caamaño, for example, noted in 1792 that "the natives were greatly surprised at our abstaining from any commerce with their women, whom they brought with them, so we understood, for that purpose, since they are accustomed to the English and others who trade in these parts, not only accepting, but also demanding, and choosing them" (Wagner and Newcombe 1938:207).

Caamaño's remark is verified by another account, from the ship *Eliza*. Describing events at the village of Kiusta in the northwest corner of the Queen Charlotte Islands, the log keeper relates: "The old woman proceeded to the last offer of friendship, which was a lady for the night, out of her numerous seraglio, with which she accommodates all vessells (sic) that stop here" (cited in Duff n.d.). Caamaño's account suggests that women offered by trading chiefs were not of high rank but were perhaps slaves. Anchored at the village of Dadens on North Island in 1792, he reports that he was offered the chief's daughter "so that I might enjoy her." It seems doubtful that the girl in question was the chief's daughter as Caamaño adds, "She had no tablet [labret] in in her lower lip and was quite pleasing in appearance" (Wagner and Newcombe 1938:207). The social status of women mentioned in other accounts is not clear.

The negative effects of late eighteenth- and early nineteenth-century prostitution are pointedly noted by Jonathan Green, a Methodist missionary who visited the Queen Charlottes and southeastern Alaska in 1829, just after the decline of the sea otter trade. Green remarks that he learned from a Kaigani (Alaskan) Haida chief "that all the young women of the [Kaigani] tribe visit ships for the purpose of gain by prostitution, and in most cases destroy their children, the fruit of this infamous intercourse" (1915:68).

After the turn of the nineteenth century the economic position of Haida women was likely affected by the addition of the potato to the native economy. Introduced by traders in the late eighteenth century, the potato was intensively cultivated by Queen Charlotte Haida women, and by the 1840s several hundred bushels were being traded annually to the Tsimshian and the Hudson's Bay Company at Fort Simpson (Dunn 1846:41). The potato trade for the Haida was relatively short-lived, however, when after 1850 potato cultivation was undertaken by Hudson's Bay Company employees at Fort Simpson.

The Contact Culture in Mid-century Victoria

By the late 1850s the Haida were increasingly frequenting Victoria where they traded at the Hudson's Bay Company post, availed themselves of a supply of illegal liquor from "whiskey traders," traded and feuded with local as well as other northern native groups, and found themselves entangled in scuffles with the law. Along with groups of Tlingit and Tsimshian, as many as several hundred Haida wintered over in Victoria encamped in the vicinity of the Hudson's Bay Company post. These migrations must have disrupted winter village life as large numbers of natives, normally resident in winter settlements on the Queen Charlottes, now opted for a winter of urban squatting. Though ceremonial patterns that were part of village life may have carried over to the urban camps, there is no reporting of Haida ceremonial activities in the local Victoria newspaper, the *British Colonist*.

The white populace of Victoria became increasingly concerned with the large encampments of natives on the edge of town and various attempts were made to confine and curtail native activities. Many northern native women, however, spent much of their time within the town limits where they staffed the "dance halls," or houses of prostitution. Unfortunately, little mention is made of prostitution in the newspapers, save the occasional arrest of a streetwalker. Francis Poole, a civil and mining engineer who explored the Queen Charlotte Islands during 1862–63, suggests that prostitution offered certain advantages to Haida women:

> Not only does no dishonour attach to that degrading practice, but if successful in making money, it is highly honoured. I remember one singular case of this. Some Queen Charlotte women went to spend the Winter at Victoria, hoping to "earn blankets." They came back loaded with blankets, trinkets, tobacco, whiskey, and other presents, which they proceeded to distribute among their people. . . . [Poole 1872:312–13]

Though evidently in some instances new economic wealth from prostitution allowed women to participate independently in potlatching, other writers of the time, such as Krause (1885:207) and Jackson (1880:118), paint a much grimmer picture, which emphasizes the exploitation of native women by both native and white men. Jackson, for example, describes the fate of Kaigani Haida and Tlingit women: "They are sometimes . . . sent to the mines, while the husband lives in idleness at home on the wages of their immorality." In the long run, the effects of prostitution were disastrous, for the tolls exacted in population costs far offset any immediate economic gains. Wilson Duff describes the general trend: "Venereal disease, a result of prevalent prostitution, killed many and rendered infertile many more" (1964:43).

Life in Victoria and large-scale prostitution came to an end in the years following the smallpox epidemic of 1862. Introduced by a miner from San Francisco, the disease had a devastating effect upon the vulnerable, unvaccinated natives but left the white population of the area virtually untouched. Florence Davidson's narrative touches on the personal tragedy of the smallpox epidemic.

The Population Decline and After

The population decline resulting from the smallpox epidemic was swift and dramatic in its proportions. By 1885 the Haida population was down to 13 percent of its former numbers (Duff 1964:39). This reduction had a significant effect upon the status of women, who, on the one hand, found their traditional roles of childbearing and rearing ever more critical as numerous lineages were threatened with extinction, while on the other hand, they began assuming positions of authority outside the domestic realm, taking up chieftainships when there were no male heirs to fill the positions. The ascendancy they may have enjoyed as chiefs, however, was short-lived. The combined effects of the Indian Act,[13] which allowed for a system of elected band councilors, the Indian Reserve Commission, which divided up lineage land holdings, and the missionaries, who persuaded several leading chiefs to forego potlatching, conspired to reduce the power and authority of the hereditary chiefs (see Blackman 1977 for discussion of these factors). Furthermore, as previously noted, a woman chief was regarded as an anomaly and every effort was made to transfer the position to a male.

The missionaries who arrived among the Haida in 1876 brought to the native culture a domestic structure which more accurately reflected that of the acculturating society. Heretofore, white women had not really been part of the contact culture, except perhaps peripherally in Victoria. But missionaries came to the native communities with wives and families. Though the culture and religion they brought were patriarchal, several of the changes they wrought among the Haida affected the status of native women positively. The missionary wife, for example, created a special interest group of Haida women. An auxiliary to the newly founded mission church, the "White Cross *jade* [women]" regularly met for Bible readings, hymn singing, sewing, and handiwork, put on basket socials to raise money for the church, tended to the dead, and assisted bereaved families. The group later evolved into the Women's Auxiliary of the Anglican Church (today the Anglican Church Women). The founding of this social group set up a communication network among community women which had not existed previously.

13. The Indian Act, originally enacted in 1876 and revised several times (most recently in 1951), is a sweeping piece of legislation outlining the

Masset in 1879 (photograph by O. C. Hastings, courtesy, Glenbow-Alberta Institute)

Ceremonial patterns were also greatly altered by the missionaries (see Blackman 1973, 1977). For example, the Anglican missionaries undercut the male emphasis present in feasting. They stressed commensality among men and women and set an example by inviting couples to the mission house to dine. Now in the 1980s, feasts are typically hosted by married couples. One missionary, J. H. Keen, attempted in the 1890s to break the pattern of feasting large numbers of guests by encouraging only small dinner parties. The feasting complex held sway, however, though superficially it came to resemble the Sunday mission-house dinners. By the end of the nineteenth century, feasts were given not only for traditional reasons (taking and keeping the chief's place, marriage, death), but also in celebration of Christian holidays. A significant material cultural change was a factor in the acculturation of feasting and in the increasingly important role women came to play in it. Traditional feasting utensils—carved spoons, grease bowls, and the larger carved feast bowls—were men's property, created by male artists and carvers for male patrons. These items were replaced in the latter part of the nineteenth century by bone china, silverware, and tablecloths, all women's property.

Cultural changes of the late nineteenth century also included the

Canadian government's responsibilities to and control over Canadian Indian bands.

expanded participation of women in the potlatching complex. This can be seen as the result of two seemingly opposing phenomena. On the one hand, the hosting of the potlatches by women is a logical consequence of their assumption of chieftainships, and is, therefore, traditional. On the other hand, women's more active roles in potlatching were a product of acculturation, possibly related to Anglican influences on the traditional mortuary potlatch and very definitely linked to changes in marriage patterns. I suspect that the active role women played in the church as fundraisers and sponsors of social events carried over to their assumption of more active roles in Anglicized mortuary potlatches as organizers, as speechmakers, and, eventually, as hosts. This was facilitated by the abolishment of the levirate and changes in inheritance patterns promoted by Reverend Charles Harrison, missionary at Masset in the early 1880s. Harrison recognized that traditional marriage practices discriminated against widows. As noted earlier, an unremarried widow was customarily forced to vacate her deceased husband's home and seek refuge in a house owned by her own lineage. Many of these widows were not only dependent but destitute. As a result of missionary efforts and, later, the application of the Indian Act, women were allowed a share of their husbands' estates. This, in turn, has provided the means for the participation of elderly women, such as Florence Davidson, in the ceremonial complex.

By no means did all missionary endeavors or all government decisions pertaining to the Haida improve the status of women. After all, agents of both the church and the government were male members of a male-dominant society. The Indian Act, as a product of that society, is a classic case in point. Several writers, most recently Kathleen Jamieson (1978), have pointed out that the Indian Act, particularly in its definition of band membership, is flagrantly biased against native women. It revokes band membership from native women marrying whites or non-status natives and denies band membership to the subsequently born offspring of these women. Simultaneously the Act confers band membership on white wives of male band members and on the offspring born of such marriages. The noticeable rise in premarital births among the Haida during the twentieth century (Stearns 1981) may be in part attributable to this sex discriminatory feature of the Indian Act. Having children out of wedlock has been an intentional strategy on the part of some Haida women whose mates are not band members.[14]

14. Mitchell (1976:383) suggests that the same strategy has been employed by Coast Salish women.

By not marrying, a woman can keep her band membership and enroll her children on the band list.

The changes that occurred in the female puberty potlatch (təgwəná) are illustrative of further negative effects of the infliction of Victorian values upon a native society. By the 1920s the puberty potlatch and its attendant seclusion had ceased. The former significance of this potlatch for Haida women is exemplified in the last large təgwəná given—for a girl who at age seventeen had not yet begun to menstruate. The girl's mother believed the rite of passage so important that she gave the potlatch anyway and, as if to compensate for what everyone knew had not occurred, invited men as well as women and distributed large quantities of property. When I asked her why the Haida discontinued the təgwəná, Florence Davidson replied, "They became ashamed of it." As in many other traditional cultures, menstruation, while dangerous and powerful, was not regarded as shameful by the Haida. In traditional Haida society, the monthly seclusions, the concealment of the hunting and fishing gear, the active avoidance of male possessions by menstruating women, and the təgwəná celebration were all public advertisements of femaleness. Menstruation was not cloaked in secrecy; rather, public knowledge of it was to everyone's advantage. The repression of these pollution taboos and the consequent repression of natural female power are reflective of the Haida adoption of Euro-Canadian values, the values of a Victorian and patriarchal society.

Missionary emphasis upon nuclear family units and the government's Indian Act affected the status of women by gradually eroding matrilineal descent. Although today matrilineal descent is still acknowledged to exist by the older generation and is traced for certain purposes, bilateral English kin terms prevail, lineage exogamy is no longer practiced, and most younger people do not know their lineage membership. Moiety affiliation is generally known and functions on ceremonial occasions, though moiety exogamy has also broken down. Application of the Indian Act early in the twentieth century furthered this trend by altering traditional patterns of matrilineal inheritance and wresting traditional authority from the lineage and placing it in the hands of an elected group of band councilors. With the undercutting of lineage authority, women lost the formal input they once had into the political realm of lineage councils. Elected band councilors have almost invariably been male, resulting, I suspect, in a considerable decline of female input into community and band politics. In the ceremonial realm, however, the input of older women is still considerable, as they play an active role in the planning and execution of feasts and potlatches. Florence Davidson's role in the pre-potlatch meetings for Oliver Adams' installation as town chief is exemplary of this function of older women (see chap. 9).

Florence Davidson's narrative suggests that during the twentieth century women have become more domestically isolated than traditionally. Though the Haida population was still quite mobile in the early years of Florence's marriage as evidenced in the fact that people left the village to work in mainland canneries, camped with families at North Island, or traveled upriver for salmon, Florence lamented that having a large family often kept her tied to the house. She had no time for clam digging, for example, and viewed as a holiday the opportunity to leave the house for a few hours to help with the hard work of preparing a feast. With decreasing reliance on native foods, women became more homebound, and expeditions to collect seaweed, chitons, wild rhubarb, and other foods became luxuries, not necessities.

Traditional ideas about the domestic division of labor were not all that incongruous with the division of labor in white society. Nonetheless, Indian agent and missionary families provided new role models for male/female relationships. That white ideals were absorbed, at least by some Haida, fairly early in the twentieth century is indicated in the following speech Florence's uncle, Henry Edenshaw, gave at the wedding of his eldest daughter in 1913:

> . . . I have done my utmost to act in my family as a White man, and my children, when of a suitable age, have been sent to the White children's school to finish their education. . . . The ideals concerning excellence in men and women's character have always risen or fallen together. . . . it has often been assumed that next to the Christian religion, humanity has no other so precious inheritance as Shakespeare's divine gallery of womanhood which I hope my daughter, now Mrs. Nash, will inspire and follow. The books that I have read teach me that during the past fifty years the ideals of womanly excellence and of marriage have risen, and that the practical observance of those ideals by men has risen and is likely to rise.

Perhaps more a reflection of the changing status of Haida art than of the changing status of Haida women are the inroads females have made into the once exclusively male visual arts. Paralleling, but not necessarily caused by, the evolution of Haida art from ceremonial to commercial, has been the emergence of women argillite, wood, and silver carvers and graphics artists. In 1977, following a meeting of Haida artists at Florence Davidson's home, I wondered though just how much women's roles had changed when I found myself together with a woman artist in the kitchen doing the dishes and discussing the maternal themes prevalent in her art.

THE STATUS OF HAIDA WOMEN: A SUMMARY

A common theme running through the analysis of matrilineal societies is that women enjoy, if not external authority, culturally favorable status simply by virtue of the fact that descent is traced through females who are seen as the focus of the entire social structure (Martin and Voorhies 1975:224–25). Quinn's review of the data (1977:211–14), on the contrary, brings together evidence that the status of women in matrilineal societies is a function of several variables, among them residence patterns, the organization of the domestic group, and the division of domestic authority. In the case of the Haida, the decision-making powers women had in lineage councils, their property-holding rights, and the potential for female succession to chieftainships can all be related to an ideology of matrilineal descent. Other variables which suggest a lowering of female status (personality attributes, physical and mental inferiority to men, pollution taboos) can perhaps be seen as indirect consequences of the status benefits of matrilineal descent. In this respect, Quinn remarks that "male dominance myths, far from reflecting women's overall low status, arise precisely because women have considerable economic importance, personal autonomy, and domestic influence" (1977:219).

In her review of the anthropological literature dealing with women's status, Quinn has pointed out, furthermore, that the status of women may vary within a culture, being relatively high in some cultural domains and low in others. It may also fluctuate throughout the life cycle. For the Haida female, status was perhaps lowest at the time of marriage and during the early childbearing years when she was a member of an extended family household under the authority of both older men and women. The status of a Haida woman was highest when she occupied a specialist role such as shaman; when she contributed property to and participated in her husband's potlatches or hosted other types of potlatches on her own; when she performed ritual acts as a father's sister (*sqaʔan*); and when, as a widow, she remarried her husband's nephew over whom she had virtually complete control. Though aboriginal Haida women occupied a relatively high overall status as demonstrated in their access to numerous domains of the culture, Haida society was still a male dominated one. Men were the final authorities of the household and the holders of positions of political authority. They alone were the hosts of the most important types of potlatches, the owners of the most important property (houses and totem poles), the performers of the most prestigious rituals (dances), the creators and monopolizers of an art form whose symbols represented the matrilineal groups they dominated.

Acculturation both enhanced and undermined the status of women. Their position was strengthened at times when new economic opportunities were opened to them (potato cultivation and, later, perhaps prostitution) and when certain changes were effected in the social order (the creation of a women's interest group under missionization and changes in marriage practices). Demographic changes facilitated the entry of women into positions that were formerly male prerogatives, and women's greater leadership roles in potlatching and feasting derived in part from those same changes. The increasingly active role of women in the ceremonial complex was also encouraged by material changes, which (1) gave women the means (through the inheritance of husbands' estates) with which to host potlatches and feasts, and (2) identified the symbols of feasting as women's property.

The status of women was detrimentally affected by other acculturative processes. The Indian Act, a product of a patriarchal Victorian society, undermined traditional hereditary authority and effectively placed all decision-making in the hands of an elected male council. Criteria for Indian band membership, defined by the Act, made women's legal status much less secure (Mitchell 1976:172). The same acculturative philosophy that created the Indian Act deemed the public acknowledgment of women's natural reproductive functions shameful, and while this marked an end to pollution taboos and possibly to certain antagonisms between males and females, it also meant an end to the natural power that women enjoyed and the special public recognition of their femaleness.

The status of older women, always high, was both intentionally and unintentionally elevated with acculturation. Abolishment of the levirate and securement of the inheritance rights of widows gave these women the basic economic means to be full participants in the ceremonial culture. Their ceremonial and symbolic status has become increasingly important in the present day, as by virtue of age and survivorship they have become the final repositories of the native language, of ceremonial etiquette, of kinship, and of a heritage fast disappearing in the latter part of the twentieth century. Florence Davidson, respected and admired in her own community and by all outside of it who know her, is one of the last legatees. ·

CHAPTER 3

Florence Edenshaw Davidson:
A Biographical Sketch

The village of Masset was virtually deserted on the morning of September 15, 1896, when Florence Edenshaw was born in her father's house. Her "grandmother," Amy Edenshaw, who assisted at the birth, and her mother, Isabella, were among the few villagers who remained behind when the Masset people departed for the Ain River dog salmon fishery in early September.

Charles and Isabella Edenshaw already had two older daughters, Emily (Wałał gidák), sixteen years of age, and Agnes (Kwənt qayngás), eight.[1] Three other daughters, born in 1885, 1886, and 1891, had died in infancy.[2] Only a month before Florence's birth, Robert (Ginάwən), the eldest son and a promising carver, had drowned at Rivers Inlet cannery. A second son, Albert Edward (Gusáwak), born in 1889, died at nine months of age. The family was eager for another son, but their disappointment was assuaged when the birth went without incident and the infant girl was healthy. Charles Edenshaw named his new daughter Jadał q'egəngá ("Story Maid"); her maternal uncle, Henry Edenshaw, who selected all the children's Christian names, called her Florence. Charles and Isabella had converted to Christianity and been baptized in the Anglican Church at Masset several years before, and so, on

---

1. Agnes' name describes a beached whale so large that all of it could not be used. Emily's name means "lots of things for the potlatch."
2. Florence only knew about the brothers who had preceded her. The female births were discovered in missionary records.

November 15, 1896, they took the infant Florence to be christened by the missionary. Prior to her baptism, Florence underwent a traditional Haida ritual: when four days old, her grandmother pierced her ears.

Charles Edenshaw adored his new daughter. "My Dad used to favor me," Nani says of their relationship. This was perhaps in part because she was believed to be the reincarnation of his own mother Qawkúna. "*Hada, ding awu di ijing*" ("Dad, I'm your mother") were Florence's first spoken words.[3]

Florence Davidson comes from a long line of distinguished Haida people (see genealogy). Her father was Chief Idínsaw, hereditary chief of the populous and powerful *Sdaɫdás* Eagle lineage. He also bore the Haida names of Skiɫ'wxan jas ("Fairies coming to you as in a big wave"), Dahʔégin ("Noise in the housepit"), the name bestowed in 1970 on the new elementary school at New Masset, and Nangkwigetklaɫs ("They gave ten potlatches for him"), conferred at his parents' final potlatch. The name Charles Edenshaw has become legendary in Northwest Coast art circles and his work has been the subject of intense scrutiny by scholars (see, for example, Barbeau 1944; Appleton 1970; Holm 1981). During his long and prolific artistic career from 1853 when he was fourteen years of age until a few years before his death in 1920, he produced scores of painted bentwood boxes, rattles, masks, miniature and large cedar totem poles, carved chief's staffs, argillite totem poles and sculptures, and gold and silver jewelry.

Though working within the confines of a longstanding Haida art tradition, Charles Edenshaw's work is distinctive and he is credited with several innovations, among them the introduction of carved gold and silver bracelets to the Haida. Edenshaw produced art for native use, including major works commissioned by natives of other tribes as well as jewelry purchased by local Haida at Masset and Skidegate on the Queen Charlotte Islands. He also carved for his family, making earrings and brooches for his young daughters out of the filings left from commissioned bracelets, and he fashioned a cedar chief's seat with his wife's crests (dogfish, grizzly bear, and killerwhale), which served as a divan in the family home during Florence's childhood.

Much of Charles Edenshaw's work, however, was commissioned by collectors for major museums whose orders kept the artist busy year-round. Dr. C. F. Newcombe, who collected for the Provincial

---

3. Traditionally, reincarnation was within the moiety if not the lineage. In this instance it was cross-moiety.

Museum in Victoria and Chicago's Field Museum, regularly purchased pieces from Edenshaw; Franz Boas bought some of Edenshaw's work at Port Essington in 1897 for the American Museum of Natural History in New York; John Swanton had Edenshaw carve numerous model totem poles and several model houses in 1901 to accompany his monograph on Haida culture; and, some of Edenshaw's last work was purchased by Masset Indian Agent Thomas Deasy, who later sold his entire collection to a wealthy eastern U.S. buyer.

Born at Skidegate in 1839, Charles Edenshaw was the heir of another prominent artist who bore the title of Chief Idínsaw before him. This was Albert Edward Edenshaw, Charles's mother's brother. Born around the year 1812, the elder Edenshaw had a reputation among his own people for being somewhat bellicose and was both respected and feared by white visitors to the islands. An extremely wealthy and powerful chief, he was frequently contacted by whites to lead exploring parties around the islands. In 1852 he earned the gratitude of the Hudson's Bay Company when he rescued the captain and crew of the ship *Susan Sturgis*, which had been looted and burned by a party under the leadership of Chief Weah, town chief at Masset. Edenshaw had houses at the northern Haida villages of Hiellen, Kung, and at Kiusta (see map) where he was town chief, but by the early 1880s, along with Haida from other outlying northern settlements, he moved to Masset.

Isabella Edenshaw (K'woiyang) and her mother's sister Amy Edenshaw (Sinlágutgang) were members of the Shark House (*Q'ad nas*) *Y'akwə'lanas* Raven lineage originally of Klinkwan, Alaska. This lineage shows a long history of intermarriage with the *Sdəłdás* lineage from the Queen Charlotte Islands, and Isabella and Amy in time followed the tradition. Isabella's mother, Ilsgide, for example, was married to Albert Edward Edenshaw's younger brother, and Amy's mother was married to a "brother" (lineage mate and perhaps actual brother) of Albert Edward Edenshaw's mother (see genealogy).

In the spring of 1862, Isabella, her Aunt Amy, and Wiba, a slave girl adopted as a playmate for Isabella who was an only child, were enroute home from Masset with their parents and a party of Kiusta Haida when the smallpox epidemic reached the Queen Charlottes. The two canoeloads of people had camped at Jalun River for the night, but by early morning when they were to depart for Kiusta, everyone but the three young girls had fallen ill with smallpox. Two *Y'akwə'lanas* uncles from Klinkwan who passed by Jalun River on their way home from Masset were able to rescue only Amy and Isabella. Wiba and the others at the camp perished with the disease.

Three or four years later when Amy reached marriageable age, she was taken by Albert Edward Edenshaw as his second wife. At the same time, the orphaned Isabella was fetched from Klinkwan and adopted by Edenshaw as his daughter. Albert and Amy Edenshaw had only one child, Henry, Florence Davidson's maternal uncle who is frequently mentioned in her narrative. Albert Edward Edenshaw died in 1894 and Amy was married in accordance with Haida tradition to his young lineage nephew, Phillip White, who looked after the aging lady until her death in 1922. Around 1873, Isabella Edenshaw was wed to Charles Edenshaw in a traditional Haida ceremony, and later, on December 27, 1885, following their conversion to Christianity, they were married in an Anglican service at St. Johns Church in Masset.

Charles Edenshaw inherited a traditional plank house from his uncle, but along with other Masset Haida, he soon built a Victorian-style cottage for his family.[4] Only the large grizzly bear mortuary pole honoring Isabella's mother's mother's sister, which stood in the front yard, bespoke the Haida affiliations of the new house's occupants.

The Edenshaws, like other Masset Haida of the time, moved about fairly frequently, remaining in Masset only during the late fall and winter months. For Florence and the other Masset children, wintertime meant school and Sunday school. Charlie Edenshaw spent the short winter days in his carving shed adjoining the house, and Isabella, having put up the family's winter supply of food, devoted her spare time to weaving the spruce root hats and baskets she would sell the following summer. She turned many of the completed hats and baskets over to her husband, who painted Haida designs on them. Florence often followed her father to his carving shed, accompanying him not so much because she admired his consummate skill as a carver, but because he always began his workday with prayer and she liked the way he prayed. Throughout the winter months there were "doings" of various kinds held in Masset: church gatherings, feasts, weddings, mortuary potlatches, welcome dances (*s'aʿgá*), and a masked dance performance called *ḵłiyá*, which Florence recalls seeing as a small child.

During her childhood years, Florence accompanied her parents at the end of February to Kung, the site of an old village in Naden Harbour; there they camped for a month or more to dry halibut. Returning only briefly to Masset, at the beginning of April (*t'aawkanut*,

---

4. Florence is not certain but thinks that all of her older siblings were born after Charles and Isabella moved into this white-style house.

Charles Edenshaw's house, c. 1900 (courtesy, British Columbia Provincial Museum)

or "gardening time") they left for Yatz, a former seal hunters' camp where the Haida now cultivated potato gardens. Here the men fished for halibut (except Charlie Edenshaw who continued to carve), while the women planted their gardens. From Yatz, the Edenshaws returned again to Masset. Early May brought the women and children briefly back to Yatz where they picked and dried seaweed. During much of May, though, the Edenshaws resided in Masset, and Florence accompanied her mother on frequent treks to North Beach to gather and process the spruce roots for Isabella's weaving. In June the Edenshaw family often left Masset on the steamer *Prince John* for the mainland. Isabella sold her baskets and hats at George Cunningham's store in Port Essington and there purchased yard goods for the family's winter wardrobe. Charles Edenshaw took his carving tools with him and continued to carve while his wife worked at Inverness Cannery on the Skeena River.

Some summers the Edenshaws went instead to Alaska and Isabella worked at the cannery in New Kasaan. In 1902 C. F. Newcombe visited them there, purchasing a spruce root cradle-liner painted with a dogfish design and some baskets from Isabella Edenshaw. He commissioned several items from Charles Edenshaw for the Field Museum and paid him twenty-five cents an hour for ethnographic information. That summer at the Kasaan cannery, Isabella gave birth to her last child, Alice (Skil Jade). Florence spent that and the next few summers looking after baby Alice and Nora, a sister three years Florence's junior.

When the family returned in late summer to the islands, Isabella and Florence picked huckleberries, crabapples, and salal berries. Late in the fall they gathered cranberries, and Isabella harvested her potatoes. The Edenshaws purchased or traded for their fall salmon; not until she was an adult did Florence go upriver to the Ain and Yakoun fish camps to slice, smoke, and later can, dog salmon and sockeye.

Florence attended the mission school at Masset until the fourth level, but her parents often needed her to help at home or to assist her Uncle Henry's wife, Martha, so attendance at school was sporadic. Still there was time for play and she recalls games with her Edenshaw cousins and friends Emma Matthews and Sophie Marks.

Childhood ended abruptly and unhappily for Florence with first her puberty seclusion, *təgwəná*, and then her arranged marriage to Robert Davidson, a respected and high-ranking man of the *C'aƛ'lanas* Eagle lineage more than twice her age. Envious as a child of the older girls who were whisked from their playmates at menarche and made to lie in a back room of the house for ten days or more, Florence, knowing nothing of menstruation, was frightened when it happened to her. A year and a half later she was not yet fifteen and still attending school when a party of *C'aƚlanas* and *Stl'əng'lanas* relatives of Robert Davidson's (the latter from his father's side) appeared at Charles Edenshaw's doorstep to propose the marriage of his daughter. "They were all streaming in and I don't know what's going on so I went to my uncle's house." A few days later she learned from an older cousin that she was about to be married. Horror struck, she defiantly told her mother that she would not marry "that old man" and she tearfully threatened to run away if they followed through with the wedding. "I wish I was dead," she remarked of her feelings when the wedding plans were formalized. The ensuing years eased the pain and in retrospect she speaks fondly of her husband, but she never forgot the bitterness she felt at being dragged from the side of her childhood friends into unsolicited wedlock.

Following their marriage on February 23, 1911, Robert and Florence Davidson moved in with Charles and Isabella Edenshaw. Not until two children were born did they move into a small home of their own. Alfred, the first of thirteen children, was born one year and ten months after their wedding. In succession followed Arnold (1914), Helen (1916), Virginia (1919), Reggie (1921), Joyce (1922), Claude (1924), Primrose (1926), Emily (1930), Myrtle (1931), Aggie (1933), Merle (1935), and Clara (1938). Spaced eighteen to thirty-one months apart, the children, Nani commented, were "just like stairsteps." Several of her children she delivered herself at home, though with some she had the assistance of her mother and elder sister Emily.

Four of the thirteen children died: Joyce at age three in 1925 at Ain River fish camp; Helen at eleven in 1928, Arnold at eighteen in 1933, and Reggie at thirty-seven in 1958. Today, seven of Robert and Florence Davidson's children live on the Queen Charlotte Islands: Aggie, Claude, Primrose, and Alfred in Haida Masset, and Virginia, Emily, and Merle in New Masset. Myrtle lives in Quesnel, and Clara, in Vancouver, British Columbia.

Childrearing was virtually a full-time job when the children were small. Nani lamented that while she had learned to read and write in school she had no time for either after she had young children to care for, and once she remarked that she wished she had learned all the stories and songs her husband knew. "There was no time; I always had a bunch of kids to look after." Nonetheless, she did become an active member in the Anglican Church, joining the choir and the Women's Auxiliary, and she worked to earn extra money for her growing family. She baked bread and pastries at North Island to sell to commercial fishermen; she labored summers in the canneries at Masset, Naden, Tow Hill, and Rose Inlet; and, for a number of years, she operated a small restaurant out of her home. Like her mother before her she put up food for the family's winter use. She gathered berries for jam and dried seaweed. In the fall she and her husband fished for dog salmon at Ain River and in later years they built a smokehouse and cabin on the Indian reserve at the mouth of the Yakoun River where they fished for sockeye in late May and early June. "I'm still working yet," Nani laughs, and indeed, in her ninth decade she goes upriver for the sockeye salmon run, cooks for feasts, and takes in boarders on a regular basis.

Robert Davidson was a commercial fisherman, but he also ran a trapline in the Yakoun valley and for a time he worked as a handlogger. As a young boy, he learned carpentry skills which served him well throughout his life. He helped construct several Masset houses, including his own, built fishing boats, and was among the skilled Haida carpenters who in 1919 built the present Anglican Church. Twice he rehoned old skills to build, with his brother Alfred, traditional Haida canoes. No longer in use by the Haida in 1909 when the first was built, the canoes were commissioned by museums. In his declining years Robert took up argillite carving, a skill he had learned years before from his father-in-law, Charles Edenshaw.

In 1929 the Davidsons moved from their small cottage into a new large two-story house designed and built by Robert. So ambitious did some villagers think Robert Davidson's plans for the house that they quipped, "Gəniyá [Robert] must be building a cannery." The Davidsons celebrated the move with a feast, and two elders named the house (*Naʔa q'Enadas*, "it's like summertime inside"; *Ne gut k'i was*, "the main road runs by the house"). In 1952 the house was destroyed in a fire and the Davidsons escaped with little more than the clothes they were wearing. The laborious process of rebuilding began, and two years later the family moved into the present spacious one-story home. Robert Davidson finally paid off the loan on the house with several of his argillite carvings.

The new house witnessed many celebrations as the years passed: winter feasts, the wedding celebrations of Aggie, Merle, Myrtle, and Clara, the golden wedding anniversary of Florence and Robert, and the wedding feasts for several grandchildren. There were sad

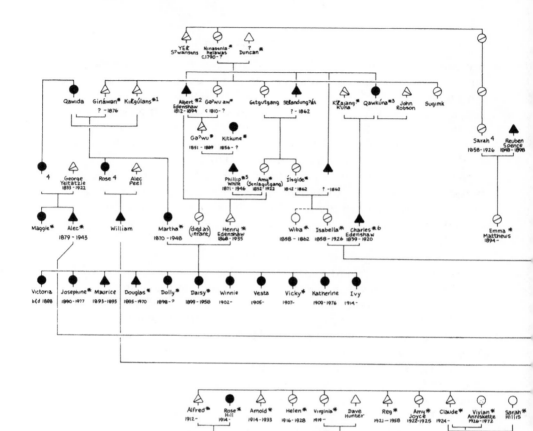

1. Kiłgúlans married Qáwida upon Gináwən's death, as was the practice under the levirate.

2. Albert Edenshaw had two older brothers and three sisters, not shown here. Gəʔwu aw was Albert Edenshaw's mother's brother's widow. Edenshaw married Amy while Gəʔwu aw was still living.

3. Qawkúna married John Robson of Skidegate after K'łajangk'una's death.

4. Not all the offspring of these individuals are shown; furthermore, grandchildren's spouses and great-grandchildren are not shown on the genealogy.

Genealogy of Florence Edenshaw Davidson

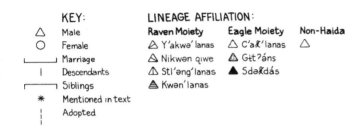

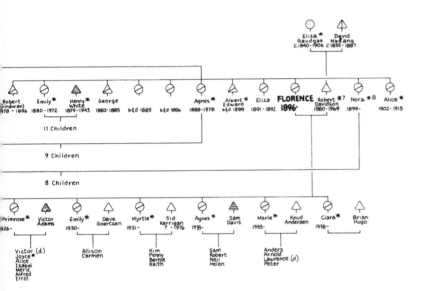

5. Phillip White married Amy Edenshaw after the death of Albert Edenshaw.

6. Charles Edenshaw had three sisters, according to Florence Davidson.

7. Robert Davidson was a widower when he married Florence.

8. Florence's sisters, Nora and Agnes, both remarried later in life after they were widowed. Their second husbands, Robert Cogo and George Jones, are not shown on the genealogy.

celebrations in the large front room, too: memorial feasts and headstone raisings (mortuary potlatches) honoring deceased relatives.

Robert Davidson lived to see his namesake and grandson carve the first totem pole on the islands erected in the twentieth century; he died only a month later in September 1969, at the age of eighty-nine. Disconsolate for many months after her husband's death, Nani seldom left the house, but finally at the encouragement of the minister, she began taking in boarders. In short order there was a steady stream of teachers, nurses, visiting doctors and dentists, tourists, and researchers who stayed and enjoyed the comforts of her home and her Haida-Canadian cooking. Their names now fill Nani's several guest books and their enthusiastic comments express their warm regard for her.

CHAPTER 4

Those Before Me
(1862–1896)

The Northern Indians will be sent from the Reserve today to one of the islands in the Straits—there to rot and die with the loathsome disease which is now destroying the poor wretches at the rate of six each day. [*British Colonist*, May 13, 1862]

Forty out of sixty Hydahs who left Victoria for the North about one month ago, had died. The sick and dead with their canoes, blankets, guns, etc., were left along the coast. In one encampment, about twelve miles above Nanaimo, Capt. Osgood counted twelve dead Indians—the bodies festering in the noonday sun. [*British Colonist*, June 21, 1862]

They say a man saw the smallpox long before it happened. This man had a tent way before the white man came; my dad used to say he didn't know where the tent came from. The man was in his tent and someone who came near it said it smelled like perfume there. Something took the man up in the air; he must have dreamt he was in the air above all the island. He saw all the villages, but they were torn up and they looked empty. Just Masset and Skidegate were all right. The ones who took the man up told him just two villages would be left and the rest would be wiped out because the people were getting too bad. Two men would be leaders of these villages, they said. They meant Alfred Adams and Peter Kelly.

Smallpox came from Victoria. On the way home where the people camped overnight, some would get sick and they'd leave the sick ones there. It spread all over the islands. Both of my mother's parents died in the smallpox epidemic and my grandmother's parents, too. They were going home to Kiusta from Masset. My mother's parents were on one canoe, my grandmother's on the other. There were some other people from Kiusta with them. They stayed overnight at Jalun River and put up cedar-bark tents. They were supposed to leave right away the next morning but they took sick. They all got sick at once. My mother's mother, Ílsgide, was a young woman with just one child, a four-year-old girl, my mother. Ílsgide was married to Albert Edward Edenshaw's younger brother; I don't even know his name. When Ílsgide took sick, she went into the water up to her chest. Then she went back to the lean-to where they had built a big fire. She went underneath her blanket and right away she went to sleep and died.

My "grandmother," Amy, was about ten years old then. She was really Ílsgide's sister, but ever since I can remember my mother never told us Amy was her aunt; we used to think Amy was her mother. Amy and my mother and Wiba, my mother's playmate, were the only ones who didn't take sick. My mother's parents bought a playmate for my mother because she's alone, the only child. Wiba's parents were slaves, but my mother's parents bought her so my mother would have someone to play with; they didn't buy her for a slave. They were going to adopt her. The little girls were playing on the beach when their uncles, Gináwən and Kiłgúlans, came by from Masset on their way to Klinkwan [Alaska]. Amy's father saw the canoe landing and told them not to stop because they were all sick; he didn't want them to catch smallpox. The uncles grabbed the two little girls, my mother and Amy. Wiba was a little ways from them, and they couldn't get to her because my grandmother's father had a gun. He was shooting at them, trying to kill them because they took the two girls. When my mother talked about Wiba she used to cry. Wiba ran after them but they couldn't rescue her because Amy's father had the gun. She got left there and she wasn't even sick. I guess she died with the rest. They were all wiped out; no one was saved from there. My grandmother used to tell me the story of it when I was little.

My "Grandfather": Albert Edward Edenshaw

This worthy Haida Chief died at Masset November 16, 1894. He was a great friend of mine and one for whom I had greatest respect. He practically did his utmost to promote a feeling of good fellowship between the whites and the Haidas. . . . From the first day of my arrival I had his support and influence, and it was through his untiring energy that the Haidas finally cast off heathenism. . . . He did not receive [the] name [Edenshaw] at his birth, but when he succeeded his uncle as the chief of the Shongalth Lennas[1], who had their headquarters at Dadens, near North Island. His birth name was Gwai-gu-unlthin, which means according to a recent interpretation, the man who rests his head on an island. The village in which he was born had disappeared, but if reports be true it was situated near Cape Ball on the eastern shore of Graham Island about 40 to 45 miles from Skidegate. . . . Edenshaw was an old man when I first met him, and I should have judged him to be about 70 years old. If this were correct it would give the year of his birth about 1812.

His early youth was spent during the time the Haidas were at the zenith of their power. . . . He has often told me of the many wars against the Zimshians and the Naass Indians[2] that he had been engaged in and how victorious he and his party always were. . . . Edenshaw had two brothers older than himself, and they were considered to be very brave men, and young Edenshaw did his utmost to be considered as brave as they were. . . . He made Skidegate, I think, his home until he was appointed chief. . . . The uncle he succeeded was a most powerful chief at Dadens near Cape Knox, and bore the hereditary name of Edinso. . . . A few years prior to his being called to prepare for the chieftainship his two eldest brothers had died. According to Haida descent he had to marry the chief's, i.e. his uncle's, daughter, but his uncle had no daughter in his family, consequently it was arranged that he should marry a daughter of an excellent and powerful chief in Alaska. His uncle finally died and Edenshaw succeeded to his property and chieftainship, and at his succession the grandest and largest distribution of goods and articles of great value including slaves took place that has ever been known on these islands. [Harrison, August 26, 1912]

Young Chief Edenshaw's property included 12 slaves, male and female, and when he became united to his wife, his wife's father gave his daughter 10 more slaves to take with her to her new home. . . . [Harrison, September 2, 1912] Edenshaw's friends say that he never captured slaves himself, though he constantly bought and sold them. He obtained them chiefly from Skidegate and often went as far as Sitka to sell them. He used to travel in state in a dugout canoe twelve fathoms long, elaborately painted at both ends, manned by a large number of slaves and dependents. By means of constant trading he accumulated a large quantity of property, and in the course of his life made no less than seven large potlatches. [Harrison, September 16, 1912]

When [the Hudson's Bay] company had their store opened at

1. Or, *Sdałdás*, Swanton's E 21 (1909:275).
2. Tsimshian and Nass (River) Indians. The latter are usually referred to as the Nishga.

Massett, Edenshaw and his followers were amongst the first to come together and form one united settlement of the Northern Haidas at Massett. I had the privilege of baptising him and his wife and of receiving them into the church. They were afterwards confirmed by Bishop Ridley and became communicants. When baptised he received the name Albert Edward, the Christian name of the late King Edward. [Edenshaw's] eldest son, George Cowhoe, was the first native teacher on these Islands, and I also had the privilege of baptising him, his wife, and family. He [Edenshaw] had only two sons and the other is so well known that he needs no recommendation from me. His name is Henry Edenshaw. I baptised him also. After his brother's death he succeeded him in his chieftainship and also became the teacher of the Masset Indian school, which position he filled remarkably well for several years. He is now franchised and entitled to all the privileges of the white man, and no better business man can be met with on this entire coast . . . .

I have no hesitation in saying that it is principally due to his [Edenshaw's] manlike ways, his influence, and example that the Haidas have taken so readily to the ways and customs of the whites, and that at the present moment they are one of the most advanced and law-abiding races on the coast. [Harrison, October 21, 1912]

My grandmother didn't tell me about my grandfather; I didn't even know till much later that he was the chief.

After the smallpox Albert Edenshaw took his uncle's place. His uncle at Kiusta sent for him; he was away at Port Simpson. That old man must have been living yet while everyone else was wiped out with smallpox. When the old man died, Albert Edward married his wife. She was my grandmother's aunt [Amy's mother's sister]. They lived at Kiusta and there Albert Edenshaw built a house with ten *day* [steps down to the housepit].[3] In the mornings when the sun used to come up his wife liked to sit at the front of the house with her elbows on her knees and her face in her hands, enjoying the sunshine. She had copper and gold bracelets from her wrists to her elbows and copper ones even on her ankles. The sun made them really shiny. She used to sit like that before the house because she was so precious. They called her Gəʔwu aw, "Gəʔwu's mother." Gəʔwu was her only son.[4] Gəʔwu aw was kind of old, older than her husband, and it's hard for her that my mother and grandmother were in Klinkwan with their uncles. The little girls were far away from her that's why it's hard for her. Albert Edward wanted to go for

3. The number "10," a ritual number in Haida, recurs throughout Florence's narrative.

4. Gəʔwu is the George Cowhoe (a corruption of the Haida "Gəʔwu") referred to in Harrison's account.

Albert Edward Edenshaw, *far right*, 1890 (courtesy, Public Archives of Canada, C60824)

them and bring them to Kiusta, and Gəʔwu aw agreed with him that he should marry Amy, too.

Albert Edward didn't want Amy and my mother to be poor, so when Amy was old enough to marry, my grandfather went to get her on a canoe with ten slaves to paddle for him. He took the girls from Klinkwan to Kung in Naden Harbour where he had a new house. There they had a wedding ceremony and for days and days they potlatched. Albert Edward potlatched for the girls because they were orphans. He married my grandmother and adopted my mother as his daughter. He had a big pole raising and *watəɬ* [potlatch] for the young girls. Maybe my grandmother's parents had potlatched for Amy, but my mother was too small yet. Her parents were still gathering things to potlatch when they died; they were just a young couple.

My mother was tattooed at the doing my grandfather held; she had a long dogfish on one leg, a grizzly bear on the other, and a quarter moon and lady on each arm.[5] The tattoos were done in red and blue. They tried to put a tattoo on her chest but she didn't want it and wouldn't let them do it. Maggie Yeltatzie [Florence's sister's husband's sister] was one of the last people tattooed. She was real ashamed of the tattoos on her hands. She used to wear gloves to hide them whenever she went out. "I wonder why I let them do this to me," she used to say.

Albert Edward Edenshaw had houses in several villages besides Kiusta and they kept moving around. His house at Kiusta with ten *day* was the biggest house, they say. He was a sea otter hunter and he used to hang the furs up at the back of the house, *t'acgwa*, the chief's place. My mother used to like to lie by the furs and run her hands over them and blow on them. They were so nice, just like silk, she said.

Amy and my grandfather had one child, Henry Edenshaw. When he was born, my grandfather's other wife, Gəʔwu aw, used to look after him real good. When Henry was old enough to get married, he had a girlfriend here in Masset, but she wasn't near enough [in terms of kinship]. My grandmother wanted him to marry Martha Duncan because that was her uncle's daughter, and he did.

My Parents

My mother and Emma Matthews' mother used to play together at Kiusta. They're related; their mothers were cousins. My grandfather

5. Isabella's tattoos are depicted in Swanton (1909:Pl. XXI).

had never seen a doll before but he used to make dolls for my
mother. Near Kiusta there's a cave with stalactites and stalagmites
growing in it. They used to believe it was a "ghost house"; if you
couldn't get babies you and your husband go in there and you start
getting babies after that. My grandfather took the stalactites and
carved the face and arms and legs on them. He collected hair from
my mother's comb and he glued it on the doll's head. My mother
said she used to wash the doll's hair all the time when she was little.

Emma's mother and my mother used to play on a *t'aawɂk'a* a lot.
It's a big dugout dish they put steamed food in to cool off before
serving. I never saw one; they didn't use them during my time.
They made a little paddle for the girls so they could paddle around
in the water on the *t'aawɂk'a*. One slave sat on each side of the
dugout to watch over them. They were ready to jump in and grab
the little girls right away in case they tipped over.

My mother's name was K'woiyəng. "K'woiyəng," I wonder what
it means? She was named after her *nanləng* who belonged to
Kwən'lanas.[6] She had her own name too; I think it was Ś'it kwuns,
"Red Moon." She got the name Isabella just before she and my dad
were married in the church. My mother had light brown hair and
real white skin and gray eyes. Her mother and her uncles were like
that too. Ginάwən, her uncle, had light curly hair and big blue eyes.
My grandmother Amy was the same. That was because they came
from a woman who was married, in the Indian way, to a white boat
captain. Wintertime he took his wife and children down south to
Victoria, but summertime his wife was lonely for her relatives in
Klinkwan and Kiusta, so he took her home every summer. The
lady's name was Ninasɨnlahelawas. She had about five children from
that captain. My mother was so light-skinned that after she married
my dad and went to Skidegate, my dad's auntie and his parents got
medicine for her. They were afraid she was going to have a short life
because she was so white, so they made her take Indian medicine. I
used to have a picture of my mother when she was a young woman.
The picture was taken in Victoria. She's standing with a fern beside
her and she looks just like a white lady. The picture was on tin.

My dad's father, K'łajangk'una, belonged to *Nikwən qiwe*;
Qawkúna, his wife, was *Sdəłdás.*[7] K'łajangk'una was a real good
carver and canoe builder from Skidegate. Qawkúna used to go with
her husband when he cut trees for canoes. She had lots of names,

---

6. *Nanləng* (or "grandmothers") are women of father's father's lineage.
7. Swanton's R 13 and E 21, respectively (1909:270, 275).

but I only know one other one—Itłgujatgut'aas. It means a rich woman grabs heavy things with her claws like an eagle.

Qawkúna and her husband used to take Indian medicine all the time. Once she went out with her husband and they found a s'it [cryptochiton] at the bottom of a tree. That's a lucky sign, so she took it. If you come across anything from the sea in the woods, it's a lucky sign. You eat it for luck and you keep the shells in a bentwood box. After that it's easy to get anything; you become richer and richer. My grandfather, Albert Edward, once found a lucky sign, too. He was going up into the woods: it wasn't summertime yet but the bluebottles were clustered on some halibut gills, haagu c'an. They were moving, just like a killerwhale sounding. Kwaagíndal, they call it. Amongst the moss it went. Albert Edward grabbed it and he became s̲kiłiłdá, "lucky."[8]

When my dad was first born they gave him the name Dahʔégin ["noise in the housepit"]. While he was growing up his parents potlatched for him ten times. He had lots of names; the last one he got—Nəngkwigetkłałs—means "they gave ten potlatches for him." When he was little his parents thought he was so precious that when he was sleeping they left the longhouse door open so they don't make any noise going in and out. They had a stick to push the door up so he won't wake up.

My dad was tattooed at his parents' potlatches. He had no clean skin he was so tattooed. Even his back, his arms, his legs, his chest, his hands were tattooed. I don't remember all the crests he's got tattooed, just eagle, sea wolf, and frog. My grandmother [Amy Edenshaw] thought my dad wasn't healthy because he's got so many tattoos on his body. She used to call him "paysen"; she meant "poison," germy.

> There was also a native jeweller in each village who made from half dollar and dollar silver coins, and also from gold coins, bracelets, bangles, finger rings and earrings. The first man to attempt the manipulation of the silver and gold was chief Edenshaw. [Harrison, May 27, 1912]

8. Other examples of lucky signs mentioned by Florence include frog nests, hummingbird nests, and owl skins (taken from an owl that has landed on one's head). If one ignores a lucky sign and does not take the object home, it is believed that misfortune will follow and one will have a short life. Swanton (1909:30) describes a creature similar to the halibut gills found by Albert Edenshaw.

Masset lay readers, c. 1910. *Left to right, seated*: Richard Russ, Charles Edenshaw, Rev. William E. Collison, James Stanley, Thomas Weir; *standing*: Sam Davis, Henry Edenshaw, Robert Ridley, Frederick Young (courtesy, Provincial Archives of British Columbia)

My father started carving one winter when he was sick. When he was about fourteen he was sick all winter long. He was in bed, but he got some argillite and started carving a totem pole. He was so sick he didn't want to eat anything, but his mother had an iron pot and she put hot water, seaweed, and grease in it, and she made my dad eat it. In May he got better. He took a walk and something came out from his chest right up his throat. He spit it in the creek. It looked like a devilfish with legs on it. That's what made him sick, and as soon as he got rid of it he got better. After that he carved his first bracelet, out of five silver-dollar pieces melted together. Later, after he married my mother but before my time, he used to go to Victoria and carve all winter long.

Maybe my dad was about eighteen or nineteen when he came to Masset. His uncle, Albert Edward Edenshaw, wanted him, so he came here. And when it was time, he married my mother. They were married in the Indian way before the missionaries came.

When Mr. Harrison [Rev. Charles Harrison, missionary] came here, he married my parents in the church. Just before they got married, Mr. Harrison baptized them. My mother didn't read so Mr. Harrison mentioned lots of names to her. When he said "Isabella," she said "yes." He told her it was a queen's name; that's why she likes it, I guess. Albert Edward put my dad in his [Albert Edward's] place while he was still living. When my dad married my mother in the church that's when his uncle gave him the name Edenshaw. When the missionary called my mother Isabella Edenshaw, she wouldn't take the "Edenshaw" for a long time. She couldn't understand it; "How can I take Eagle's name?" she kept asking. Finally she gave up.

A lady named Kwoiyat gudang awu ["Kwoiyat's mother"] willed my dad a longhouse in Masset after her husband died. Her husband was my dad's tribe [lineage], one of his uncles. That was the time that my dad gave a big potlatch for his two children, Emily and Gináwən, my older sister and brother. By the time my parents had Agnes, they moved to a white man's [style] house. My mother had another boy, born before me. His name was Gusáwak, Albert Edward. His neck swelled up and he died when he was nine months old. My parents lost the only boys in the family.

CHAPTER 5

Before I Could Walk
(1896–1897)

What I think would most forcibly strike a stranger visiting our village for the first time is its civilized aspect. A formidable line of totem poles running along the main street still indeed proclaims the place an Indian settlement: but the Indian lodges which once stood behind each of these poles have almost disappeared and shapely wooden cottages—all built by the natives themselves—have taken their place. At the back of almost every house is a garden where the owner grows sufficient potatoes to supply his wants. A few of the Indians also keep horses and cows.

The interior of the houses, it must be confessed, are not yet what one would wish to see them. The habits of the lodge are still in several cases retained. . . . However, things are improving and many of the younger people now take their meals at tables and sleep on bedsteads instead of passing their existence like their forefathers on the floor. [Keen 1894]

When I was on the way [summer 1896], my mother and dad and the whole family—Gináwən [Robert], Emily, Agnes—went to Juneau, Alaska. It was springtime and they went by canoe. My brother had the navigation chart and he used to tell dad how they're going to come across a camp or something. They'd stay at the camp overnight and start again to Juneau. My brother would look at the chart and say, "we're going to come across an iceberg tomorrow," and my dad would be real surprised when he saw it.

My dad went to Alaska to carve. Gináwən was a carver, too, and my dad used to say that his son's work was the best of all. When they finished working, they sold the canoe and they took the steamer, *c'an khuwe* [sea canoe], to Victoria. My mother wanted a treadle sewing machine. My dad said, "We'll go down to Victoria to buy it," and the whole family went to Victoria to buy this treadle machine. They bought a lot of things there. On the way back the steamer stopped at Rivers Inlet where most of the Masset people were working in the cannery. My grandmother [Amy Edenshaw] and my step-grandfather [Phillip White] were there. Gináwǝn used to love his grandmother and she used to love him so much. "I'm going to stay with my grandmother," he told his parents. "I'll come home with them when they're through working."

When they were done working in the cannery and almost ready to go home, Gináwǝn went out swimming. He dived in and didn't come up for a long time. My husband, who was only twelve or thirteen then, watched him for a long time and got worried when he didn't come up. A good diver came around and he found Gináwǝn on the bottom, face down. They worked on him for a long time. Finally they quit and took the body home.

My grandmother had gone to the inlet where the stream was to wash clothes. She and Phillip were there and you could hear her laughing clear from the mouth of the bay when they came with the bad news. "Sɨnlagutgang!" They called her name real loud and she stopped laughing. "Something terrible happened. Your Gináwǝn drowned." Then they took my grandmother and her husband home, towing their little boat.

In those days when someone died at the cannery, the Chinamen would build the casket, nail the box up, and put a nice expensive cover on it. Sarah Brooks's brother [from Masset] died the same time as Gináwǝn, and there were two caskets on the steamer when the Masset people came home from Rivers Inlet.

My mother and dad were staying in a tent at Fort Simpson waiting for the steamer and their son. When the steamer was coming my mother started cooking and Emily and Agnes put nice dresses and summer hats on to meet their brother. But there's no Gináwǝn. My dad was coming, too, and he stopped halfway there, feeling that something happened to his son because nobody was getting off the boat. Finally, Agnes Williams' father walked up to my dad and just hugged him. "*Kilsle* [chief], something terrible happened to you." And he grabbed him because he knew my dad was going to jump off the wharf and drown himself. All the people around cried with my dad and tried to get him and the family on the boat to go across to Masset. My mother and grandmother ran and threw themselves in the water; it was so hard for them. They tried to stop them, and finally they got them on the steamer.

They came home in late August. My uncle, Henry Edenshaw, was

Masset in 1911

anxious for his nephew. He was going to cut hay across the inlet for his cows and when his wife Martha asked him when he was going to cut hay, he said, "I'm waiting for Gináwən; we'll work together." He made Martha put all kinds of food together to take across. When my parents and grandmother got home and told him the bad news he took it as hard as they did. He cried and no one could stop him.

I was born in September. People had gone up the inlet [Masset Inlet] to dry fish and pick berries; there were hardly any people here. All the people were wishing my mother would get a boy but I disappointed them. And I'm still living. When I was born my grandmother was real happy. Even though I was a girl she was happy because the trouble [labor] was over. When a baby is born the first mess it makes is black. They used to take this, get a stick, and paint eyebrows on with it. They did it so the baby's eyebrows don't point down. My grandmother made my eyebrows like that. She pierced my ears when I was four days old. The *sqa ʔanlang*[1] used to do it in the olden days, but my grandmother was so happy that I was born and that my mother was safe. They called me Jadał q'egəngá right away after my *nanlang*. My father gave me my Indian name and my uncle called me Florence. My mother and dad didn't read, that's why Henry Edenshaw gave all of us names. Mr. Keen, the missionary, baptized me.

I don't know the story of my name well. There was a young lady. They say she was a "princess" [*y'aʔᴄEyt*, high ranking]. She came on a small canoe and drifted ashore at Rose Spit. A young man found her and asked her name. "Just holler '*jadał q'egnadła gEl go-oooo*,' 'the story maid arrives,' and say '*s'aan jat gu sandlan tla gEl go-oooo*,' 'the killerwhale maid arrives.'"[2] He kept on hollering the names because she was *y'aʔᴄEyt* and didn't want to come into shore quietly. She told the man to hide her underneath the canoe; she put it upside down and she used to lie underneath it. That's all I know; I don't know how they found out about her. She was *Nikwən qiwe*, my dad's father's tribe [lineage], the very first one. My name means "Story Maid"—that generations after, the story of that woman will be known. Because I got the name I hate it when they talk about it; it

1. *Sqaʔanlang* are women of father's matrilineage. The English term "auntie" is often given today as an equivalent.
2. The second name, according to Peter Kelly (Morley 1967:32), translates "Women on Whom the First Dawn Came." This woman was the ancestress of the *Nikwən qiwe*; no one knows where she came from. This second name was given to Nora, Florence's younger sister.

sounds awful to me because she drifted ashore and a man found her.

I don't know who had the name before me. Henry Young from Skidegate told me no one could be fit enough to be named after this y'aʔˣEyt girl; no one could be like her. "First time someone is named after her and you're the only one who fits it," he said to me.

After I was born, I used a cradle for about one year, I guess, and my sister Nora used the cradle after me. It was carved by my dad, with a dogfish on the bottom. In 1903 when my parents were in Victoria, they sold the cradle to Mr. Newcombe.[3]

3. The cradle is shown in color in N. Bancroft-Hunt's *People of the Totem* (1979:46 [New York: Orbis Publishing]).

CHAPTER 6

I Am Yet a Girl
(1897–1909)

I find it a good plan to stay long enough in a mission to thoroughly enter into the life of the people so as to be able to understand the conditions which prevail.

It is a pity though the people do not stay longer at a time in their village. All summer most of them are on the coast of the mainland working at the canneries . . . so it is from October to February that most of the work must be done among them here.

The last time there was confirmation in this church was when it was opened *eighteen* years ago.

Before long there may be a white settlement on Masset Inlet.

Sunday services are attended by 150–200 people (350 population). The morning service is in Haida—except the hymns and chants, and the evening service (as is the custom in the diocese) is in English. The young people all much prefer the English service. It is much better attended than the other. [Du Vernet 1906]

My mother said I was real fast in everything. I walked around real early and I started talking when I was small. My dad used to favor me because I used to tell him, *"Hada, ding awu di ijing,"* "Dad, I'm your mother."[1] They used to believe in second-birth [reincarnation]. *"Hada ding awu di ijing,"* I kept on saying. Those were my first words.

---

1. Favorite children are quite common among the Haida. Florence noted that Aggie was her husband's favorite child, but in regard to her own preferences said, "I love them all."

I don't remember when my sister Emily got married; I was too small, I guess. She must have been about fifteen when she married Henry White, and right after, Agnes got married.[2] They came for Agnes from Alaska. When there's no one to marry at home, chiefs' children marry someone from a different village. Agnes married Alec Yeltatzie from Howkan. They even cooked for the wedding at my dad's house, but I can't remember anything of it. I didn't know they were married but I remember when Carrie [Agnes' first child] was born. I remember Emily's first baby, too. When Emily had her first boy, Gusáwak, I said to my mother, "Why don't you call me by Emily's name, then I could be having a baby now, too." My mother laughed about it for a long time.

Ever since I can remember I'd go with my dad to watch him carve. Wintertime he used to work in the shed behind our house. When we were all grown up he started carving in the house. As soon as he finished breakfast he'd be ready to go out and I'd be ready to go with him. He sat on a little armchair with the legs cut off so it was low to the ground. He had a little box beside him where I used to sit. Soon as he sat down at his carving table, he'd take off his cap and he'd pray every morning. That's why I used to go out with him; I enjoyed his praying so much. When he was through, he'd start carving. I'd sit there for awhile and I'd say, "Dad, I'm going now," and he'd say, "Oh." Kindly, he said it.

My dad used to make little longhouses, and I used to want them real bad to play with, but I didn't tell him. He used to make all kinds of earrings for me. I would lose just one earring all the time and he'd make a new one. "Your dad will fix another earring for you because you look like a boy," my mother would say. She used to get kind of mad at me when I'd lose my earrings. My dad made just gold earrings for me, because I was his favorite, his mother's second birth.

My parents didn't own much of my dad's work. What they had they sold. My mother even sold her bracelets when people wanted them. We had a chesterfield in our house that my dad carved for my mother. It was like a chief's seat, with a *q'ad* [dogfish] on it and a *xudj* [grizzly bear]. It had *xudj* tracks on it—*st'asəl*, we call the tracks. My mother put a feather mattress on it and we used it for a

---

2. Emily married in 1900 at age twenty (Florence was four years old at the time). Agnes married in 1902. Information on both marriages comes from the St. John's Anglican Church marriage register.

Chief's seat carved by Charles Edenshaw (courtesy, Museum of the American Indian, Heye Foundation)

chesterfield. It went to Alec [Yeltatzie] when he took my dad's place, and he and Agnes sold it for $150 to buy a casket for their son who died.[3]

My dad used to get orders for things, poles and jewelry, and he would work on them all the time. When my mother went to work in the cannery my dad would stay home to work on his carving. When I was little we went to Ketchikan summers so my dad could carve and my mother work at the saltery there. When my dad finished his work he'd always tell me, "I'm going to sell my things," and I'd wash my hair and put clean clothes on. I'd get ready real quick and I wouldn't play around after so I could be clean when I went to town. The people would give him money for his work and we'd go to the grocery store. "Dad, can you give me five cents?" I would say. He always gave me a quarter. I bought a "prize" box, little candy box with a prize in it. I used to collect it for my friends. I gave the prizes to my friends but I ate the candy.

I liked going to the store. My mother used to buy all her woolen

3. The chief's seat is on display in the Museum of the American Indian in New York.

material in Ketchikan and she made our clothes from that. She
bought coats for us from George Cunningham's store in Port
Essington on the mainland. James Martin was the first one to have a
store in New Masset, here on the islands. When my mother and dad
and I would go up to New Masset on a row boat I thought I was
going to a city. I just saw one store there but I enjoyed it very much.

When my parents went to Ketchikan I used to look after my
youngest sister Alice while my mother worked at the cannery. My
mother used to feed her with condensed milk. She had a big bottle
with a long rubber tube to it. I gave Alice the milk, and soon as she
was finished I filled the bottle up with milk for myself. I made it real
strong and real hot so I could taste the rubber tube. I was sucking
away at the bottle when my dad turned around from his carving and
looked at me. "*Um-uh, um-uh*," he said. He was surprised, that's
what that means. My sister Nora was younger than me, but she was
gentle. She never did anything crazy like that.

One time when my mother was working at the saltery in
Ketchikan salting spring salmon, she told me to cook rice for her
and have it ready when she got home. I took the bag of rice out to
the tap to wash it, but instead of washing it I threw two handfuls on
the walk. "Don't, don't do that, sister," Nora said. "I'm doing it so
Mum will think it's snowing when she gets back." When my mother
came in the door she said, "Why's there so much rice on the walk?"
I didn't say anything, just pretended to be busy. Nora told her I did
it. My mother told me not to do it again; she said they're going to
call me crazy if I do it again, and I was real scared.

When we went to Inverness cannery summers I used to pick
berries there. "I'm going to pick berries for my dad," I always said.
I picked blueberries and salmonberries. When I came home from
picking berries, Eliza Naɫang, my husband's mother, would be going
for water. "I'll go for your water," I said, and she would be real
happy. I was about ten when she died and they had the doing at
Masset to pay people who looked after the body.[4] Because I used to
pack water for her they paid me. They asked my mother to bring me
along to the doing. I was so proud; you know how little girls are.
They don't invite kids my age and I was the only little girl there.
They passed tobacco to the men to smoke and they gave out dishes,

---

4. Florence refers here to the mortuary potlatch given after the death
of a person when the tombstone (formerly mortuary totem pole) is lifted
into place. Members of the moiety opposite the deceased's perform the
important mortuary rituals and are reimbursed for their services at the
potlatch that follows.

blankets, and yard goods. The men got about five blankets, the small Hudson's Bay ones with black stripes. They gave me four fathoms of dress goods. They used to use Tommy Nutcome's house for doings because it had a big room. When I was young they passed soda pop [ginålga hawla, "something sweet"] around at doings. Strawberry, raspberry, any kind of berry flavor. Wintertime they would put it in big pots and one or two people packed it around. They scooped it up in a dipper and gave it to you to drink. When you gave the dipper back they'd get some for the next person. They didn't think about germs in those days.

About a year after that doing I started working in the cannery at Inverness. I was eleven. We piled empty cans in the trays. When we'd filled all the trays we left work. We'd go out for awhile and we'd forget to come back. We'd come back to work whenever we remembered it. I used to get five cents an hour, but I enjoyed that time.

When we came back to Masset from the cannery I used to pick berries with my mother. We went up to New Masset for salal. There weren't any white people there then, just all kinds of berries. My mother also used to go to Watun River for red huckleberries and I went with her. She'd bring the berries home and cook them with salmon eggs for thickening. She boiled them till they were dry. She put the berries in a bentwood box with a cloth covering over them, then thimbleberry leaves and skunk cabbage leaves on top before she put the lid on. She cooked her berries in the shed behind the house where my dad carved and she stored them there, too. She cooked salal berries the same way. My mother put up huckleberries, salal, and cranberries in boxes, five or six of them, for the winter. She used to jam blueberries in big jars and she preserved maltberries and crabapples in water. My dad had a little dugout [qʷotłu, "sea otter canoe"], and my mother, Emma Matthews' mother, and Alfred Adams' mother used to paddle out to Tow Hill to pick crabapples in October. I didn't go with them; I guess they didn't want to take me. They'd spend days and days there and get real lots of crabapples. Sometimes they'd pick the stems off and preserve the apples in a barrel. Other times they'd cook the apples, just simmer them, and put them in a barrel. Wintertime they'd take the juice out. It tastes like apple cider. Then they'd whip up grease and mix the apples with grease and sugar. K'oi qayudiya, they called it. They put the mixture in a bent box, put a clean flour sack on top, and put roasted thimbleberry leaves and roasted skunk cabbage leaves on top of that cloth. They packed clean sand on top of the leaves so air doesn't get in.

Falltime my parents didn't go with the other people up to Ain River to fish for salmon. We used to buy our salmon from other people. I didn't go to Ain River fish camp until after I was married.

Fall and winter I spent most of my time helping my uncle, Henry Edenshaw, and his wife. I liked working with Martha. My mother loved her brother [Henry] so much; she thinks highly of him, so I helped them. Young girls used to help their uncle's wife all the time. I was supposed to be going to school but my uncle's wife needed me, so instead of going to school I stayed home to wash diapers by Martha. I was staying by my uncle falltime when I was about eleven and he told me, "Florence, you get up early in the morning and cook porridge." So I got up around six o'clock to cook the porridge. First time I ever cooked porridge, so I was rushing around. I boiled water in the kettle and I took the big pot out and I put rolled oats in it. While the porridge was cooking I was real tired so I lay down in the kitchen and I went off to sleep. My uncle came in and said, "EH!" and I woke up. I got up to see the porridge and it was real hard. My, I was scared of my uncle. "Did you cook porridge before?" he asked me. "No." "Just your mother cooks it?" "Yes." "No wonder it's so good!" I don't remember if they ate it or not.

I used to stay home from school most of the time to help my uncle. Their house was kind of like a hotel—they had about eight rooms for guests. I looked after their dining room when white people used to stay there and I fixed the beds and cleaned up the rooms.

I was a handyman for my parents, too. I used to go out with my dad to get wood in the wintertime, just like a boy can do. Soon as I can pull a handsaw I'd go with him. I felt sorry for my dad; I didn't want him to go alone so we cut wood together.[5] I was a strong little girl, I guess. I used to pack the wood out with him to the boat. One time we went and I saw a bunch of snow there. "Dad," I said, "I'm going to take this home to eat it with milk." He said it's all right, so I took off my kerchief and put lots of snow in it. When I got home I got the chills and next day I caught pneumonia. I was sick for more than one month. I don't think my dad took me out after that to go for wood again.

Once when I was real small my dad went down past where the cemetery is to collect some driftwood. His dugout was too full, I guess, and he tipped over. Robert Williams' dad and Tl'aʔɢuntz, a [former] slave, saved him. Because they were the opposite tribe

5. A man was usually assisted by his nephews, but Charles Edenshaw had none in Masset.

[moiety] from my dad, there's a big doing. *ʕansangáda*, they call it. All the Eagle tribe gave money to my dad.[6] John Robson, my dad's stepfather, made a big paper eagle and they nailed it up on the wall. They paid Robert Williams' dad and Tl'aʔʕuntz lots of money and they had a feast and Indian dancing. I was there but that's all I remember; it was just like a dream to me.

Wintertime when I was small they used to dance so much: The *s'aʕgá*,[7] they called the dances. They just did them for fun so they don't forget them. Some used to wear masks but after white people come around here they cleaned out all the masks. Too bad I didn't learn the songs. I used to see it in Tommy Nutcome's house; they used to dance there all the time. I remember when they used to dance *ƚiyá*. *Ƚiyá* wasn't part of the *s'aʕgá*. They used to go around the village saying, "We're going to see *ƚiyá* tonight," and all the children would be real excited. The mask was real big and wide with a big nose and mouth. The eyes were red and behind the mouth was red. Little kids used to be really scared of it. I don't know what *ƚiyá* means in English.[8]

In February we used to go to Gwas, near Kung. We stayed there for a long time until we got lots of halibut and dried it. We used to barbecue the halibut, the bony neck part. The tail and the head were boiled, to eat with seaweed.

April they call *t'aawkanut*, "gardening time." My grandparents [Amy and Phillip], my parents, my sisters, and I would go on a little canoe to Yatz to plant gardens. Lots of people from Masset went there to garden. They cut the eyes out of the potatoes to plant and we ate the middle part; they called that part *scusid stƚuʔEl*, "potato's

6. *ʕansangáda*, which Murdock (1936) refers to as a facesaving potlatch, was given when an individual suffered embarrassment before a member of the opposite moiety. Members of the moiety of the embarrassed person contributed wealth to the potlatch, thus the contributions of the "Eagle tribe" to Charles Edenshaw. This wealth was distributed to members of the opposite moiety and served to erase the memory of the embarrassing event.

7. *S'aʕga*, the word for shaman, also refers to individuals who performed in the Haida version of the winter ceremonial dances. The word root, *s'aʕ*, denotes "power." Both shamans and dancing society members were believed to be possessed by spirits. By the time Florence was a child, these dances, as she notes, were being performed strictly for entertainment. The *s'aʕgá* is described by Swanton (1909:160–176).

8. I have been unable to determine the significance of *ƚiyá* as it is not mentioned in any of the usual sources on the Haida. Harrison (1925:87), however, describes a mask (Lthwō-gī-gē or Stlē-whul) which resembles in one feature ("its big red eyes") the mask that Florence calls *ƚiya*.

bottom." I used to really enjoy eating it. At gardening time the men would go fishing for halibut. The women dried the halibut there and used the guts for fertilizer on the gardens. Falltime, in November, they'd go to dig the potatoes up. They only grew potatoes at Yatz because they thought the ground was too precious for anything else. My mother grew turnips in Masset, nothing but turnips, and she used to sell her turnip seeds. After they planted their gardens at Yatz they'd gather seaweed and dry it on the rocks. We'd go back home for awhile after potato planting and then we'd come back to collect seaweed in May.

Near the end of May, ladies would go on boats across Yan to get wild rhubarb [western dock, *k'la q'os*], just like they'd go for seaweed. When I was old enough to pull some, I'd go with my mother. I used to *ɫkuju* [desire] it so much. I worked fast to collect it and I used to try all my best to get real lots. We'd carry home bundles of wild rhubarb tied up in a tablecloth. My mother cut the rhubarb up and boiled it for dessert. We ate it with lots of sugar and grease.

Ever since I can remember, I used to go with my mother in May for spruce roots [*ɫing*]. Every fine day we'd go out to North Beach early in the morning before sunrise. We'd pack water and food with us and mother would cook our breakfast in the woods. She used to have kindling ready and she left her pots and dishes there. We'd collect *ɫing* all day long.

Sometimes, just to do something different from getting *ɫing* I'd ask my mother if I could get some *xigə* [hemlock cambium] and she'd agree to it. They used to pound and dry it for winter and soak it overnight in hot water before they'd eat it. We ate it for dessert, with sugar and grease. I would just collect a little bit.

When it was noontime, we'd quit collecting *ɫing* and my mother would make lunch. Sometimes other ladies would come along and we'd have a nice time together—it was just like a picnic. Then we'd gather driftwood from the beach and make a big fire to "cook" the roots. My mother roasted them and I pulled the skin [bark] off. We'd collect piles and piles of them. My mother would know when to quit, when we had enough. The sun would be going down when we started for home. The bundles of roots were all tied together and we each packed a big bundle of roots. When we got part way home I'd make my mother rest so I could pick *sqəltó* [false lady's slipper]. There was just a carpet of it. It was so pretty. I picked all I wanted and when we got home I put the flowers in bowls of water. They smelled so nice in the house. When we got home my dad would cook for us. We didn't want to eat, but we would just to please my dad. Soon as my mother finished eating she'd start splitting the roots in half. She bundled them up and put all the same size ones together in a bent box. She packed them in real tight. She used to have so many boxes to keep the *ting* in. If you don't cover it, the roots turn brown, so she kept them in boxes.

My mother used to weave baskets and hats all winter long. When she was going to start her weaving she soaked the roots overnight, so they'd be easy to work. She'd get up early in the morning and cook and, after everyone was finished eating, she'd go to work splitting the roots again and weaving them into a hat or basket. She worked all day long, day after day, from the time she finished picking and putting up berries till the spring. It was just like having a business. When she finished a hat she put it in a dark place and then my dad would paint a design on it. Sometimes he painted mother's baskets, too. My mother used to weave everything— placemats, hats, baskets with covers, seaweed baskets, baskets for carrying water. She even used to weave around bottles. She learned to decorate her baskets with grass [false embroidery] from a Tlingit lady in Ketchikan. What my mother wove all winter long she sold in June when we went to the mainland to work in the canneries. She sold her work at Cunningham's store in Port Essington. She used to get five dollars for a finely woven, painted hat. Mr. Cunningham paid her cash for her work and she bought our winter coats there. Mr. Newcombe used to come here from Victoria to buy things from my parents, too.

The summer I was eleven, my Uncle Henry Edenshaw had a big doing at Dadens on North Island. The big old totem pole in front of my grandmother's [Amy Edenshaw's] house blew down during the wintertime. The pole had a grizzly bear on it, at the bottom. Jitkanj'əs [a girl of the C'ał'lanas Eagle lineage] made fun of the bear, poking it in the bottom. They said so much about it that my uncle took lots of food to North Island and invited the whole town. They had a big feast with stew and lots of oranges and apples. They gave Jitkanj'əs a big bowl of oranges mixed with grease and sugar. Her mother told her to say "Haadé" ["people"] real loud as they gave it to her. They wiped her mouth with a kerchief and then she gave ten dollars to ten men of the opposite tribe, one dollar to each. The doing lasted for two days, the ṣansəngáda. The second day my uncle had a picnic across at Kiusta. He made Emma Matthews and me make sandwiches, ham sandwiches with hot mustard on them. Even though we were little girls, we were real busy. They had soda pop there, too. The bottles used to come in barrels—real big barrels just full of soda pop and funny bottles with round bottoms. The whole town had a picnic with my uncle. My mother and grandmother helped my uncle with the food and they gave him money toward his ɢansangáda. After it was all over they cut the totem pole up for firewood.

When I was little they had strong Church Army here. There was a Church Army hall down by the beach. I used to go there all the time with other kids. I liked to sing and I liked to watch the ladies in the Church Army. We used to go to church every Sunday. Saturday night we used to bathe and wash our hair, and I'd braid my hair in all kinds of braids. Sunday morning when I'd comb it out my dad used to say, "Jadał q'egəngá, your hair's so big you can't go through the church door." My dad told us if there was any wrong-doing the devil would punish us and that would make me real scared. "Someday the world's going to end and the bad ones are going to get punished," he said. At church, they used to have just men's choir and I thought men in the choir were the very best kind. None of them were bad. When I went to church with my parents I used to pray that when I grew up I'd get married to someone in the choir. So the devil wouldn't punish me.

I used to play with Phoebe Stanley and Josephine Ridley all the time. My cousin, Douglas Edenshaw, used to play with us sometimes, too.

During my time boys used to play together and girls played together, but Douglas played with us because his parents didn't allow him to go away from home. Other boys would go to North Beach or anyplace they wanted to. Once I went to North Beach when I was about ten and my mother spanked me for it. It was my dad's idea for us to stay by home because of what happened to my older brother Ginawən.

We used to play dolls and we played hʔəntz gudangan, "pretend." We pretended to talk like grownups. I don't think we pretended at things like watəł [potlatching] or s'aɢgá [winter dancing]. During my time all the older people were Christians and they don't even joke about things like that. They were scared to joke because it was just like doing it. So they don't pretend. They're scared of God, I guess.

One time we were playing together, hiding, and Douglas came to us with a dead cat. Soon as he brought this cat to us Phoebe suggested, "Let's pretend to have a funeral." Daisy and Dolly Edenshaw, my cousins, and Nora, my sister, were with us then, too. Four of us carried that dead cat and we made ourselves real sad singing "Roll On, Dark Stream." Whenever there was a funeral the Church Army used to sing this hymn. We were all singing and going down toward the cemetery real slow. We heard someone yelling at us so we looked and my uncle's wife was coming at us with a big stick. We dropped the cat and we all ran home.

Once Phoebe, Emma [Matthews], Douglas, and I decided to play wedding in the woods. "You want to marry Douglas?" "No." They ask another one. "No." They were all shy. "Who's going to marry Douglas?" No one said anything. "Florence, you marry him." "OK." We got somebody's veil to take to the woods. Phoebe and Emma put flowers at the front of the veil. They worked at it for quite a while and then they put flowers on their hats that they made out of skunk cabbage leaves, and they made bouquets. All the bridesmaids followed me down to the village. I don't remember if we pretended to have a feast or not. I must have been ten or eleven.

Below the hill called Hijaw there was an old longhouse with three old people staying there. My mother used to cook for them and she had us bring the food to them because they were so old. One time my mother soaked real lots of k'aw [herring spawn] that she had dried at Skidegate and put it in a big preserving kettle. "You girls go bring this to the old man," she said to us. Dolly [Edenshaw] and I and Douglas and Nora went to bring the k'aw there. "Florence, you sit down and rest," Douglas said to me. So we all sat down around that kettle and started eating the k'aw to make it lighter. We did that twice and my mother came out of the house screaming: "Hurry up, before you finish it, and bring it to the old people!" We got real scared and brought it to them right away.

We used to make our own dolls because there's no store here with dolls. The head was made of colored cloth and the eyes, nose, and mouth were embroidered on. We stuffed the head with rags or anything. When I started going to school the missionaries gave the kids Christmas presents, toys and things. They gave all the girls my age pretty wax dolls; we were so proud of the dolls. The missionaries had a Christmas tree and they gave coffee to the adults and cocoa to the kids; they baked all kinds of cakes to eat, and cookies. We sang Christmas carols that the missionary's wife taught us. When someone broke her wax doll she used to bring the broken parts and give the pieces of wax to her best friends to chew. Just like chewing gum. I used to wish for it but nobody gave me any.

When I was a little girl my Uncle Henry Edenshaw used to play Santa Claus for us. "Christmas Song," "Father Christmas," we used to call it. We hung up stockings and around midnight he'd come and fill them up with all kinds of things: nuts, raisins, oranges, apples, and bottles of fruit syrup. We hung our stockings in the front room by the door.

At Yatz where my mother used to garden I played with Sophie Marks. We used to make boats out of driftwood bark. We put a stick on the boat for a mast and cloth for a sail. I would sit a rag doll in the boat and sail it in a puddle across to the other side. When the boat landed Phoebe would welcome it. She used to sing while we were playing. She sang all kinds of Haida songs. Sophie used to enjoy the Haida songs very much, but not me. My mother used to sing hymns all the time when she was weaving, I didn't learn Haida songs until I was old. Sophie and I also used to collect chitons at Yatz. She was real active, but I wasn't; I was real clumsy compared to her. My parents used to keep me at home so much, that's why I'm not like her. We pried the chitons off the rocks with a butcher knife and when we came home we cooked them in the fire.

When I was little we played a ball game. We called the ball *sqwəsqáajaw* ["round thing they throw"]. I gathered moss and stuffed it in a little bag made from a clean flour sack. Then my mother would sew up the bag and crochet pretty colored wool around it. We'd throw the ball over the smokehouse roof and as soon as someone on the other side caught it he'd run around the house and try to hit someone with it. The one who was hit was out of the game.

My grandmother used to love us just like any grandmother does. I thought no one could be like my grandmother. She used to like combing my hair when I went to visit her. She used to ask me what I want to eat and she let me eat anything I wished when I visited her.

The summer they first started handtrolling I must have been about twelve years old, and I went with my grandparents to North Island where they camped while my step-grandfather [Phillip White] fished. It was my dad's idea, because my grandmother was sick with rheumatism and couldn't walk anymore. They were living in a tent at North Island and I looked after my grandmother while her husband went fishing. I was real surprised that my parents let me go because they didn't used to let us out of their sight. One day at North Island my grandfather asked me if I wanted to go out fishing the next day. I gladly said yes. I went out three times with him and he didn't catch anything. When Sophie went fishing with her father they caught lots of spring salmon. "You're just unlucky, that's why we don't catch anything," my grandfather said to me. It made me feel real bad. He used to kind of pick on me. At home my mother and dad never said a mean word to us, that's why I couldn't stand it when my grandfather talked like that. Just then my Uncle Henry came to North Island on his gas boat. "I want to go home with you," I told him. So I asked my grandmother and she agreed. "You do that," she said, "you're getting homesick for your parents." I was real happy to get home. I spent three weeks with my grandmother at North Island.

Chapter 7

I Become a Woman and Marry (1909–1911)

I was thirteen. My mother didn't tell me what *təgwəná* [menstruation] was. All I knew was "*təgwəná*," I didn't know how *təgwəná* goes. I was real scared. You don't know anything about the blood and you bleed so much. Young girls used to be real shy. They thought that what happened to you was bad and so they don't talk about it; they just kept it to themselves. Lots of girls I knew had theirs way before me. I used to wish I was them. I wished I was lying down like them. Emma had hers before me and I thought she was so lucky (she was two years older). When it happened to me my mother told me not to say a word and to lie down and relax. I didn't mind, I felt bigger. They hung the sheets close to the bed and I lay down for ten days.

During that time I couldn't drink water because it would bring me bad luck for the rest of my life. I couldn't look at the sea because they say if you do, when you're older your face twitches. Eating shellfish also brings bad luck. As much as you try to get food, you can't. During my *təgwəná* they don't let a girl eat anything fresh. You're not supposed to eat much. In the old days they used to give young girls black cod [but not during the *təgwəná*]; they made them eat the whole fish so that afterwards the girls wouldn't be hoggy. They didn't let me talk much because I would get the habit of talking all the time. You have to have respect for yourself, my mother told me.

My younger sisters, Nora and Alice, came to visit me. When they were around they were shy because my parents don't let me talk. I remember someone who was *təgwəná* and she told her sisters to get water, to sneak water to her. The people laughed at her so I tried all my best not to do that. Sophie Marks came to visit me once during that time. Just she and my sisters visited me.

At the end of ten days or two weeks they let me get up and sit around the house. I was kind of shy because I went like that; I was the "talk of the town" because I *təgwəná*. My mother gathered bowls[1] until my *təgwəná*. Afterwards she gave them out to those she loves, I guess. She gave Sophie material and something else because she came to see me.[2] My mother didn't call the women together because of the missionary; she just gave the bowls out in a secret way. My grandmother called the women together when Emily went like that, and for Agnes too. I don't think they did it for Nora; she's three years younger than me; we became like a white people then. They quit it because it's not a nice thing to do to spread the news around.

When I was still a small girl, a girl from Masset had a big potlatch at her *təgwəná*. She was sixteen or seventeen and never got her period, so they pretended and had a doing anyway. She was the only girl in the family and her mother was a rich woman; she owned a store. They invited all the Eagle tribe, even men, and gave out lots of things. Everybody knew it was pretend. Not long after, the girl got quinsy and died with it.

My grandmother used to tell me how I was supposed to act. She'd call me if I did anything wrong and say, "Florence if you keep doing that no one's going to marry you," and I'd get real scared. I don't want to be single. I was small but I thought she meant something real terrible. Here when I got married, I felt so sorry for myself. I used to think marriage law is like tying you down with iron. Now people think nothing of it.

My grandmother used to tell me not to stand up and drink water: "Before you drink water, you sit down." Just men and boys were supposed to stand up to drink water. I guess she wanted me to be a lady. She told me a white people's story about what I should do. A young girl baked bread and had dough under her fingernails.

1. China washbowls were typically distributed at late nineteenth- and early twentieth-century potlatches.

2. Traditionally, a girl was visited during her seclusion by her *sqaʔanləng* (women of father's lineage), who instructed and advised her. Sophie Marks and the other women Florence mentioned who received property following her *təgwəná* were all members of Florence's father's lineage.

Florence Davidson, c. 1919

Her boyfriend asked her when she had baked bread. "Two days ago," she said. And the dough was still on her fingernails so her boyfriend quit her. That's why you're supposed to wash your hands real clean right after you fix bread, she told me. And one time she told me about a young girl and boy who were going to get married. The young boy came to the door and the girl's shoes weren't laced up! Both of her shoes were untied and untidy. "Did you just get up?" he asked her. "No, a long time ago." The next day when he went to see her she was dressed the same. He found out she wasn't sensible so he quit her. "So, soon as you get up, you lace your shoes," my grandmother said to me. She also used to tell me a story about the olden days. In the old days a girl married her dad's nephew [father's sister son]. Before they were married the boy would get wood for her dad, his uncle. And the girl would cook seaweed for her dad's nephew. When the older boy put the spoon to his mouth the seaweed was hanging off and it spilled on his front. The younger nephew was able to keep it on the spoon so it doesn't spill. When she found out the older boy wasn't sensible she told her dad she wasn't going to marry him; so they let her marry the younger one. Sure enough, the older one got married to a different girl and he couldn't get much of anything, but the younger boy used to know how to get things and he and his wife became rich.

Before I got married my mother used to tell me to have respect for my husband. Don't let him wash dishes or his own clothes. She told me not to wash my husband's clothes with mine, to keep his separate. Also she said you're not supposed to wash kids' clothes with grownups' clothes because kids wet the bed. You're not supposed to mix pillow cases or sheets with the clothes, and you have to wash dish cloths and towels separate from the clothing. If you mix them it brings you bad luck. You're not even supposed to wash your face in the dish pan. You have your wash basin separate from what you wash your face in, and when you spill the water out, you don't spill face water where you spill the dish water. If you spill the face water in the pail for the dirty dish water it will cloud your eyes and you can't see clearly. My dad told all of us not to eat too much shellfish or drink too much water. It brings you bad luck, he said; you become poor.

THE MARRIAGE PROPOSAL

When the Indians lived on these islands, and no white settlers were present, their marriage customs were altogether different from ours.

The missionaries came among them, and married all of those living under the tribal custom. The older people have, since that time, arranged all marriages, and this custom is only another form of carrying out the Indian way of years ago. The result has not been to bring happiness to the families. . . . [Deasy, 1915:95]

The girls look for a home, with the surroundings they have been brought up in. The eligible young men are few, and a great number have no homes of their own. There is a custom, among the Indians, of the friends and relatives selecting the bride and groom. In some cases, unhappy marriages are the result. If the girl does not marry, what is there for her to do but to return to the old home, where the elderly people talk the language of the tribe, and where she must again take her place as a helper. She is then taken to the cannery, where nothing good is learned, and many fall away. [Deasy 1917:98]

I was still going to school yet when several people came into my dad's house to propose for my husband-to-be. I was wondering what was going on when all these people came in. The women all belonged to *C'al'lanas*, my husband's tribe [lineage], and the men all belonged to my husband's dad's tribe *Stl'ang'lanas*, except for my husband's brother. They were all streaming in and I didn't know what was going on so I ran to my uncle's house. I told my cousin Josie who all came in to my dad's house and she started laughing. She didn't tell me what was happening. Maybe a week later her sister Dolly got some ammonia in a quart bottle and she opened it and said, "You smell this, Florence, sniff it real hard." I sniffed it and I almost fell down. I didn't know ammonia before that. "You know why I made you smell it?" she asked me. "No," I said. "When you don't want to get married you smell it and you really want to get married afterwards." I didn't know why she said that to me.

"Don't say anything when I tell you something," my mother said to me. "Those who came in last week proposed to you." I didn't know what to say. Propose! Why? I thought. I was just a kid yet. I didn't know what to say and mother advised me not to say anything about the proposal because they were high-class [*y'aʔᵪEyt*] people.

The next week Josie said to me in English, "Florence, you know they proposed to you?" I don't know anything, I don't know English. "No, I don't know what you're talking about," I said. "They want you to marry Robert Davidson," she said. And she laughed and laughed. I thought she was just teasing me. I told my mother what my cousin said. "Did you say yes?" I asked her. "No, your dad sent them to your uncle. Your dad says he's got nothing to do with it; it has to go through your uncle. You have more respect for your uncle than for us," she told me. "That's the only brother I have." "You're going to make me marry," I said. "Yes, you're going to marry him." "I'm not going to marry him," I said. "Don't say that, Florence, he's a real prince [y'aʔɢEyt]".

It bothered me so much. For a long time I couldn'ʈ sleep when I went to bed. Every day I bothered mother. "I'm not going to marry that old man. I'm not. If you make me marry him, summertime I'll run away. You won't see me again." My mother didn't say anything though every day I used to bother her. My dad didn't say a word to me about it. Finally, my mother said, "Don't say anything dear. Your uncle thinks it's best for you to marry him. He's a prince. He's going to respect you all your life and if you don't want to marry him you're going to feel bad all your life. He belongs to clever people; you're not going to be hard up for anything. We need a young man's help, too. You must remember that. We belong to chiefs too and you're not supposed to talk any old way. You have to respect yourself more than what you worry about." I don't want to say any more because my mother said I'd be sorry for the rest of my life if I didn't marry him. I made up my mind not to say anything much as I disliked it.

The night after my husband's relatives came to my dad's house they went to see my uncle. They asked someone to go there first and my uncle said they could all come in and talk to him. So they went in and my uncle agreed with it right away. In the olden days it was a disgrace for a girl to get a baby without a husband so they married the girls early. It was a disgrace for the girl's uncle and her parents, too. They went to my uncle because he's head of the family. My dad put it into my uncle's hands too because my uncle knew about the ways of white people. My dad thought I was too young and was hoping that my uncle would tell them to wait for another year or two years time. When my uncle agreed with it right away my dad was kind of disappointed. My uncle thought it was all right for me to get married because they don't want to lose out on Robert Davidson. He's sensible and clever and he's y'aʔɢEyt.

It was around Christmas time when they came in to propose. I was fourteen that September. They proposed for the next year, summertime, but soon as my uncle agreed to it they wanted to have the doing right away. It makes me wish I was dead. We got married February 23, 1911.

I went to school until just a few days before I got married. After they decide to make me marry, while I'm still going to school, my mother made long skirts for me. Gee, it was embarrassing. Young schoolgirls don't used to wear long dresses; they have short dresses. You know how it could be. I was ashamed to go out.

THE WEDDING

It has been usual for the White race to imagine that the aborigines of this coast are lacking in many ways from the customs of our people and particularly in the manner in which they take to themselves life partners . . . it might prove interesting to describe the ceremonies which [mark Haida weddings].

. . . usually in the afternoon the wedding party starts from the house of the bride for the church, headed by a brass band in full uniform, and accompanied by the men, women and children of the reserve. The groom is dressed in the latest fashion, with a white flower in his buttonhole, and is accompanied by his best man. The bride, attired in white, with a bridal veil and orange blossoms, is accompanied by a party of bridesmaids, all looking charming in their white costumes.

A choir, comprising the membership of the tribe, await the entry of the wedding party, when they sing some appropriate hymn, accompanied on the organ by the choirmaster, who is also a native.

After the ceremony, which is carried out in the English language, the bridal party is escorted to the town hall, where tables are groaning under the delicacies of the season.

On a raised platform the principal wedding guests take their seats with the bride and groom. Tables are ranged along the entire length of the hall, for the whole of the members of the band, comprising 350 people.

At a given signal, grace is sung by the assemblage, and the wedding dinner, which has taken many days to prepare, is indulged in.

It has always been the custom to provide everything new for the invited Whites. The tableware is of the best, and the culinary art of those who prepared the edibles, must be seen to be appreciated. Frosted cakes, jellies, fruits, nuts, and every conceivable delicacy is present. In order to provide the necessary beef for so large a crowd, one of the many cattle, owned by the Indians is slaughtered some days before, and served at the commencement of the repast.

In the centre of the table occupied by the invited guests is the proverbial wedding cake, which is afterward cut and distributed to all present. Again at the close of the supper thanks are given for the good things provided, and oratory is indulged in.

Relatives of the contracting parties open the speech-making by wishing long life and prosperity to the happy couple. All of the white persons present are expected to speak on the occasion, which some do in English and others in Haida or Chinook. After all who desire have expended the necessary number of felicitations, the hall is cleared and dancing is indulged in. . . . An orchestra, consisting of natives, provides the latest music to which the young men and women dance two-steps, waltzes and modern measures. The evening passes in merriment and good feeling. [Deasy 1913:4]

My husband-to-be was married before, to Alfred Adams' niece [sister's daughter]. His wife wasn't healthy; she got TB and died young. I thought Robert Davidson was a real old man. One time before we were married he took me to New Masset to do some shopping. He told me I could buy anything I wanted to. It was snowing, lots of snow on the ground. We went by the beach to town. I walked real fast so I don't go close to him.

After the proposal the men on my husband's side held lots of meetings. After my uncle said "yes," they're the ones who had to do the worrying. My dad sent for my husband's older brother, T'ak [Alfred Davidson], and he told him not to make the wedding too big. "It's not lucky to have too big a doing," my dad said. If the doing was too big I might have a short life; that's what they believed. My dad got ten boxes of pilot bread and lots of apples, maybe ten of that too. Alfred Davidson bought the rest; lots of apples and bundles of "Jap" oranges. The women of my husband's side baked lots of pies and cakes by Alfred Davidson's place. But they forgot to order the wedding cake. Emma Matthews was supposed to get married at the same time but she got a sore throat and they postponed her wedding. So they tried to borrow Emma's wedding cake while she was sick.

The day of the wedding they started cooking beef stew. The young men of my husband's side looked after the big pots of stew cooking outside, but the Raven side helped, too.

Kate Jones made my wedding dress and she wanted to give it to me because she and my husband were closely related, *gudʔał qiwa*.[3] The day of the wedding the village band came to get me; they divided the band and half went to get the groom and half picked up the bride. Charlotte Marks's father, Thomas Weah, gave me away, not my dad. That's how they used to do it in the olden days.[4] The band played the wedding march as we went down to the church. The groom is supposed to go with his dad's relatives, same as the girl. I don't remember who went with my husband, maybe his stepfather, Richard Naylans, and James Jones. Reverend Hogan

3. This is an important kinship relationship in Haida culture. Individuals who are *gudʔał qiwa* (*ał qiwa*, for short) have fathers who belong to the same lineage. The two *ał qiwa* individuals do not belong to the same lineage, though they would, of course, belong to the same moiety. The relationship is likened to siblingship. Kate Jones later requested payment for the wedding dress.

4. Thomas Weah (also referred to as Thomas Weir in census records) belonged to *Sdəłdás*, Florence's father's lineage.

married us. I was stubborn; I wouldn't say the promises. I guess I thought I wouldn't be really married if I didn't answer when they asked me. I felt bad the whole time. Right after, we went to the community hall. It was full of people. They made all kinds of speeches, the *Stl'əng'lanas*, my husband's dad's relatives. They even sang a song for me composed by my husband's stepfather. I don't remember the song. Alfred Adams stood up and adopted me at the wedding dinner because his niece used to be married to my husband. He said he thought of me just like his own niece. He kept his promise—he treated me nice all of his life.

The people brought their own dishes to the feast. They ate stew with lots of pilot crackers. There were apples and oranges in front of each plate, just like now, and lots of *qawqEł* [food to be taken home by each guest]. They brought empty fifty-pound flour sacks to take the things home in. After they cleared the hall, they started dancing—waltzes, quadrilles, real lively songs.

I didn't enjoy any of it. I felt real bad because I was a married woman. Everybody but me was real happy. I don't remember any more about the wedding, it was too awful.

CHAPTER 8

I Become a Mother and Have Lots of Children (1912–1938)

. . . there is no doubt that the Hydah nation is ambitious to become a part of the British nation freed from wardship, and capable of exercising the franchise, on this side of the line as their brethren are on United States territory. Individually, a large percentage of them read and write. They take a keen interest in everything that goes on around them. Their internal affairs are managed by councils, elected annually, and working under by-laws, approved by the department. They have their churches, town halls, good streets, presentable residences, wharves, brass bands, gasoline launches, row-boats, cattle, horses, and all modern improvements including water-works. When at their home towns, the school-houses are filled with pupils, and they are asking for a boarding school, to which they guarantee to send every eligible girl and boy. They all dress well, and the able-bodied Indian asks for no relief, earning a living for himself and his family.

. . . The women are the principal gardeners. They prepare small gardens, before the fishing season, and grow vegetables for winter use. The women and children work in the canneries, for about two months, and the whole family make enough to carry them through the winter.

. . . The Massets did not construct many new houses. They made an improvement as good, in tearing down all the old shacks, along the waterfront, formerly occupied as dwellings, and in removing the signs of former times, the "totem" poles. . . . Since the introduction of the councils, the Indians are doing away with old ideas and customs. The former chiefs are no longer the official heads of the band. In place of the "totem" pole, they have erected flagstaffs, from which they float the British flag. If all Indians disposed of the "totem" poles, and the hereditary chiefs were eliminated, it would go a great way towards suppressing the "potlatch" and the "feast." [Deasy 1917:96–97]

After we married we stayed with my parents for quite a while, till I had two kids. My grandmother Amy helped us buy our first little house. I told my grandmother, "Joshua Collison wants to sell his house. I really want it but we can't buy it." "It's all right, dear, I'll buy it for you," she said. The house was one hundred dollars. She gave me fifty dollars in gold and we paid the rest when my husband went trapping. Summertime we paid my grandmother back. We gave her paper money but she didn't care. We were real happy to move into that small house. It had just one bedroom and the kitchen, but in two years time my husband bought some lumber and added on a sixteen-by-sixteen-foot front room. *Q'atgusge*, we call it. That's where the honored guests are seated.[1]

My husband used to work hard for my parents. He cut logs for them for the winter. Ever since I married I don't think my dad ever worried about having wood. When my husband went hunting he used to get enough for my parents, and we used to fish for them, too. My dad gave my husband money all the time or bought him clothes.

After I was married I used to pack my sister Emily's little girl, Effie, around. "Emily, let me have this baby," I said. I used to dress her up and take her for walks all the time. I pretended to look like a mother.

People here thought I wasn't going to get babies, that I was *q'eq'ala* [barren] because I didn't have my first baby for a long time. When I got married I didn't know anything about men. My mother used to tell me before I got married to keep away from boys. "Soon as you go with boys," she said, "you get pregnant." That's why I used to be so scared of boys. I didn't let my husband touch me for a long time. He told someone I didn't want babies because he's not handsome. Finally, I gave in. All day long the next day I was ashamed; I don't know what to think. Here it wasn't that difficult!

My mother wanted me to have a big family so I'd have lots of kids

---

1. On social/ceremonial occasions the "front room" is the modern equivalent of the interior of the traditional Haida house. The focal point of the house, this room is used for feasts, meetings, and mortuary potlatches ("memorials"). The two critical directional terms applied to the traditional house interior—*k'iaʔgaga* (the door side) and *t'ʔacgwa* (the chief's side or place)—are reference points in the front room as well.

to help Henry Edenshaw. Two of my boys used to help him, and Agnes' and Emily's older boys. My grandmother was so happy because all of us had lots of children. In the olden days, they used to give young girls little birds like sea gulls to eat so they'll have lots of kids.[2] My mother used to say, "I want those little birds for you so you'll have a big family." She wanted them for me too because I acted like a boy when I was little. I don't want to eat them so I refused her. I wanted to be a mother for a bunch of kids; as many children as I have I accept it. Today they have two or three kids and they quit. I don't understand it. I wanted a boy first because we had no brother. When I got pregnant for the first time, whoever saw me said, "I wish you have a boy." And I got a boy.

When I was ready to deliver, my mother, my aunt, Martha Edenshaw, and my sister Emily looked after me. In the olden days, my mother told me, women used to take four stones from the corners of the fire and put them under the waistband of their skirts. They get up early and walk toward the beach and every few steps they drop a stone till they're all gone. It makes them get their babies easier.[3] I don't know if my mother did it when she was pregnant with me; I didn't want to do it. My mother was real scared when I was about to deliver; she rushed around, preparing things. I wasn't scared. I didn't know anything about delivering babies. All night long I was in labor and toward morning Alfred was born. He was so big and my mother was real happy. My sister Emily had a baby born the same day, Dora. As long as my mother was living she and Emily helped me deliver my babies. But after my mother died, I got them all by myself.

I didn't have morning sickness when I was pregnant, but I didn't enjoy pregnancy either. You can't do as much work then. When you get the baby, though, it's the happiest time you have.

Two years after Alfred, I got another boy, Arnold. Arnold died when he was eighteen, in 1933. He was at boarding school painting the school building and he fell from the scaffold and landed on a can of paint. He started hemorrhaging. He got TB and he knew he wasn't going to get well. We brought him home and he died in October.

Helen was born after Arnold. She died in 1926 with black measles when she was eleven years old. She was at boarding school at Sardis, and when she took sick her dad went to get her and brought

2. Florence could not remember the English or Haida name for these birds; they are not reported in the literature.
3. Charlie Nowell (Ford 1941:157) notes that the Kwakiutl do the same.

Florence and her sisters, 1940s (*left to right*: Emily, Nora, Florence, and Agnes)

her home. She died here in February. Virginia was born next, and then Reggie. Reggie was a small baby; I was only seven months pregnant when he was born. Because he was born way ahead of time we used to keep the fire going all night long for two months. I kept him close by me and pulled the sheets around us. Reggie was killed in 1958 launching a boat. I used to worry about him so much and I used to pray for him all the time because he drank. I was away visiting at the time, in Hydaburg, when I got the news. When I first heard it I thought he'd been drinking and was killed on the highway.

After Reggie, Claude was born, at Watun cannery. Joyce came after Claude—Amy Joyce. After I got up I went to my grandmother with this baby and asked her if I could call the little girl after her. "I think a lot of your baby because you ask me for the name," she said. She was so happy that I asked to use her name. When Joyce was three years old we went up to Ain River camp to dry fish and she took sick. We had been there for one week and got lots of dog salmon. I was cutting and slicing fish all day long. I guess my little girl got double pneumonia; she was foaming at the mouth. She was three years old but she didn't talk yet. That very day she said, "Mum, I want to use the pot." I was real surprised. I thought she was so cute, talking real plain. Here she died that very night.

Primrose was next. When she was almost due I went berry picking with my friend Emily Parnell at Kayang, near Masset. It had been raining real hard and it was just like a lake in the woods. Right above the water there were lots of blueberry bushes. I was up to my chest in water so I could pick those big berries hanging over the water. I kept on picking and filled up a big preserving kettle with blueberries. We walked home with the big pot of berries. Next day I didn't feel like preserving it, I was too tired. In the evening Primrose was born. I had no time to work on the berries and Emily was too busy in the cannery to take them. The kids didn't care to eat them, so all my hard work got thrown out.

My mother died the year Primrose was born. She died in May and in August when Primrose was born I was all alone; I got her by myself. Emma Alexander came to see me right after Primrose was born. She picked the baby up and said, "Oh, I dreamt my sister [Isabella Edenshaw][4] came back." That's why she was so happy,

4. Emma Alexander and Isabella Edenshaw were *gudʔał qiwa* (see note 3, chap. 7), thus the former's use of the term "sister." The pattern of reincarnation here is much more traditional, occurring within the same lineage.

because Primrose was the second birth of my mother. Just Primrose, Reggie, and Claude were second births. Claude used to say he was the second birth of David Bell. David Bell drowned and Claude, when he was about four or five, used to say to me, "Mum, under the water it's just like on earth. Just trees and flowers on the ground—that's how it looks under the water." Mary Bell used to love him just like her own son. Reggie was supposed to be the second birth of my dad. When he was about one month old he looked at his hands just like he was carving; but when he started using his hands he was left-handed. My dad was right-handed and he said before he died he was tired of carving and wouldn't carve when he came back. People used to believe in second birth [*cants*] so much.

After Primrose I had a miscarriage. Nothing caused it. I didn't work too hard. I was alone then, too. Four months pregnant. Emily, my sister, looked after me. I cried real hard, just like I lost a big baby.

There were five years between Primrose and my next baby, Emily. Emily was born here, in February. I don't know who was by me when I had Emily, nobody I guess. I used to be all alone after my mother died. Gee, that's crazy, being all alone, just like an animal. I was a kind of nurse, I guess, delivering my babies. I could have been a nurse if I'd gone to school.

Myrtle was next, born here in the house, then Aggie. Aggie was born the summer that Arnold was sick with TB. When she was due, I put my bedding in the back room so Arnold wouldn't know what was going on, and I hid myself away in labor. Soon as the pain went away I got up and walked around. I went to where he was to see how he was doing. "What's wrong with you, Mother, you're so quiet." "Nothing," I said, "I was just doing some work in the other room." I got my baby all alone. As soon as she was born I cut the cord and I had everything ready with me. I tied the cord and wrapped her in nice clean diapers, and put blankets around her. Mary Ridley used to come in all the time and see how I was doing. She told me to send the kids to her if I needed help. After I had the baby, I sent Primrose to get Mary Ridley. "Tell her to come in the back door because my son is lying in the front room." When she came in she felt sorry for me because I was all alone. "Why did you do that, dear?" she asked. "I don't want to bother you. I thought I didn't need help so I just wanted to be alone." Everything was all right so they fixed up a bed in the other room for me and put me there. I was staying there for over a week when my husband came home from fishing. He looked after the house and worked just like a woman would work, setting bread, baking, cooking for the kids.

Merle was born after Aggie. We were at fishing camp, Dadens, on North Island. Clara, the youngest was born at Naden. I was working in the cannery there. I was all alone again with both Merle and Clara.

After your baby is born you're supposed to stay in bed for four weeks.[5] My Aunt Martha Edenshaw did that. When I got older I used to stay in bed for only two weeks, but at first I stayed in bed for three weeks time. Right after the baby is born the mother is supposed to drink [eulachon] grease, nothing else. I did that; I love it [grease]. I nursed my babies for a year and a half, till I got pregnant again. Soon as I get pregnant, I quit nursing them. When I had my babies they were no longer painting the eyebrows like they did when I was born. And I didn't pierce my girls' ears when they were tiny. They did their own or each other's when they were small kids, I guess.

From Emily on down my children talked English. I thought it was real smart that they were talking English. My sister Nora told me, "You talk English to them when they're three months old, then they'll talk English, nothing but English."

Emily George, who was maid of honor at my wedding, didn't get her own children. She adopted one of her sister's boys, and her sister Margaret used to advise me: "Dear, you're young and get children so often; whenever someone wants to adopt one, don't let the child go. Hang on to it. It's all right when the child dies because when they bury it you know where it goes, but when it's living, if your child lives with your sister, it makes you feel worse than anything else." That's why I've got a bunch of children; I don't want anyone else to keep them for me. I'm glad she used to say that to me. We always tried all our best for our children. We weren't stingy with things, but we had to look after money or anything else real good. All my life when my kids were small, we managed to get by. We don't bother other people. We used to put up so much food; we worked hard together, my husband and I. I don't think I ever rested to be a lady. Sometimes I used to wash till three o'clock in the morning. Now the government spoils people. If you don't work you get welfare. That's what makes everything different nowadays. Now every month, even if you're not working, you can get lots of money. Life is real easy now, but we used to live good.

5. Four is also a ritual number in Haida.

Florence and daughter Clara, c. 1940

My dad used to advise me not to talk about my children, what they do or how they act. "Don't waste other people's time," he said. "Just a mother thinks her children are cute; other people don't care. You waste their time and they dislike it, especially if your children are ugly." I found that out, because Alfred was ugly when he was little. I used to obey my dad and not say anything about my children when I see other mothers talking about theirs.

My mother used to tell me all the time to have respect for my husband, not to let him wash clothes or cook for himself because he was out working for his living. "When your husband comes home, you have to serve him," she said. "If you think low of your husband and don't do those things, everyone thinks nothing of you. No one cares for you if you don't treat your husband right."

Our great grandmothers believed that even if they don't make enough for a living, they don't tell anybody. If they say anything about it they become like that [poor] for the rest of their lives; it brings bad luck. That's why all our grandmothers were rich. Even though they were rich they keep it a secret. They don't want to tell anybody how much they make. If you're poor and you have rich relatives you don't tell them you're poor; it brings bad luck. Haidas are too proud to tell others they're poor. We just believe in helping other people. My mother and grandmother used to tell us that it pays to be kind. What you give away, it comes back to you. When you give food to others, more will come back to you.

My Uncle Henry Edenshaw used to say to my oldest sister Emily, "I'm old and when anything happens to me, don't be like a girl." Girls are supposed to be helpless; if they want to do anything, the people thought they can't do it. My sister used to say to me all the time: "Don't be hopeless when there's anything to be done. Do like a man would do."

My Husband

My husband's father, Nałang, was chief at Yan [village across the inlet from Masset] and his uncle was chief in Alaska, at Cape Chacon. My husband had ten Indian names, but I only know one of them, Itłagitgwinəng q'Endlas, his uncle's name. My husband gave the name to Father Kreager [minister at Masset, 1965–69]. It means the totem pole, the biggest pole among the Haidas, was so tall and the eagle on top of it was looking down at all the chiefs. That was his real [i.e., inherited] name, but they called him Gəniyá, after his grandfather.

He was real strong and ambitious, my husband. What other men couldn't do, he could. Even when he was old he was the same. He was real clever. He was a fisherman and a carpenter. We got lots of fish but when there was no fish he used to work wintertime for white men, building boats, repairing boats. He built houses in the village, too. Once he made a bed for the children with a headboard and he painted flower and leaf designs on it. My dad used to admire the bed when he came in. "Why doesn't your husband come and carve with me. I could leave him all my tools," my dad said. My husband just laughed. "I can't sit down and do anything," he said. "I'd rather run around fishing; I like going out." If he'd worked with my dad I could have a carved wall now! My husband didn't start carving until he was an old man.

When we first got married, my husband used to run a trapline with his brother Alfred. They trapped land otter and marten, but when World War I started, they worked at a logging camp doing handlogging. My husband and his cousins (George Jones, David Jones, and George Brooks) checked around to get a real good spot to do handlogging. The government scaler would come around to measure all their logs and each one knew how much he was going to get. They made real lots of money. When they finished the trees there we went to get my teeth fixed. They used to make fun of me. "Tree-money teeth. She's real proud of her tree-money teeth," they used to say.

We had about three kids when my husband was handlogging and we used to enjoy camping near where they worked at Awun. I used to save the money my husband made to buy material and make clothes for the kids, dresses and shirts. It was wintertime when we stayed at camp and everything froze up. I washed clothes in the washtub in the shed where we were living and then took them to the creek to rinse. It was quite a ways to the creek. I wrung the water out with my hands and kept myself warm by putting my hands under my arms every little while. When I finished rinsing, I took the clothes back to the shed to hang up. I used to keep the fire real hot so things will get dry quick.

My husband liked working. He used to smoke when we still had only a few kids and then he quit smoking, to save money. He was thinking of me and the children, so he quit smoking. He liked me to dress up all the time and he didn't want me to have my hair any old way. Even two weeks before he died he kept on telling me to get dressed the proper way. So I combed my hair and put makeup on. I put my best dress on. Soon as I came out of the bedroom he was smiling away. "*Wha!*" he said. When you like something best of all you say "*Wha!*"

FRIENDS

> Today at a family gathering I watched Nani and Selina Peratrovich
> sitting beside each other in animated conversation. They speak, they
> listen and respond with youthful energy, but between them they have
> accumulated a total of nearly 175 years, more than two dozen children,
> over 100 grandchildren and great-grandchildren, and more years of
> marriage than probably either would care to tally. Their friendship
> alone spans some 70 years. They are absorbed in each other's words,
> now laughing, now touching the other on the arm. I wonder if their
> Haida conversation reminisces about the early days when they picked
> berries together, the later years when Selina encouraged Nani to take
> up weaving again; do they lament arthritic hands, Nani's "head full
> of batteries," and other liabilities of old age? Somehow I think their
> conversation must be ageless. "We're just like schoolgirls together,"
> Nani once noted. Theirs has been a rich and rewarding friendship.
> [Field notes, July 13, 1980]

Selina Peratrovich, Emily Parnell, Maggie Weir, Emma Matthews,
Martha Williams (my husband's sister), and two of my older sisters
were my friends. We talk to each other about our children, I guess,
nothing else much. I don't talk much to Martha because she's way
older than me. I have more respect for her than that. All my friends
were in the choir and we picked berries together, too.

Women didn't have men for friends. If a man and woman even
talk to each other, the people say that they "go together." Even
today they say that when they know better.

WORKING

The summer after I was married they began work on the cannery at
Naden. The whole town moved there to build the cannery, but we
stayed here. Just my husband, myself, my grandmother next door,
and my uncle and his family stayed. We lived in my mother's house
while she was at Naden with my dad. Much as I wanted to go with
my parents, I couldn't. I was a married woman, no longer a little
girl. The next March someone came around and hired the men to
build the lighthouse at North Island. They hired my husband and
Henry Edenshaw moved us to North Island on his gas boat. We
lived in a tent and I took a little dog, Gwuls, that belonged to my
sister Nora, to keep the rats and mice away. My husband used to
eat in the mess house on North Island while he worked on the
lighthouse but later on I used to cook for him.

In April I wanted to go and see my mother and dad. I was so

Florence and Selina Peratrovich in Florence's kitchen (photograph by Ulli Steltzer)

young and I got lonely. My grandmother said, "If you could row, we could go to Naden." We got a boat and Mariah Smith came with us. She was kind of lazy, this Mariah Smith; she got tired of rowing real quick, and she wrapped herself in a blanket and went to sleep. My grandmother paddled, but I was the only one rowing this fourteen-foot boat. We left North Island early in the morning and it was after midnight when we got to Shag Rock [Yatz]. It looked like my parents had just been there. There was lots of food and dry wood in the house but it was empty. We camped there for the night and early the next morning I rowed us to Naden where my parents had gone. I was sixteen then.

After I was married we went away once to work in the mainland cannery, and after that we didn't go there anymore. When Alfred was about two years old we went to Alaska, Rose Inlet, with my sister's husband, Alec Yeltatzie. There were no fish there. There used to be lots, but when we went, there were no fish and the cannery didn't operate that summer. Usually we'd go at the end of May and come home at the end of September. Everybody else came home earlier from fish camp, but we were still living there with a bunch of children. We were thinking of our children, to earn a little bit more money.

My husband handtrolled at North Island and I enjoyed myself there very much. A Jew came there to sell things like tablecloths, bedspreads, sheets, pins, and towels. The ladies were really excited—it seemed like we were in a city. Everyone bought lots of things.

I used to bake all the time at North Island. We took our kitchen stove with us for the summer and I baked bread and pies to sell to the fishermen. I used to be real busy doing it. Some summers I baked at Yatz instead. Lots of fishermen went there so my husband built us a one-room shack and he moved us there. I had four girls with me, Emily, Myrtle, Aggie, and Clara. Two of the girls slept by me and the other two on another bunk. We used to enjoy ourselves there. The girls picked up small sticks of driftwood for the oven and I used to bake every day: bread, apple pies, lemon pies. It used to be ten cents for a loaf of bread and two bits for the pies. My husband used to bring us supplies for baking.

While we were living in our first house I used to serve coffee and dessert in the front room. I always made pies or cakes, whatever people wanted. It used to be fifteen cents for pie and coffee. Wintertime one year I got a 2½-gallon freezer. I made ice cream and sold it for five cents a cone. I enjoy my life, doing that. Even after I had lots of children, I was still doing that. I don't want just my

husband to work for our clothes and everything. I buy the dessert
and I get things for my kids, Sunday clothes.

I served coffee and dessert in our second home, too. I quit when
the girls were going to high school; it was too much work for me
and I was thinking of my girls. But I still baked bread, and cakes
when people ordered them. During the last war I used to bake a
hundred loaves of bread a day. Sometimes fifty pounds of flour
lasted me only three days.

I think just ladies have always sliced fish. The men clean the fish
and help with the heavy things. Men think a lot of their wives. They
don't want them to get hurt or lift anything heavy. The first time I
sliced halibut after I got married, I hung it outside our house to dry
and my step-grandfather, Phillip White, came along and teased
me: "Qa, qa, qa! Florence, a big *yEł* [raven] has been eating your
halibut." He said that to me because it was all raggy looking. Here
when it got dried I gave them some. Emily George, my mother's
cousin, taught me how to slice fish. We were at Ain River fishing for
dog salmon in 1917, the first year we went there. Emily asked me if I
had a *tákadaaw*, a slicing knife.[6] "No," I said. "I've got quite a few,"
she told me, "so I'll give you one." I learned quickly and started
slicing away on what my husband brought me.

At Ain, my husband and his brother Alfred used to look after
smoking the salmon we sliced. They hung it up for us. We had a
real big smokehouse. Alfred and his wife Phoebe had one side and
we had the other. Each of us used to dry five hundred fish for the
winter. We went up Ain River at the end of September and we came
home around the middle of November. We went there during the
War years. We were drying fish there in 1918 when everyone took
sick with the bad flu. Emily George and lots of others died there. I
got the flu real bad then, too.

At the end of April we quit eating dried fish. We soaked it in
water and used it for fertilizer, what's left over from winter. We used
to go out and make gardens, past Yan but before Yatz. My husband's
sister used to go there, that's why we gardened there. Two years
after I was married we made a garden there. We also had a garden
at Yan and grew turnips, cabbage, and potatoes.

In April when we were at North Island my husband used to go
out nighttime for *s'adana* [cassin auklets]. The birds come up on land
nighttime and the people make a fire so the *s'adana* comes toward
the flame. They kill lots of it, all they want. The whole village used

6. The *tákadaaw* has a semilunar-shaped blade and is considered to be a
woman's knife.

to get lots. Sometimes young women go and get lots and give it to their friends. I didn't have much time to go out for anything except berries because I was busy with my children and washing. So my husband did it himself. When he got a hundred he thought that was plenty enough. He used to pluck the birds and clean them for me, and I would make stew from them. We looked for eggs too, in the holes [burrows] on the hillsides. I told my husband, "I don't think I could put my arms in the hole. I'm scared of a mouse or something else." "Once you take one out," he said, "you can't help yourself and you'll get carried away." Sure enough, he was right. We used to boil the eggs for a long time before we ate them. My husband would collect the eggs when he was out trolling and there were no fish. Sometimes he'd fill a pail up with eggs. He was so happy when he came home with something, all smiles. I used to like it. It made him feel good when he got anything and I was always happy then, too.

ENTERTAINMENT

> On New Year's Eve Mr and Mrs Henry Edenshaw (Christian Hydahs) were the entertainers of the largest party that ever assembled on the shores of Masset Inlet.
>
> In their large hotel, 26 guests sat down to a sumptuous repast, while the town hall was used for the entertainment of 300 of the people of the Hydah nation. The Masset Brass Band, under the leadership of Alfred Adams provided music during the dinner and for the concert which followed. On New Years' Day football teams of the white settlers and the Hydahs competed on the reserve. After playing for an hour, without either team making a goal, the umpire . . . declared that the two "clans" must meet again in the near future to settle in the same friendly way the supremacy. From all sections of Masset Inlet the settlers gathered in the town and were entertained royally by the townspeople and the Hydahs. [*North British Columbia News*, April 1911]

When I was a young kid they used to get me for a bridesmaid all the time, so I got to dance at all the weddings. My parents didn't believe, though, in letting young girls go out alone, so when I danced at weddings my mother would wait for me. That's why after I got married I enjoyed the dances so much. The winter after we were first married my husband and I used to go ballroom dancing all the time. I don't think we ever missed a dance.

We bought a player piano and at big doings the people used to borrow it. I let them use it in the town hall for weddings and dances. That's the only time we let it out, for real big doings. We bought it when we were still in our first house.

They used to invite just men to feasts. During my dad's time they used to invite people with their wives but not too often. When I was young whenever they had a real big feast just the men were invited. My dad started inviting couples to feasts. The first time my husband and I invited the people in we already had children. We invited about ten people. My husband went out hunting and got lots of ducks and geese. We cooked them, and the people we invited were real happy. They enjoyed themselves so we started inviting people in after that.

Once when I was little yet, my sister Emily invited a few people in, including Chief Weah, the town chief. They had a small dining room and I sat the people. I made a mistake and told someone else besides the chief to sit at the head of the table, and Chief Weah went away mad while they were eating.

I used to help everywhere they were making a feast. I'd bake pies and cakes. We used to use lard for cakes in the old days. I wasn't hired,[7] I just helped out. I was real glad to do it. I'm getting a rest from the house, I thought. It was just like a holiday, going out from the house. I stayed out all day long, coming home to feed four or five kids at noon, and then going back. Even before I got married I used to help at feasts, and I'm still baking.

THE NEW HOUSE

Our first little house had three rooms, a kitchen, a front room, and a bedroom. It was kind of hard for us when we had about three kids and so we started thinking about building.

In 1928 we built a new house. My husband designed and built it. It had seven bedrooms upstairs, and downstairs a sitting room, dining room, front room, and kitchen. My husband used to pile the lumber for the house on the beach. He cut the logs for the house and Mr. Robson from New Masset cut the logs at his sawmill. The people used to tease my husband. They saw the big pile of lumber and they said, "Looks like Gəniyá's going to build a cannery." I tried all my best not to buy things, to keep money toward the house. When I buy stockings I keep them just for Sundays. We had a bunch of children and I don't want to run short because we're building. We

---

7. For certain festivities, such as large feasts and mortuary potlatches, people of the opposite moiety are "hired"; that is, their services are requested and at the "doing" they are reimbursed. It is considered improper to refuse such a request.

had lots of cows at that time. We killed three big cows that winter we were building and we hung the meat on the little porch behind our house.

When the house was finished my husband invited the people in for a feast. His uncle from Skidegate called the house *Naʔa q'Enadas*. "This house is a great house," he said. "The inside is just like summertime; they don't know it's winter out there" [that is, there was so much food, as if it were summer]. That's what the name means. My husband's "grandfather," Robert Ridley, called the house *Ne gut k'iwas*, "the house is right at the road." We kept our home like new all the time. When we had company we served them in the dining room. I used to sew flour sacks for tablecloths. I put two fifty-pound bags together and crocheted lace around the edges. We used up more than fifty pounds of flour a week in those days. We stayed in that house until 1952, when we lost everything in a fire.

THE CHURCH

A reverent congregation fills the Church on the Lord's Day. There is a surpliced choir, and hearty singing. The people have the Bible in their own language and some of the prayer Book. Most of the men, and nearly all the younger people, speak good English; the children are taught English in the School. The men hold Church Army Meetings in their Hall, and Bible Classes are held during the winter. [*North British Columbia News*]

My grandmother used to take me to the White Cross ladies' meetings of the church. Because her legs were weak I went with her to the school where they held the meetings. It used to cost a dime to join and my grandmother paid my fee because I helped her. That was in 1911. I was married in February and I joined the White Cross in November. The White Cross ladies raised money for the church and looked after the church building. Whenever there was a death in the village, the White Cross looked after the casket. They made it look nice and nailed lace around it. Later the White Cross became the Women's Auxiliary and now they call them "Anglican Church Women" or ACW.

When they started the White Cross, all of the members said promises, my mother told me. They had to put their hands up and say "love your neighbor as yourself" in Haida. They also promised not to drink. The ladies used to bring their sewing to the meeting. They sewed things to sell so they could raise money for the church.

We also held basket socials to raise money for a new church.

Sometimes they would pay forty dollars for one basket of dinner.
They think nothing of doing that because they want to have a nice
church.

I got married in the old church. In 1919 the people started
building a new one. There were lots of carpenters in the village and
they were all willing to help. I told my mother I wanted to help
cook for the carpenters. They made a big kitchen at the old trading
company and the women made stew for the men in big pots. My
mother looked after my kids while I cooked; I don't think I missed a
single day. After dinner I used to go home to wash and my husband
would hang the clothes out on the line for me. Sometimes when I
was too tired he'd even do the wash on the washboard and I'd hang
it out next morning. When the church was finished they had a big
doing for the opening.

All my life I've been singing in the church choir. I don't think I
missed any choir practices or church services. My husband used to
stay home and cook lunch; just once in a great while I stayed home.
In the evening we all went to church. Those days young boys and
girls used to fill the church so there was just standing room. Nothing
else was going on at the same time as church. At Christmas time the
choir would start caroling at 10 P.M. and wouldn't finish until four in
the morning. Everyone would invite us in. We weren't tired, we'd go
to church again at eleven in the morning. It's not like that anymore.

In 1923 they elected me president of the WA [Women's Auxiliary].
After that I was always president, vice-president, secretary, or
treasurer. I can't do it anymore, though. I'm too deaf now. When I
became president in 1923 they asked me to look after the body of a
small kid who died. When Emma Matthews was president of the
WA before me she used to say, "I wonder why I'm the only one who
looks after the dead bodies?" I knew what she meant when I became
president. Maybe I've looked after a hundred dead bodies. Ethel
Jones used to help me for a long time. First time I had help was
about fifteen years ago when Thomas Marks died. My back was sore
and it was hard for me to work on him so Mary Stanley and Emma
Alexander, her sister, helped me. They bought everything for the
coffin and I lined it and we made the cover. We lined that, too, and I
put the lid on the coffin. We put a satin ribbon and cross on the lid,
and pleated lace and put it around the lid with thumbtacks. We put
the body in the coffin. Whenever I start nailing it up, it's hard for
me, thinking of when the person was alive. Even now the minister
calls me to go and see the body when there's a death. I go with him
to pray for the body.

DEATHS

> For many years now the Haidas have practiced burial beneath the ground, a special enclosure some distance from the village being set apart for that purpose. When a death takes place, the body is now placed in a coffin, and reverently borne to the mission church, where the beautiful burial service proceeds as in England. It is customary for the village brass band to head funeral processions, playing suitable hymns, even sometimes a dead march. When a death occurs, all the nearer relatives break forth in distressing wail, which is renewed when the corpse leaves the house, and again when it is being lowered into the grave. In some cases, wailing is expressive of real grief; in others merely conventional. Sometimes to the wail is added blackening of the face and tearing of the hair, for these Indians . . . are essentially emotional. Occasionally, parents will bury toys and even clothes with a dead child, alleging as a reason that they do not wish their grief to be aggravated by sight of these things lying around. These extravagances are, of course, discouraged by the missionaries, and are gradually dying out. [Keen 1914]

There have been lots of sudden deaths in my family, my grandmother, my uncle, his wife. . . . I was married and Virginia, my daughter, was about four when my grandmother died. She was looking after my little girl while I was working at Watun River cannery. She asked her husband to call Elizabeth Stanley to bathe her. I don't know why she knew she was going to die. She died sudden death.

My Uncle Henry Edenshaw died far from home, in Bellingham, Washington. He was riding in a car and when he got off, he raised his hands over his head and flopped over dead. It was real hard for me; that's the only uncle I have and he died far away from home. Alaskans and Skidegates came for the funeral and afterwards they had a feast. My uncle's wife said to me, "Florence, you have a nice husband, have respect for yourself and show appreciation to the people who came from everywhere and invite them in." I told my husband and he went out and found our cow on North Beach. He went there in the evening when the tide was coming in. He killed the cow and loaded the meat on his boat; it was 4 A.M. when he got home. Emily invited the people in first, then we invited the whole town and all the visitors like my aunt wished us to do.

After fishing that year [1935], Emily called me, Agnes, my grown son Alfred, my sister's son Ernie, and Jeffrey White, her own son. Jeffrey gave his mother $100, Alfred gave her $100, and Ernie gave her $100. I gave her $50 and Agnes gave $50, and Emily gave $50 herself. She took all the money to my cousin Douglas and falltime he went down south to buy the headstone. A few years later when they took the stone down to the cemetery right after New Year's, they invited people from Skidegate and had a big doing.[8] They even had Indian dancing and the Ravens and Eagles had a contest to see who danced the best. The invited guests judged the dancing. That's the first time we had danced for a long time. They gave away lots of things; it was a real big doing. That summer Henry White, my sister's husband, got sick and died. People say it was because we had such a big doing. Too much, it was too big. That's why he died.

My Aunt Martha took sick after she lost a grandson in a house fire and she died while we were down south fall fishing. We came home just before Christmas and there was no Martha. I took it really hard. I was at the WA meeting and when I talked to the ladies, I couldn't help talking about her, too. I started crying. Emma Alexander told me to quit crying for her. "She's Eagle and you're Raven and you're not supposed to take it hard. You've got lots of children. It might happen to one of your own if you grieve too much for the opposite tribe [moiety]." You mourn for your dad or your husband but not someone of the opposite tribe like an auntie.

8. Headstones are not taken down to the cemetery until the day of the potlatch; consequently, many sit before the homes of the deceased's relatives during the time they are saving and preparing for the potlatch. In some instances several years pass before the stone is placed on the grave.

CHAPTER 9

I Quit Having Babies: My Later Years (1939–1979)

I didn't even feel it [menopause]. If you have lots of children, you don't feel it. Every two years I got my babies. You lose so much blood [through menstruation] and you build up new blood every two years when you get pregnant. That's why older ladies are healthy. Today ladies get some kind of medicine from the doctor or else they make them close up the womb so they don't have any more kids. It's not good for their health, I don't believe in that. So many young ladies died of cancer or other kinds of sickness. The ones who get lots of children, they live to be old. Selina Peratrovich and Emma Matthews are older than me and still strong yet; that's because they had lots of children. After I had Primrose, the doctor wanted me to stop, but I wouldn't agree to it. My mother wanted me to get lots of kids, that's why I say no. Way after my mother died, I said no. I could have been dead a long time ago if I had agreed with that doctor.

I told my children not to get married like me. I got married when I was real young. I kept on telling them to marry when they were older. All my girls were over twenty when they married and Alfred was twenty-five. Claude got married young, though; he was only eighteen. He went to Alaska to work and before he went I told him not to get married. I was working at the Masset cannery then, cooking. The local workers all went home to eat but some white men were staying in a house near the cannery and I cooked three meals a day for them. I was hired at sixty-five cents an hour which was real lots of money then because women cannery workers only got two bits an hour. It was during the war [WWII].

One morning, after I finished cooking breakfast for the men, the steamer came. I thought nothing of it but soon after I heard a knock at the door. I opened it and Claude was standing there with a young girl beside him. "Meet my wife, Mom." I didn't know what to do, I thought he was teasing me. I looked at him. He looked so serious. I grabbed Vivian and kissed her. Claude pulled a big box of chocolates from under his coat and gave it to me. "Here, Mom, you have this. Whoever kissed my wife first was going to get this box of chocolates." I felt real bad because I wasn't there when they got married. Vivian's mother didn't know she got married either. Just like they got no parents. I felt real bad thinking about that. Vivian was about sixteen, I guess. They got married in Ketchikan and they moved in upstairs with us.

WE LOSE OUR HOUSE AND REBUILD

In 1952 we lost our home in a fire. I lost everything, even my shoes. No pillows, no blankets, no shoes, no sweaters. All of us lost everything. We had all kinds of clothes and the upstairs was full of groceries we had received from Woodwards in Vancouver.

I was knitting. We just finished eating lunch when I heard a funny sound; it caught my nerves so I looked out the window and saw the shadow of a flame. It was coming from the spare bedroom upstairs. It was Clara's, our youngest's, birthday and we had bought lots of chicken to have a birthday dinner. But the house started burning and by four o'clock in the afternoon it was all burnt down. Joshua Collison came by and chased us all out of the house because the ceiling was going to collapse. After a while, someone came to us all dressed in a white shirt and dark pants, a tall slim boy. I didn't know him, but he asked me, "Mom, do you want anything from the house?" "Yes, in the kitchen there's a blue box, a little box with jewelry in it." The boy didn't come back to me, but later, when my sister Agnes invited us to dinner, I discovered the little box of jewels in my brassiere. A couple of days after, a Seventh Day Adventist minister told me that was an angel. God had sent an angel to me because he wanted me to be happy with at least a little bit. Two of my dad's bracelets were in that little box.

When everything was over we started staying by Primrose and her husband Victor. We had nothing. I was dressed in a housedress and I lost my shoes. I wore Clara's shoes.

The next day after the fire the whole town collected $400 for us.

They gave us clothes, they gave us food, and the Indian agent gave us food. He wrote on a slip of paper that whatever we needed we could get from the store. We saved the $400 for windows. I told my girls we would all work in the cannery to earn money to build a new house. Aggie and Myrtle quit going to school after the house burned; they lost all their clothes in the fire. They started working for the house and gave us $800 toward building.

The fall after our house burned we went fishing with my cousin Douglas Edenshaw on his big seine boat. I cooked for the crew. One day when I was in the galley my husband yelled that they needed me to look after the winch. So I looked after the winch while they were brailling the fish on. I was real proud that I was doing men's work. We didn't make any money fishing that fall, just enough for gas and groceries. We fished around Comox [on the east coast of Vancouver Island] and in the evenings we went into town. I really enjoyed the trip after we had lost everything.

When we finished fishing in November we went to Vancouver to buy supplies for our new house. We bought windows, doors, plywood, insulation, flooring, everything but shingles. We were planning to buy shingles but we ran out of money. We took all our money out of the Fishermen's Credit Union to buy materials and the manager said we could borrow more if we needed it. Because we were old we decided to borrow only $1,000. Even that makes my husband worry so much. We used to pay the loan off whenever we had money and when it was down to about $200 my husband asked if he could pay off the rest with some of his argillite carvings. The manager accepted it and the totem poles are still there in the window of the Credit Union in Prince Rupert.

For a time after we lost our house we stayed in the cannery house where I used to cook for the cannery workers. Right after that they sent my husband away to the hospital; there's something wrong with him, doctors say. They think it's TB, yet he was so fat. They put him in Miller Bay [Indian] Hospital in Prince Rupert for about eight months. When he came home he was real fat and there was nothing wrong with him. He didn't have TB.

I used to pray that we would get a home. I prayed for my whole family because Claude and Alfred and Victor [Primrose's husband] were going to build houses, too. We all started building at the same time.

I used to help my husband on the house. When he was up on top of the house and wanted something, he'd stick a piece of lumber down to me marked where he wanted it cut. I had a sawhorse and saw and I cut it where it was marked. I was young and strong yet. When I gave the cut wood back to him he'd laugh and laugh. "Why are you laughing, did I cut it short?" "No, just like I'd cut it myself, you make it so neat." After the rafters were up the girls did the shingling. Our son Reggie gave us $500 to send for shingles and when the shingles came from Vancouver, the girls started shingling away. They don't let Clara go up though because she's fat and they don't want her to fall down. As much as she wanted to nail shingles with the rest, they don't let her.

My husband and I designed the house. I wanted the front room twenty feet long and twenty feet wide, big enough to invite all the people in. We had lots of girls and when they got married I wanted to use our home for the wedding dinner. Men used to come to my husband and say, "Gəniyá, you're making such a big house. What are you going to do in it?" "Son," he used to say, "I know what I'm doing. Where we're staying now, the whole family comes in and they have to stand around having coffee. No room to sit down. that's why I plan a big house, so they'll be comfortable when they come home and sit around."

I designed the kitchen. At first we had the sink right by the window and when I do the dishes I can see the people going to church. I hated to stand there every Sunday morning doing dishes while people are walking to church. Maybe they think I'm standing there just because I'm curious. Maybe they think I'm staring at them when all I'm doing is my dishwashing. It made me feel bad so I asked my husband to move the sink to another wall, away from the window. "You always make me do something again. Maybe you're thinking I'm your second husband," he said to tease me. "I'm old and you make me work so hard on the house. It's already done and you want everything changed around all the time." When I told Claude and Alfred about it, how my husband teased me, they laughed and they moved the sink right away.

After we moved into the new house my husband said, "My uncle gave my house a name; the name's still warm yet. This house will be called the same."[1]

1. The same two names were given the new house; traditionally house names were the property of individuals. Thus, a house name could be applied to a later structure that occupied the same site or to a new house in a different location if the owner of the house name moved.

Making things

> I have to give Nani a lot of credit for my inspirations. I have a theory
> that the women always kind of kept the art alive because they always
> bugged their husbands to do this, do that. . . . Every time I come home
> Nani bugs me about something. "When will you do my bracelet, when
> will you do my ring? I need another blanket design." Everytime I come
> home she bugs me for a new button blanket design. [Robert Davidson,
> August 1978]

After we lost our home in 1952 when we went fall fishing with my
cousin Douglas, I bought material and pearl buttons from Eaton's in
Vancouver so I could make a button blanket. I was the first person
from Masset to make button blankets in recent years. I had no home
so I wanted to do something. I made just one then, working on it for
two years in my spare time. My husband drew a grizzly bear design
for it. I kept it secret because I thought someone might laugh at
me for doing such an old-fashioned thing. They thought nothing
of button blankets during my time. My grandmother used to cut
buttons off her blankets and give them to my sisters and me. As
soon as we got babies she'd give us a big bunch of small buttons for
baby clothes. When I was a little girl and people did Indian dances,
most of them used shawls, wool shawls, when they danced, not
button blankets. Now everyone uses button blankets again.

Haida began making button blankets after the missionaries came,
after they quit raising poles. The missionary stopped them from
doing it and my grandfather was very sad about it. His son, Gəʔwu,
suggested to my grandfather that instead of worrying about totem
poles they should make designs on blankets they got from traders
and put the traders' buttons around the design. My grandfather
agreed with his son, and that's when they made one. I don't know
if that was the first one, but that was when they started making
button blankets around here. Maybe other people, mainland people,
made button blankets before that time.

I've made lots of button blankets. In 1975 when they had the
opening of the National Museum in Ottawa [opening of the
Northwest Coast gallery] they invited me, and my daughter Emily
suggested I give Prime Minister Trudeau a button blanket at the
doing. "You have to do something because they invite you," she
said. "You have to show your respect." I was very glad I got a
daughter to advise me. Robert drew the design for the blanket. I
already had the design and I was making the blanket for Robert, but
when Emily wants me to give a blanket to Trudeau, I used the
blanket I was making for Robert. I worked on it day and night,

Making a button blanket (photograph by Marjorie Mitchell)

about eighty hours in all. I put the blanket around Trudeau when he got off the elevator at the museum. He was real surprised. I gave him a Haida name, Kiłgúlans. He was smiling real hard. "Mrs. Davidson, will you tell me what it means?" "It means your speech is good as gold." "I appreciate that," he said. He was wearing the blanket all evening.

Painting a Canoe

Way before I began making blankets, in 1939, I painted a Haida canoe.[2] A man from the States had ordered the canoe from my husband and his older brother. My brother-in-law was an old man then; he supervised the work and my husband and son Alfred made the canoe. I used to go and watch them work on it, and my brother-in-law said to me, "Florence, you paint our canoe; your dad was clever, you must be clever." I told him I'd paint it. I was just joking but he believed me.

Someone happened to give me a picture of a small canoe with a painted bow so my husband and I started copying it on paper. "We'll make the pattern here at home and we'll go there to put it on the canoe when everybody's sleeping," I said. We measured the bow and made the pattern, on cardboard, in the house. It looked all right. I tacked it on the canoe with thumbtacks and drew a line around each pattern piece. I finished quite a bit and when I started painting it looked real nice. My husband was happy. Every time I finished one part of the pattern, like an eye, he said, "*xwuh!*" He was proud of it.

I don't think women ever used to draw designs in the old days, just men. That's why I was scared when I started painting the canoe. I used to get up early in the morning before anyone else was up. I was ashamed if they saw me doing that and made fun of me, that's why. When it's possible for me, I can do it. All the people were surprised when I was done. Older people came around and said, "Of course, of course, her dad was clever."

When the canoe was finished the ones who ordered it didn't want it, I guess. Someone else came to see it and bought it. My husband and his brother got just five hundred dollars for that big thing. It

2. In 1981 Florence corrected her earlier statement, noting that she believed she painted the canoe in 1936 or 1937. H. B. Phillips, who took these photographs, agreed that 1939 was incorrect and believes the year was 1937, as he was not on the islands in 1936. Because the narrative has been reorganized topically within the life cycle, discussion of the canoe was left in this chapter.

Canoe painted by Florence (photograph by Howard Phillips)

Launching the canoe

was very sad. We didn't have enough money for our food and they had spent so much time making that canoe.

Weaving Baskets and Hats

I don't know how old I was when I started weaving small baskets. When I was young I wove one little basket with a cover for my cousin Josie to keep hairpins in; that was the first one. I learned by watching my mother weave. After I got married I wove a little bit at North Island. Emily Thompson, my husband's cousin, gave me a big bundle of spruce roots. She told me to soak it and she'd help me split it. I made a small basket with a fancy stand and a handle. Emily Thompson gave me grass to decorate it with, too. I made a design with the grass, something like leaves, and sold it to a mainland woman for a dollar. After a while I started making little baskets with covers on them and I sold them to Alfred Adams for his store. In the summertime he moved his store to North Island where the people camped. He paid me $1.25 for each one. I was so happy when I sold him two baskets and brought $2.50 home. I still had some roots, but I didn't make any more baskets because I started knitting sweaters.

My husband was still living when I began to weave cedar bark. I told him I wanted to start a basket and our daughter Myrtle took us along the highway to get some bark. We got lots, but I didn't touch it for two years. When my friend Selina came in I gave her two rolled-up bundles of bark. "Why don't you start weaving," she asked. I knew how to weave but I got no time to do it. Selina started a little hat for me one afternoon. I started working on it and really enjoyed it. Then I made tea while she worked on it. We kept on taking turns and finished it at two o'clock in the morning. We were just like little kids we enjoyed it so much. I made Claude paint the hat and I sold it for thirty-five dollars. I was so happy I felt like I got three hundred dollars for my hat. The next hat I made all by myself. In the old days they used to make hats just out of spruce roots.

YAKOUN RIVER FISH CAMP

When we were young we didn't go to the Yakoun to fish; we got no time. My husband was trolling all the time. He brought me spring salmon from trolling and we canned that. When we got old, that's when we started canning fish up the Yakoun.

We built our cabin and smokehouse at the Yakoun in the forties, I guess. That's when we first started going there. We got ten cases of number 2 cans to start canning with. I sliced and dried real lots of sockeye, maybe more than three hundred. That year we filled a thousand cans, too.

One summer when we were slicing fish, my husband dropped a big butcher knife he was using. I heard it drop, but we couldn't find it. They say it's bad luck to lose something; it means there's going to be a death. The same time my husband lost a sweater. And when we came home from canning, Johnny Hunter, our eighteen-year-old grandson, got killed at logging camp. Not long after that, the summer our grandson Robert's pole was raised in the village, my husband died.

Our Golden Wedding Anniversary (1961)

When it was our golden wedding anniversary we presented the church with a big Bible because of our thanksgiving. My husband was the minister's warden at that time; before him, his uncle, Robert Ridley,[3] had been the warden. All our children were going to give us a surprise doing for our anniversary but it was impossible to keep it to themselves. They all donated money toward it and cooked the food. We invited the Skidegates and people from Port Clements and New Masset as well as the village. We had a hundred and fifty people in the front room and ninety in the other room. We got so many presents they filled up the big kitchen. We unwrapped them for two days.

Springtime the same year the log carrier *Haida Nation* was built and they wanted someone respectful from the village to go to Victoria and christen it. The councilors decided that my husband was the best one to go. My husband said he was too old to go alone but that if they let me go too he would do it. Someone met us in Victoria and took us to the motel. They even used to serve us meals in our room. I wanted to go out shopping the next day and I told my husband, so we go to the hallway to go down in the elevator. "You know how to do it?" he asked me. "Yes, it's written here," I said. I pushed the button and the elevator opened. "*Haw'it,*" I said, "Come on." He was scared getting in and the door closed on him. I went down and left him there. I pushed the button to go back up. "It's open," I said to him, "Hurry, get on." Though everything was free for us in the motel we went out to eat in a restaurant. The day we

---

3. Robert Ridley belonged to Robert Davidson's father's father's lineage; thus, in Haida, he is a "grandfather" to Robert Davidson. At the same time he was Robert Davidson's mother's uncle (a "mother's brother"), and appropriately referred to as "uncle" by Robert.

Robert and Florence Davidson, 1961

christened the ship my husband told me, "Make yourself look real neat, you're going to see all kinds of cameras today." "I don't think so," I said. "We're so old and we're just Indians." I didn't believe him. They got all kinds of cameras and there were about two hundred people at the dock. The log carrier still goes from the islands. The children used to call it *cini* [grandfather] Robert's boat.

The Totem Pole Raising and Robert Davidson's Death (1969)

My grandson Robert got married in Vancouver not long before he came here to carve a totem pole. When he came home to work on the pole I made a big wedding cake for him and his wife and we had a big party. The hall was real full of people and they had a dance. We served lots of things; we gave out fruit and all kinds of cakes and cookies. After that he started carving the pole and his grandfather used to go to where he was working and advise him. When he finished the pole we made a long list of food for the doing—half a side of beef, apples and oranges, grapefruit. The band councilors asked Robert if we could let the feast go and let them do it because we were old. I'm sorry now I let it go; we could have done it, but they asked for it.

I bought lots of towels, all kinds of cups, mugs, aprons, and nylons. We spent about a thousand dollars on little presents. Vivian [Robert's mother] spent about five hundred dollars on hers and Robert about six hundred dollars on towels and things. We weren't going to do it but Phoebe and Charlotte Marks told me, "Florence, don't think too little of this doing. This is the biggest thing your grandson is going to do. You'll feel sorry afterwards when you think of it; all your life you'll feel bad over it. You're wise, but I want to give you advice." I thanked them for it and so we sent for things. The house was full of everything. I could hardly get around there were so many things in the front room. But I needed another big pot. I was the chief cook and I had people help me cut the meat and vegetables for the stew. I wanted to phone a Chinese store in Vancouver where we got pots. Just then Susan, Robert's wife, came in and she phoned for me right away. "Tell him to send it in the air," I said. Next day we got the big pot and all the towels that we ordered. All we had to do was phone for it. At the doing they gave out the towels to the men and the aprons and nylons to the ladies.

Two weeks after the doing my husband took sick. Dora and I had gone to the church to clean. We ate lunch with my husband and I told him not to bother about the dishes. He agreed. When we came back he was real tired. "I'm not feeling well," he said. And I helped him to bed, put pajamas on the wood heater to take the dampness out, and helped him put them on. After I put him to bed I phoned Dixie [the nurse]. After she looked at him she phoned the doctor in Queen Charlotte City and I went with him in the taxi to the hospital there. I stayed with him; I didn't want him to wake up and be all alone. Next morning the doctor came around at ten o'clock with the big machine to check his heart. "Mrs. Davidson, you got nothing to worry about. Your husband's normal today." "Why don't you go shopping," my husband said to me. I only had two dollars with me but I don't want to worry him so I said ok. When they fed him lunch I went to visit his relatives who lived close to the hospital. They asked me to stay by them and fixed me a real comfortable bed. When I went back to the hospital and told my husband what they said he was real happy. Then I went to visit Vicky [a first cousin] for a few minutes. She was in a nearby room. I went back to my husband's room and it's so quiet in there. He was hanging on the railing of the bed and leaning over. I ran to him and I grabbed his forehead. It was cold as ice. "I wonder why you are so cold," I said to him and I looked at him. He didn't breathe. I ran out but I couldn't find anybody. I heard someone in the kitchen so I ran there. "I want a nurse," I said. "My husband just passed away."

At first I just can't cry, it's too hard for me. My husband's relatives came for me and they took me out. I don't know where they took me but soon as I hit the fresh air, I started screaming. I can't stop crying. I didn't go back to the hospital. My, that was hard. He just went to sleep and then he was gone, like nothing. He used to tell me all the time, "I'm old and you should think nothing of it when I'm gone, but you're too precious (*kwoiyas*) to think nothing of me. I know you're going to take it hard," he said. "Don't go out when you feel lonely, just stay at home and try to tough it out." That's our belief, Indian belief. They call it *inda*, denying yourself. You have to keep to yourself, after your husband or wife or sister or brother or parent dies. Not for a little one, though. You have to be alone for a long time, a year or two. My husband died in September and in March the minister told me to go out. He took me uptown to shop for groceries. When I was in the store and looked at friends it made me real nervous. I don't want to talk to them and I turned the other way. I don't get used to seeing other people for a long time. As long as my husband's headstone is by the house,[4] I don't want to go out. When I go out it's like he's there staring at me. It makes me feel bad.

---

4. The mortuary potlatch or "headstone raising" for Robert Davidson was held in December 1970.

He was eighty-nine when he died. He was a real good Christian;
that's why he didn't suffer.

The summer after my husband died, Father Kreager came in and
advised me to take in boarders. So I started taking people in; I enjoy
anybody's company. I know I've got a blessing, just like my husband
left me lots of money. Whoever stays in here gives me money and I
can manage for my living.

Right before my husband died, he said to our granddaughter who
was pregnant. "Joy, I'm coming back to you. I'm going to be real
handsome and real smart, too." Craig, her son, is the second birth
of my husband.

Songs

For a long time the Haida quit Indian dancing, but then the
fishermen used to try it all the time even though they didn't sing
Indian songs. They didn't know the songs. My husband used to
know lots of songs and once I pleaded with him to teach me how to
sing Indian songs. I was president of the Church Women and I
wanted to make money for the church. He thought I was teasing
him about wanting to learn. Finally he started singing for me and I
learned. I used to ask him to sing for me late at night after we went
to bed. Reggie, our late son, used to ask, "Mother, what are you
people up to singing so many Indian songs?" When I told him he
said, "I thought you both were crazy." Mother and grandmother
didn't teach me any Indian songs, just my husband. When my
mother used to weave, she sang hymns. I used to know lots of
songs but too many sudden deaths in the family makes me forget.

Recent Doings[5]

In 1976 when Oliver Adams was to become chief of the village I
decided to donate buns. I baked a thousand dinner rolls for him and
put them in the freezer, because his dad was *ał qiwa* with my mother.
Their fathers belonged to the same tribe, *Sdəłdás*, that's what *ał qiwa*
means. My mother thought of his dad [Alfred Adams] just like a
brother, that's why Oliver thinks of me like his *sqaʔan*.[6] That's why I

5. Other, more recent doings, which we did not pursue, include Bill
Reid's totem pole raising at Skidegate and the dedication of the Charles
Edenshaw memorial housefront at Masset, both in 1978.

6. This illustrates the permutations of the *ał qiwa* relationship in
successive generations. Florence Davidson is not a member of Oliver

promised lots of buns. Near the time of his doing he came in with
my daughter Primrose, his sister-in-law. He asked me if I'd be in
charge of his doing, supervise the cooking. "I'll try all my best for
you, Oliver," I said. I told him he should ask the people to have
a meeting for his doing. They always used to do that, invite the
people in to decide what they are going to do. He invited the people
in here for a meeting, the whole town. Just the Eagle tribe [moiety],
his tribe, was supposed to come, but everybody was so anxious
they all came. I went to Rose, my son Alfred's wife, and said to her,
"Rose, you're his 'grandmother' [woman of father's father's lineage],
and you're the ones who are supposed to be real excited over all
this. Why don't you donate money, then everybody will copy you."
So Rose stood up and said, "Oliver's older than me, but my mother
told me I'm his grandmother." And everyone was laughing really
hard. Someone else stood up and gave him twenty dollars and then
everybody donated twenty dollars. After awhile we had another
meeting in here to plan for the doing. I felt real bad because two of
his daughters refused to take part. They're real religious [Jehovah's
Witness] and they were against the doing.

When they prepared for Oliver's doing they cut up vegetables for
two days and they cut 220 pounds of beef into chunks. We cooked it
here in three big pots, outside. The hall was just full of people. I
was so happy, just as if it were my own doing. The next day there
was another big doing. I cooked the clams, smoked salmon, the
potatoes, the smoked seal meat. Claude barbecued the salmon. The
Skidegate people donated herring eggs.[7] At the doing I sang a
song for the two chiefs, the Skidegate chief and Oliver. The song
belonged to Richard Naylans, my husband's stepfather. I have the
rights to use it. Next time I have a doing I'm going to spend lots of
money on this song so I can keep it. At the doing the Skidegate
chief's wife gave me a crocheted bedspread. I got two envelopes
from Oliver, one with five dollars for singing the song and the other
with a hundred dollars for my two days of trouble with all the food.

Right after Oliver's doing I went to Ulli Steltzer's doing in Vancouver, the opening for her book *Indian Artists at Work*. I was real

---

Adams' father's lineage and thus, by this reckoning, not Oliver's *sqaʔan*
(woman of father's lineage). But because Isabella Edenshaw and Alfred
Adams were *ał qiwa* and thought of each other as siblings, Florence is like a
father's sister's daughter to Oliver and, hence, his *sqaʔan*.

7. Herring spawn, a native delicacy, is not found in the Masset area.
Traditionally, as well as today, it was acquired from the Skidegate people.

anxious for it. I wanted to see Carol, my niece who lives in Seattle, before the doing so I went down early and stayed by my daughter Clara in Vancouver. I phoned Carol, but no answer. The doing was to open on Sunday and I learned that Carol had been killed on Friday. I didn't feel like going to the doing but I went anyway and pretended to be happy. They had the funeral in Alaska and I flew up to Prince Rupert but I missed the ferry to Ketchikan and I missed the funeral. I went to Ketchikan anyway to stay with my sister. It was a very sad time for me. Soon as I got home I can't get up any more. I was lying around; I wasn't sick but I felt so tired.

You are cordially invited to a dinner given by Mrs. Florence Davidson in her residence on Thursday, 13 January 1977, at 5 o'clock P.M.

Feast goods for the memorial dinner for Nani's niece, Carol James, continue to pile up. Yesterday Nani removed 2 turkeys totalling 48 lbs. from the freezer to thaw, purchased 50 lbs. of apples, 50 lbs. of potatoes, some turnips, paper plates and paper bags for *qawqEł*.[8] Aggie has baked three sheet cakes, Emily came by with 10 pies and a bagful of candy, Nani made five layer cakes and over 100 tart shells. Tomorrow she says she will set 12 dozen buns and bake more pies. Primrose phoned to say she was baking 2 cakes; Virginia and Dave delivered two five gallon buckets of cookies. Nani has made at least three batches of cranberry sauce and has an enormous pork roast in the oven "because it's better to have too much than too little. I'm afraid the turkeys might not be enough." Merle Andersen, who typed and duplicated the invitations, sent five pink frosted layer cakes, and Sarah (Claude's wife) contributed 17 peach and pumpkin pies. As she was making tarts, Nani noted to me, "I don't know why I'm nervous." I asked if it was because of the doing. "No, it's not my first! I like baking; I've been doing it all my life. It's my favorite thing." Today she remarked to someone on the phone, "My niece gave me a whole case of pilot bread and I haven't used it. That's why I invite the people in tomorrow." [Field notes, January 12, 1977]

We set 80 places at the three long tables, filled cookie trays with cookies, tarts, little cakes and folded *qawqEł* bags and placed them beneath the paper *qawqEł* plates beside each place, and in accordance with Nani's instructions, put 1 apple, 1 orange, 2 buns (on most), and 4 pilot bread crackers on each paper plate. I wondered if the number 4 (a ritual number in Haida) was significant; I know the pilot bread was; it

8. As noted earlier, *qawqEł* refers to food that is taken home from the feast. Typically feast tables are laden with fruits and desserts that are intended for guests to take away. It is expected that no food will be left on the table when guests depart.

had been a gift from the late Carol James, in memory of whom the feast was being given. Nani was consulted on most matters; where certain pieces of furniture should be placed as the large room was emptied to make room for the long tables, where the pies and cakes should go; and what we didn't ask, we received instructions for: "put two buns on each plate, put lots on the cookie tray; they'll take it all. Wait till the raspberries cool more; it looks awful if it soaks into the tart."

. . . After the feast Nani fell asleep at the kitchen table warming her feet by an electric space heater and listening to the tape we made of the doing. As Alfred said in translating her feast speech: "If one doesn't give a dinner after a death one is always weeping. When one gives a dinner, it eases the mind." I think it has. [Field notes, January 13, 1977]

REFLECTIONS

We got telephones first and then electricity.[9] Howard Phillips, from New Masset, asked me after we got the telephone and lights, "How are you keeping, Mrs. Davidson?" "Not too good," I told him. "You white people should leave us alone. You gave us the telephone and you gave us lights. All we worry about is bills coming in. We like to have all the lights on and we like to phone long distance; now we have to pay for all the bills." He was laughing away at me.

We were supposed to get the lights in time for Bishop Munn's visit to the village. They promised to have the village lighted that night. Just before the Bishop came in to our house, they lighted us up. Just imagine, you haven't got lights and all of a sudden you're lighted up. That was the happiest day I ever had.

When I was young people used to think a lot of each other. They had more respect for each other than now. They used to invite people in and they used to bring home lots of food and they called each other "chief." Most of all they respected each other, not like today. When I was little I didn't see anyone drunk; that's the biggest change I see, drinking. After we come to be like a white people, that's what happened. It used to be so peaceful here. The church was full; no TV, no beer, no Canadian Legion. When someone got married, the whole town got excited. If a Yala one [member of the Raven moiety] got married, all the other Yala run around and do work for the one getting married and they give lots of donations to the doing. Today it's different.

Life changes so much. One time you're poor, one time you've got more than enough. All my life when my kids were small, we

9. Electricity was put in the village in 1964; phone service predated it by several years.

managed to get by. We didn't bother other people. Any clothes or shoes we needed we used to get from the sale catalogue in August. We used to put up so much food; we worked hard together all the time. I don't think I ever rested to be a lady, I struggled so much. Sometimes I used to wash until three o'clock in the morning. I'm just like a machine, made of iron I guess. Whenever someone comes in to visit the table was full. We always cooked more than enough and if someone comes in during mealtime, I moved away from the table and put clean dishes at my place so the person can join us. I make myself happy. Even now I still do that.

I always be happy all of my life when my husband was living, except when we lost one of the family. Seems so empty without one. When I was younger I wasn't lonely because I got my husband and lots of children around. Being lonely, that's the saddest time. If you're alone with nothing, no one cares for you, not even your children. That's why, old as I am, I'm still struggling.

One time when Selina was here with me, a nice gentleman came to visit us and he say to me, "Florence, why don't you get married; you'll have a real nice front yard." "Oh, no thank you," I say to him, "I've been married long enough, for all of my life. I don't want to try it again. I want to be a girl now."

I always admired my daughter-in-law Vivian; she looked after Claude, her husband, so much; she didn't worry about anything else but him. I thought she was so nice to do that. I always admire Selina too because she treats her grandchildren and her daughter-in-law [Primrose, Florence's daughter] so nice. I admire Clara Russ from Skidegate; she was so kind to everybody. My grandmother used to say it pays to be kind. "Don't try and save and be stingy with things. You don't get ahead that way," she said. That's why I always try all my best to be kind to everybody. I'm just like other people. I try all my best to be nice to people. Even if I don't know them I welcome them. "You don't have to call me Mrs. Davidson, call me Nani," I tell them. I feel closer when people call me Nani.

Working in the church, that's the most important thing for me. I try all my best for the church, even when I'm old.

You see how it is to be old, real hard. If my hands were all right,[10] I could do so much weaving. If my ears were all right I could be so

---

10. Florence has arthritis in her hands.

happy. *Q'edaǝng eʔdu ijing*—"old and good for nothing." I'm just like an old tree. Nothing's good for it. Sunshine makes it crack, and then the rain soaks in the cracks. But as long as you stay healthy you don't feel old. I know I'm old but I still enjoy myself. What I see still makes me happy.

*
**

CHAPTER 10

Discussion

As the personal record of a member of a culture, the life-history document gives substance and meaning to ethnographic and ethnohistorical description. In this concluding chapter, I should like to examine several facets of Florence Davidson's account which offer insight into Haida culture during her time. Her narrative provides commentary on the cultural themes and values governing her life, the options and choices open to the Haida individual, male and female roles, culture change, and the processes by which cultural information is lost.

THEMES AND VALUES

In 1975 following a visit to Nani's, my anthropologist husband was immediately struck by the visible expressions of wealth in Masset homes, noting how different this community was from the Alaskan Eskimo villages he had known. Ethnologists who have studied the traditional cultures of the Northwest Coast have often mentioned the native preoccupation with wealth, expressed most obviously and spectacularly in the distribution of goods at potlatches and in the hosting of sumptuous and extravagant feasts. Though the feasts and potlatches have been altered in both form and content, the wealth orientation is very apparent in modern Masset and has been a guiding factor in Florence Davidson's own life. Even a casual visitor to her home can see the importance of property in the rows of mugs and china cups displayed in the open shelves of her kitchen, in the armfuls of silver and gold bracelets she wears on important occasions, in the silverware and plates she can muster from her cupboards to set feast tables for over one hundred people, and in her well-stocked larder, which can accommodate a number of unexpected guests. During the ten years I have known her, Nani has accumulated goods for at least four potlatches and has given more than a dozen feasts.

The concern for wealth, however, goes far beyond the display of property and its ceremonial distribution. It finds expression in attitudes toward ritual purity, work, and economic self-sufficiency, and in attitudes toward children. These aspects of the Haida wealth orientation have been important in the shaping of Florence Davidson's life.

The relationship between ritual and wealth was made apparent to Florence early in life. Eating too much shellfish brings poverty, her father cautioned, and further dietary restrictions that insured prosperity and fertility were imposed upon her when she went through her puberty seclusion. Florence's mother and grandmother instructed her about the ritual separation of male and female clothing and the proper disposal of water used for washing dishes and for the human body. Incorrect behavior in any of these areas was causally linked to economic failure.

If proper ritual behavior insured or at least aided economic prosperity, such prosperity was also to be tempered with moderation. Florence's father did not want too big a "doing" for her wedding, as the overly ostentatious show of wealth was unlucky. Later, she attributed the death of her sister's husband to a funeral potlatch held for Henry Edenshaw that was too grandiose. This is perhaps a strange commentary on the ethos of Northwest Coast economics; there are evidently limits to the size and grandeur of ceremonial disbursement of wealth. The bigger the better, but only to a point.

If prosperity among the Haida was a function of proper ritual behavior, it was also acknowledged to be a function of hard work. The work ethic has been a driving force in Florence Davidson's life. Although John Swanton (1909:50) mentions an ideal of inactivity for a high-class woman in traditional times, I suspect it was more ideal than actual. In recounting her life history, Florence often commented on the hard physical labor that has been part of her life. As a girl she spent long days gathering spruce roots for her mother, helped her father cut firewood, worked summers in the canneries (though she did not view childhood employment in the canneries as "work"), and assisted at her Uncle Henry Edenshaw's home.

Marriage and especially children meant more work and longer hours. Pregnancy, Florence noted, was not enjoyable, because "you can't do as much," but even though she was pregnant for more than ten of her twenty-six childbearing years she managed to "do" a lot. She washed clothes into the early morning hours, sewed for her children, and prepared daily meals for ten or more people. Like many other North American women of her generation, Florence Davidson was also an energetic domestic entrepreneur, augmenting her husband's income to keep pace with her steadily increasing family. For a time she operated a coffee shop from the front room of her house. She knitted sweaters for sale and made baked goods, following Haida fishermen to purvey her bread and cakes at isolated fish camps. Today the loaves continue to flow from her bread oven. "Old as I am," she notes, "I'm still struggling." But when she says, "I don't think I ever rested to be a lady," it is not so much said wistfully as said with pride.

Florence admired the same dedication in her husband. He labored at fishing and carpentry to provide for his family; he made furniture and designed and built two homes for them. And, Florence notes, he gave up smoking when the children were small so there might be a bit of extra money. The family struggled to be economically self-sufficient. Florence remarks, in regard to their efforts, "We didn't bother other people." Economic self-sufficiency of households was the ideal in traditional times also, though I wonder if, in the context of the changing economy brought by the white man, the struggle for self-sufficiency was not greater and the lack of self-sufficiency more threatening to self-identity when the alternative was dependence upon the government and its officials.

Traditionally, much of a Haida family's economic efforts were directed toward its children. Parents worked and saved to be able to potlatch for their children. Florence refers to this when she states that her mother's parents had not potlatched for their daughter, because when they died they were just a young couple still saving toward a big potlatch. Children in Haida society acquired status and rank initially through the efforts of their parents. Those whose parents did not potlatch could not become y'aʔçEyt. The same concern for children was expressed long after the supporting potlatch form disappeared. Florence summed up this attitude in her words, "We tried all our best for our children." She sees her married years as time focused upon her children, not just in attending to their immediate needs but in providing for their futures.

"Respect for self," a phrase that recurs in Florence's life history, represents a traditional behavioral ideal in Haida culture. The concept embodies proper speech, proper etiquette, proper behavior, respectability, and self-assurance. It is a theme that not only weaves through Florence's life, but prefaces her account. Her concern for proper speech is indicated in her warning that she would not relate "what's no good." The admonition "respect yourself" was used on her by adults to elicit proper behavior as she was growing up. Florence mentions it during her puberty seclusion, and later her mother told her to say nothing of her impending marriage— "have more respect for yourself than to speak of it." Florence's grandmother advised her on respect for self in the proper treatment of her husband; her father advised her to respect herself and not bother other people with talk of her children; and her aunt advised her to show her respect for herself and others by inviting the people for a feast following the death of her uncle.

Today, Nani's respect for self is evident in her words, her bearing, her treatment of others. Unfortunately, however, respect for self does not always extend beyond the boundaries of one's own culture. This fact is poignantly expressed in Florence's comment to her husband before they christened a new log-carrying barge in Victoria. She did not expect many people at the event because "we're just Indians." James Sewid, a Kwakiutl whose life history is recorded by James Spradley (1969), provides a contrast. Spradley notes that "James Sewid commented briefly upon the importance of self-esteem with reference to his own race and their loss of pride. He stated many times that he was proud to be an Indian, and the data which have been reviewed strongly support the conclusion that he has a deep, pervasive sense of pride, or self-esteem" (1969:280). With the passage of time, as she has become more familiar with outsiders through her boarders, Florence Davidson sees herself less and less as "just an Indian." She once laughingly remarked at the increasing number of people who have come to know her as Nani, saying, "pretty soon the whole world's going to be my family."

The embracing of Christianity has been one of the most important and positive themes in Florence's life. When I asked her what she most wanted to be remembered for, she answered without hesitation, "for my work in the Church." Anthropologists have often viewed the church as a disruptive force in native cultures, for missionaries brought and usually effected great changes. The early (1870s–1890s) impact of Christianity on the Haida can be viewed similarly. Missionaries were instrumental in changing burial practices, eradicating shamanism, forbidding some forms of potlatching, changing household composition and dwelling type, and suppressing art forms. By Florence's time, however, many of these changes had been integrated into Haida culture and she

Greeting Queen Elizabeth at Sandspit, 1971

herself notes that during her childhood all the elder people were Christians.

Christian precepts of good and evil were inculcated in Florence as a child. She remembered only one occasion when she was physically punished by her parents, but she noted that her father admonished her that if she were bad the devil would punish her. So strongly was the good/evil dichotomy implanted that as a young girl Florence wished to marry a member of the choir because "they were the best ones of all." The home Florence grew up in was a Christian home. Her mother sang hymns as she worked, not Haida songs, and her father began his daily carving with prayer. Florence's uncle, Henry Edenshaw, who exerted a great influence on his sister's children, was the missionary's assistant, Sunday School teacher, translator of the Bible into Haida, and, in the words of every missionary who worked with him, a "model Christian." Florence and her sisters were baptized and confirmed into the Anglican Church, were taken to Sunday School each week by their parents, and were married in the church. At age fifteen, Florence joined the Women's Auxiliary of the church and has been an active member ever since. Her present home sits near the church and rectory and she has worked closely with the various ministers who have occupied the Masset post. Her contributions to the church have involved hard physical labor similar to that invested in her family.

Just as she has "tried all her best" for her family she has also tried all her best for the church. She has baked to raise money for the church, provided hot meals for carpenters who constructed the present church building, provisioned and opened her home for church-sponsored events, washed and waxed the church floor, and made altar cushions. She accompanies the minister when he first calls upon a bereaved family, and for more than fifty years she has tended the dead, preparing bodies for burial. Once, describing the church organization, Florence remarked, "We look up to the men as our leaders; we don't question them." While she may not be, nor want to be, a spiritual leader, Nani is regarded by both men and women of her community as an exemplary keeper of the faith and as a pillar of the Masset church.

Christianity has been compatible with certain values and practices that Florence Davidson and many other Haida espouse, and in conflict with others. Reincarnation seems to be one belief that has not met opposition from the church, although the pattern of the reincarnation belief has changed since Swanton (1909:117) wrote that reincarnation was typically within the lineage. Many Haida, Florence included, still believe in some form of reincarnation.

Florence herself is the second birth of her father's mother, and some of her children, grandchildren, and great-grandchildren are second births. Florence's artist grandson, Robert Davidson, asked her recently if she was going to "come back" and she smilingly responded that she would come back through his daughter so "that way you'll have to make lots of bracelets for me."[1]

The traditional Haida practice of denying oneself at the death of a close relative (*inda*) has been followed by Florence and others of her generation, though one does not today hear the old wailing or crying songs and the bereaved no longer blacken their faces or cut their hair as they once did. *Inda*, as practiced by Florence, seems not incompatible with her practice of Anglicanism, though it was the Anglican minister who finally persuaded her to leave her house several months after her husband's death.

Like other Haida of her time, Florence has given feasts and potlatches to mark important ceremonial occasions. In some respects, these ceremonies run counter to even modern church policy, and in other respects they and the church have accommodated one another.

Proper honoring of the dead requires, some time following burial, the giving of a memorial feast such as that described in chapter 9. The Haida long ago ceased honoring the dead with the memorial burning of food,[2] which missionaries regarded as wasteful, and instead hosted a lavish feast of non-native foods. The memorial feast is generally more ample than the ordinary feast, the extra food serving to honor the deceased. The minister, who is present on such occasions, is called upon to speak and/or pray. Feasts have even been used ceremonially within the Masset church. In 1970, for example, Florence hosted a welcome feast for a new Church Army captain and his wife, and when another Anglican minister was transferred from his Masset post in 1974, she hosted a farewell feast in his honor. While early missionaries sometimes discouraged the giving of large feasts, the church's attitude has changed in recent years; the last white minister to Haida Masset, in appreciation for having been given a Haida name, feasted the community himself.

Proper honoring of the dead among the Haida includes not only the giving of a memorial feast but the hosting of a memorial potlatch

1. The reincarnation belief does not require that one be born after the death of the reincarnate kin. Furthermore, an individual can be reincarnated into more than one person at a time.

2. Florence could not remember the practice, adding that it had disappeared by her time.

(called in English a "memorial" when I first began study in Masset, but now occasionally described as a "memorial potlatch"). Here the conflict of Christian and Haida values has been most apparent (see Blackman 1973). Though the form and content of the mortuary potlatch have adapted to Anglicanism and the minister participates in the celebration, church involvement has resulted in ambivalence toward the distribution of wealth. Following the potlatch to honor her late husband, Florence remarked to me, "we could have given away more but we were afraid to because of the church." The accommodation she and other Haida long ago made to the church and potlatching was to donate generously to the church, while keeping the distribution of food and goods at the ceremony within limits acceptable to the church. The meaning of these ceremonies, however, seems little altered from traditional times. Florence noted that one weeps for the dead until one gives a memorial feast; the feast eases one's mind and wipes away the tears. Similarly, until proper homage has been paid to the dead with a headstone (formerly a totem pole) and memorial potlatch, the living cannot rest. Florence remarked that as long as her husband's tombstone sat before the house, she felt bad. Only after she had given the potlatch, which followed placement of the stone on the grave, was her mind eased.

CHOICES AND ADAPTATIONS

The options open to Haida women of Florence Davidson's generation were few. Most women married young, remained in their village of birth,[3] and bore and reared large families. The main alternative to such a life course was to marry a white man and leave the islands, but few followed this pattern at the time Florence was married. Florence herself has always lived in Masset, although in later years she has traveled as far east as Ottawa and periodically journeys south to Vancouver, Victoria, and Seattle. Her present home sits within view of the site of her childhood home and those of her grandparents and uncle. From her kitchen window she can see the homes of her now deceased sisters, Emily and Agnes, those

3. Unless they were of very high status and no spouse of appropriate standing could be secured locally. Two of Florence's sisters (Agnes and Nora) married outside Masset, taking up residence with their Alaskan husbands. Agnes and her husband returned to Masset to live, but Nora remained in Alaska.

of some of her Edenshaw cousins and her sister's daughter, and that of childhood playmate Emma Matthews.

The lack of choice in Florence's life is most clearly seen in her arranged marriage. Even her parents felt bound in regard to her marriage since, as Florence noted, what her uncle said was "law." Her initial reaction to the marriage was that she did have a choice. She was defiant, threatening to run away if her parents carried through with the marriage. And while she acquiesced to her mother's request to respect herself and not discuss the matter, at the ceremony she refused to say the wedding vows. "I pretended not to be married, I guess," she reflected. When asked if her reaction was unique, Florence replied, "I don't think other girls were as upset as me." She recalled that her grandmother and mother remarked upon Emma Matthews' quiet acceptance of her arranged marriage to Daniel Stanley in 1911. "Emma must be wise not to say anything, my grandmother and mother were saying." Emma may not have been as vocal in her protests as Florence, but she was not eager to be married. She once noted that her wedding had to be postponed because she had a bad sore throat, and that, taking advantage of the situation, she had eaten a mixture of sugar and snow to make her throat worse and lengthen the postponement.

The Kwakiutl James Sewid, whose marriage was arranged to a young girl close to his own age, expressed in retrospect some of the same sentiments as Nani but without her defiance or bitterness. "I didn't want to get married," he said, "but of course I had no business to try to argue . . . because I knew the older people knew what was right for me" (Spradley 1969:66–67). In the end, Florence had no choice either and became at fourteen a married woman. She exercised some control by refusing for a time to sleep with her new husband, but following a discussion with her mother, she capitulated to the expected role of wife. By the time her own children approached marriageable age, marriages were seldom arranged, and Florence's children chose their own spouses. She urged them, however, "not to marry young like me" and to marry into the opposite moiety.

Despite her rebelliousness at marriage, Florence Davidson identified strongly with the Haida woman's role. As a small girl she found the idea of motherhood appealing. She pretended to be the mother of her older sister Emily's child and wished her own mother to call her by Emily's name so that she might be magically transformed into a mother. Although she refused to undergo a traditional ritual that would assure her fertility, Florence claimed she "always wanted to be a mother for a bunch of kids." Isabella Edenshaw wanted her daughter to have ten or more children; Florence had thirteen, remarking, "as many children as I have, I accept."

At the same time, Florence expresses pride in having been able to perform men's jobs, as well as ambivalence about undertaking such male roles. In explanation she noted that her sister Emily, following the advice of her uncle, urged her not to be "hopeless, like a girl." Charles and Isabella Edenshaw had no sons, so their daughters were expected to take initiative and responsibilities they might not have assumed had there been sons. Early in life Florence was doing the work of a son or nephew as she went with her father to cut firewood. She commented that she was strong, "like a boy." Later she undertook a man's task when she agreed to paint the prow of a canoe her husband and his brother had made; though she had never painted or carved before, she perhaps learned these skills in childhood through observing her artist father at work. Nonetheless, fearing public criticism both because she was inexperienced at painting and because she was performing a traditionally male activity, Florence painted in the early morning hours when no one was about. Finally, Florence expressed pride in being able to fulfill a man's job on her cousin's fishing boat. She admired similar flexibility in her husband, praising the women's work he occasionally under-took on her behalf.

The limitations imposed upon a Haida woman of Florence Davidson's generation are evident in the circumscription of her life. Rosaldo (1974:23–24) suggests that a universal characteristic distinguishing women's and men's lives is the association of the former with the domestic sphere of culture and the latter with the public sphere. While others have criticized this view as too rigid (see Quinn 1977:182), it aptly describes a major difference between the lives of Haida women and Haida men during Florence's time. The distinction may not have obtained in traditional times, but by the turn of the twentieth century men were the primary wage earners and women's lives focused almost exclusively on children and the house. Florence's domestic confinement is apparent throughout her account. Though she followed her husband to North Island and Yatz where he fished, her growing family allowed a little time for picking berries but none for hunting cassin anklets and digging clams with other women. Florence had no time to learn her husband's stories and songs when the children were young. I remember once asking her for the Haida names of birds; she replied that she knew only a few as she had always been "kind of a house cat."[4] Helping at a feast, and attending Women's Auxiliary meetings and choir practice were among the few occasions that offered a degree of freedom from home and children.

Culture Change

James Spradley, in his analysis of James Sewid's life, describes this Kwakiutl man as an individual who successfully adapted to culture conflict and change. The push and pull between the two divergent ways of life is nowhere more apparent on the Northwest Coast than in early twentieth-century Kwakiutl culture. Progressive and conservative factions of Kwakiutl society clashed over language, church, potlatching, and other issues. James Sewid, according to Spradley, successfully straddled Kwakiutl and Canadian ways of life, achieving a "bicultural adaptation" (1969:277).

Conflict is not so apparent in Haida culture of the same period. From the missionary's and the Indian agent's view, the Haida were tractable and receptive to Christianity, to white-style housing, and to the accoutrements of the "civilized" way of life. Yet these changes did not come freely. Florence's description of her friend Maggie Yeltatzie, a high-ranking woman who always wore gloves to hide her tattooed hands, recalls the personal pain that can accompany culture change. The swiftness of some cultural changes is also noted in Florence's account. The traditional *tagwaná*, or female puberty seclusion, that Florence underwent was not held for her younger sister Nora, because "we became like a white people then." With missionary suppression of the *tagwaná*, the negative values associated with female sexuality in Euro-Canadian culture were impressed upon the Haida. "We became ashamed to talk about it," Florence said of menstruation.

Florence's family—her parents, grandparents, and uncle—had taken steps to adopt a Euro-Canadian way of life. They lived in white-style houses and brought their children up as Christians. Florence's uncle Henry was looked to by the family as a model: he was enfranchised; his home resembled a white person's home; he spoke English, was well-read, understood the ways of white people, and moved easily in their company. He loomed large in Florence's life both because he was a model of the "new" Haida and because he was her closest lineage uncle.

---

4. Older Haida men, however, could recall the names of most birds.

The latter facet of Florence's relationship with her uncle serves as a reminder that the distinctively Haida aspects of her upbringing should not be underestimated. Much of a culture is transmitted in its language, and Florence has been a Haida speaker since she uttered her first words. Neither of her parents spoke English and Florence herself still speaks Haida more frequently and easily than English. The economic values she learned as a child were Haida, not Euro-Canadian, and these are the economic values that govern her life today.

Despite changes in residence patterns (from avunculocal to neolocal) and kinship terminology (from Haida to English), the social obligations and ties marking Florence's life are those of the matrilineal Haida: showing respect and obedience to mother's brother and proper etiquette to other kin; marrying a high-ranking man of the opposite moiety; performing ceremonial obligations as a *sqaʔan*; denying oneself at the death of someone close. When I asked Florence what women she admired, her answer was a very Haida one. The women she mentioned were singled out for their achievements in meeting kinship obligations—looking after a husband, showing kindness and generosity toward in-laws, grandchildren, etc. Proscriptions and rituals which Florence has followed to promote a successful life are also embedded in Haida tradition.

These Haida values and practices underlay the superposition of an increasingly Euro-Canadian way of life, but the two achieved a not inharmonious blend, or so it seems when viewed from the perspective of one woman's life. While anthropologists often speak of the "breakdown" of traditional cultures and the "disorganization" and "anomie" that ensue with acculturation (see, for example, Duff 1964), through Florence Davidson's eyes, Haida culture of her time emerges as an integrated whole, not traditionally Haida, not simply Canadian, but nonetheless a real and legitimate culture in its own right. Early twentieth-century Masset was a good place in which to grow up: community spirit was strong as evidenced in the pride in the village band, the construction and upkeep of the road, church, and community hall. The church was full on Sunday mornings and around the Anglican Church flourished a rich community life into which were incorporated older patterns of moiety reciprocity, feasting, and honoring the dead. Masset citizens were law-abiding and prosperous; they met kinship obligations; there was little drinking or antisocial behavior; parents tried all their best for their children; and the Haida looked to the future.

Florence Davidson's life history also points to some more general characteristics of acculturation. First, her account cautions that culture change may be viewed and experienced differently by males and females. In some instances differential acculturation may bear a direct relationship to traditional knowledge and sex roles. To take a simple example, Haida and other Northwest Coast men entered the commercial fishing industry as owners and operators of fishing boats, a role compatible with their traditional training as fishermen. Women, on the other hand, staffed the canneries and salteries cleaning and slicing fish, skills learned as part of their traditional upbringing. As a result of performing separate roles within the same economic system, males and females experienced an aspect of Euro-Canadian culture somewhat differently. Simultaneously, a changing culture may appear differently to males and females as each retains or acquires new knowledge and experience as a result of sex-role differences that are not traditional. Florence Davidson's unfamiliarity with the Haida names for birds provides an example. In part, one might expect a Haida male to be more knowledgeable about birds than a female, because bird hunting was traditionally a male activity. On the other hand, Florence's lack of knowledge of bird names is probably equally a product of the increasing domesticity of Haida women of her time.

The oral tradition provides another case of differential acculturation. Florence did not learn much Haida oral tradition, partly because when she was a child her parents and grandmother took their newly acquired Christianity seriously, and partly because, as a young woman, she had no time to learn stories on occasions when they might have been passed on to her. Her husband did learn stories, family history, and myths as a child from his uncles, and he passed this knowledge, or some of it, on to his sons Alfred and Claude. Florence, however, laments that she never had time to sit and listen, "because I was always too busy with a bunch of children." Later after the children were grown, she did learn her husband's songs, and from him she acquired other domains of traditional knowledge, such as Haida botanical data (Turner 1974:95). It is notable, however, that in the case of the songs, the main impetus for learning them was in order to stage a performance to raise money for the church.

A second aspect of the acculturation process appears in Florence's learning of cultural roles. We sometimes forget that a significant amount of learning takes place through the process of play. It is noteworthy that in their games of "pretending to be grown up," Florence and her friends, for the most part, did not mimic grown-up behavior that a generation earlier was probably an important part of child's play. They did not, for example, pretend at potlatching or traditional dancing; the rituals they imitated were those of white society.[5]

Furthermore, in a culture that is undergoing rapid change to the point where practices and institutions disappear within the lifespan of an individual member of that culture, much of the memory of the traditional culture is that of a child. Florence's knowledge of traditional marriage for example, is a child's memory. Arranged marriages ceased before such time as she would have been able to participate in the arranging. Thus, she cannot tell of the negotiations, the discussions, the roles the parties to the marriage arrangement played. Her only experience of such marriage was through the eyes of a frightened child whose marriage was being arranged. She has similar childlike reminiscences of performances of the "secret societies." Divorced from the house-building potlatch, which was no longer practiced when she was young, the dances were performed for public entertainment. To a child the masks were real; they frightened and inspired awe, and in that sense conveyed a reality unknown to an adult member of the culture. But the knowledge of the performances, the songs, the meaning of the masks were not imparted to the small girl who witnessed the dances. And that is how a culture, or how portions of a culture, becomes lost to its bearers; the knowledge passed on to the next generation is the knowledge of a child.

Today the childhood memories are critical to the definition and reassertion of native identity. As Pamela Amoss aptly put it in her description of Coast Salish elders, "They now find themselves in a period when people want to affirm their Indian identity and need the old to legitimize their claim to an exclusive cultural tradition" (1981:229). Haida ceremonies barely within Florence Davidson's memory are resurfacing at the instigation of artists like her grandson Robert who create masks, rattles, and drums and bring them to life in dance and song. Florence's description and enactment of dance and song inspire the carver of the mask. The mask is the impetus for the dancer to perform, to excel, and even to innovate. And Florence Davidson, and others of her generation, provide the slender threads that legitimize the masks and the performances in which they are used.

5. During Charlie Nowell's childhood, on the other hand, Kwakiutl children did play at potlatching. Nowell noted that fathers and elder brothers "teach us to give these play potlatches" (Ford 1941:85).

There is no panacea for the debilities of old age as Florence herself laments, but there are some compensations. She has not achieved the carefree state of girlhood, denied her at fourteen and jestingly sought in widowhood, but to her own people and to students of her culture she has become a fragile link to the past, a veritable cultural treasure.

CONCLUSION

Florence Davidson's life history is only a partial accounting of the experiences and feelings of an elderly Haida woman. Certain events and feelings were deleted because she did not wish them to appear in print; others escaped her memory. Nonetheless, the narrative speaks for her; she has listened to it and approved it.

My discussion of the narrative has addressed certain themes and values in Florence's life, as well as the changes her life has incorporated, but it has not probed the depths of her Haida culture, for my knowledge of her language is inadequate. The discussion has also hinted at general patterns of acculturation that may be gleaned from life-history documents.

Florence's narrative offers more than cultural themes and gleanings about cultural change. Its primary value lies in its documentation of the life of a Haida woman. Florence Davidson's life pattern, though, is representative not just of most Haida women of her generation, but the domesticity, the segregation of the sexes, the time spent in childbearing and rearing large families, the provisioning, and the never-ending labor and lack of time for self, speak to a whole generation of North American rural women. Her life history also bespeaks her tenacity and endurance, and that of other women like her. The bearing of thirteen children (some with no assistance), the suffering of many deaths of close relatives (including four children and seven grandchildren), the struggle back from adversity after having lost everything in a fire, the successful accommodation to a rapidly changing world, all testify to Florence Davidson's personal strength. Her narrative recalls the unheralded accomplishments of generations of women who have reared children and seen them to an easier life than their own and who have lived on to an often lonely widowhood.

Florence's own life's journey is perhaps aptly summarized in three statements she made: "I always tried all my best for my children. I tried all my best for the church. What I see still makes me happy."

AFTERWORD

For the last several summers I have returned again briefly to the
Misty Isles on a journey that has become an annual ritual and
renewal. My visit in August 1979 marked the official closure of my
research and writing of Florence Davidson's life history.

I left Victoria for Masset on August 2, 1979. With me I carried two
copies of the nearly completed life-history manuscript (one for
Nani), a genealogy of Florence's ancestors and descendants, and a
"final" list of questions to ask her. It would be a busy short week.
There were old family photographs I wanted to copy for inclusion in
the book, and there was more interviewing with Nani, and the
manuscript to read to her. I wanted to visit Masset friends; I needed
time to touch the sands of North Beach and feel again the magic that
the islands and their people hold for me. I needed time, too, with
Nani, to sit quietly with her at her kitchen table, to laugh with her,
to listen to her. I was accompanied by two dear friends, Marjorie
Mitchell, an anthropologist who had worked with Nani during the
summer of 1974, and Anna Franklin, an anthropology student who
had come with me to Nani's in the summer of 1978. I was eager to
share familiar haunts with them and to see Nani through their eyes.

Past and present blend as I clamber into the Grumman Goose that
is to take us from Prince Rupert to Masset. Delighted at being able to
secure the co-pilot's seat up front, I greet the pilot, Bruce Brown, a
grandnephew of Nani's, and we exchange news of our lives since
last summer. After takeoff I scan the skies for the first glimpse of the
Charlottes, and watch as the serration on the horizon takes form as
Rose Spit. We fly over the sand bluffs on the east coast, behind Tow
Hill toward Yakin Point. The skeleton of an unfinished house sits on
the Indian Reserve at Yakin Point, looking not unlike a beached,
decaying leviathan. I search below for more changes and discover a
golf course beside the Canadian Forces "elephant pen." It seems
somehow a desecration of North Beach. The Seegay Inn, New
Masset's modern hotel, lies now in a pile of charcoal rubble, the
victim of a February fire. We circle New Masset and land smoothly in
the cold waters of Masset Inlet.

Our luggage finally piled into a rented car, we drive through New
Masset toward the Haida village at the end of the peninsula. I
remember once reading an article in a Toronto magazine that
depicted Haida Masset as a rural slum. So many outsiders see the
broken windows, the faded houses, the weedy yards as signs of a
decadent welfare community. I see instead the view from the

houses: the spruce-rimmed shore of Masset Inlet, the swiftly moving water, the ever-changing, low-hung skies. Instead of weeds I see fireweed flowers, lupine, and Queen Anne's lace, and by the corners of the houses I see the ghosts of Masset past. I find here a place of indescribable beauty.

"Drive slowly, drive slowly, so I can see what's changed," I instruct Marjorie. New houses catch my eye: Willis White's opulent white house transformed from the weathered frame which stood for years in the Masset dampness, Rose and Alfred Davidson's new two-story house, a brown ranch home beside the ruins of Reuben Samuels old house, and at the point looking out toward the sea the magnificent new cedar-plank longhouse, its carved and painted front already silvered from the sun and wind. We turn down the "church road" now marked by a street sign labelled in Haida, courtesy of a linguist who entertained thoughts of reintroducing the native language. Nani peers out her kitchen window through the foliage of her many plants, and then she is at the front door her pincurled hair wrapped in a kerchief. I hold her tightly. "It's nice to have my girls back with me again," she says. A quick turn around the front room as we set down our bags and then we move into the kitchen where Nani has been frying bread. She knows it's my favorite treat. "*Shibli hʔalingá* [fried bread], Margaret," she smiles at me.

Over tea and steaming fried bread with fresh strawberry jam, I reenter the Masset of now. More of the old ones have gone since last year; the rectory sits empty, the minister having left in January for a church at a Nass River village; there is talk of a celebration this September in honor of the tenth anniversary of the raising of Robert Davidson's totem pole; plans are being made for a new recreational facility in the village and for multifamily housing. I inquire about Nani's large family and she asks of my parents, my husband and stepson. We reestablish the bonds between us.

Later that first day I explain the contents of the first three chapters of the manuscript to Nani and begin reading to her, starting with her own words in chapter 4. We sit at the kitchen table, joined by Marjorie and Anna. Nani cups her hand over her left ear and leans toward me as I slowly read in my lecture decibel voice. Marj and Anna later tell me that I slip into Nani's voice and cadence. Eyes partly closed, Nani nods, now laughing, now turning to the others breaking through my paced words to relate the story on her own. She balks at my reading of one portion of the manuscript. "It sounds funny," she says of her brief words that describe her first sexual experience with her husband. We try and reassure her that her situation was not unique and that other women would welcome hearing of her experience. "OK, its all right to leave it in," she concedes. When I finish her narrative, she approves. "It's real interesting, dear." A couple of days later I begin reading some of my own portions of the manuscript. Nani listens intently to the preface and when I finish, her only comment is an authoritative "Right."

I try to fill in gaps in the life history, clarify specific points, and get Nani to reflect on certain topics. We review the genealogy and I ask questions on kinship for a paper I am writing. Nani never misses an opportunity to poke fun. I ask for kinship terms in Haida: "What do you call your son-in-law Victor?" "I always call him Victor." "What do you mean, talk about growing old—you see how I am!" We discuss childhood play again and Nani recounts once more the pretend wedding she participated in. When she finishes, I query, "did you ever pretend to . . ." She fills in my pause, "go to bed?" "No, I never pretend to go to bed with anyone," she laughs.

Nani tells us that when she was young the Masset Haida used to greet each other in English with "Good Morning" regardless of the time of day. "All they knew was 'Good Morning,' " she says. And so, when she goes off to bed or encounters one of us anew during the day, she announces "Good Morning" and we respond in kind. We bring Nani a velour robe as a present and she says she wants to save it for winter but promises to model it for us before we leave. We return from an early morning walk our last day to find her wearing her new robe and four carved gold bracelets. "You look beautiful Nani," Marjorie tells her. "Of course," she retorts, posing among her kitchen greenery for our cameras.

In the early morning of our last day we hike to the Masset cemetery. The old tombstones are barely visible above the fireweed and beach grasses, and the new portion mostly vacant in 1970 is now nearly full. I discover here the graves of others who have died since last summer. We walk to the beach and sit on a drift log watching the tide inch silently up in the morning quiet. We hold a last communion with North Beach before returning to Nani and breakfast. Just prior to our afternoon departure we gather at the old oaken table in Nani's kitchen and I read aloud the poem I composed for her that morning on North Beach. "*Hʔaawa qʼuljat, Hʔaawa,*"[1] she says when I finish. She looks at the words for a moment, then folds the yellow sheet and tucks it into the pocket of her sweater.

We take pictures of each other standing beside Nani on the front

1. *Hʔaawa* means "thank you" in Haida. *Qʼuljat* is a term of respect used for a woman, equivalent to the male *Kilsle* (Chief).

stoop before we leave. "I don't know which way to look," she says, impatient at our focusing and metering. "All these pictures are taking my life away," she teases us. Yes, we would each take back something of Nani and the magic of her place as we try to record memories in two dimensions. We drop Nani off at a friend's house and say our goodbyes there. *"Diman əgəntł quinga, Nani"* (Look after yourself). *"Ding sin, ding sin"* (You too, you too), she replies.

We fly down Masset Inlet, cutting across the peninsula before we come to Nani's house, the land now to our south. Sundappled waves lap at the white sands of North Beach and in the distance glimmer little muskeg lakes. I tick off Chowan Brook, the Sangan River, Kliki Creek, Yakin Point. I see the flowers and moss that soften Tow's craggy stone face, and finally, the meadowland at Rose Spit. I follow the spit to the land's edge; it curls into the sea, then disappears into the mists for another year.

Florence Davidson, 1989 (photograph by Ulli Steltzer)

Epilogue 1992
"One More Time"

It has been ten years since *During My Time* went to press. Like many other life history projects, this one was reluctantly brought to closure, for its ending marked the conclusion not only to my research in Florence's community but to a very rich and personally satisfying project for both of us. But once the interviewing was complete, I was eager to finish the manuscript so that Florence might hold in hardcover the results of our efforts. My urgency was propelled by her age, for she was already elderly when we began the project. Happily, she was a vibrant eighty-seven when the final product appeared and, at this writing, she is still active in her mid-nineties.

Though I am no longer engaged in anthropological research in Florence's community, my personal relationship with Florence and her family continues. Since completion of the book I have had the pleasure of returning each year to the Queen Charlotte Islands, now as guest rather than researcher in Florence Davidson's home. These brief summer visits occasion hours at Nani's old oaken kitchen table where, over tea, dried fish, and freshly baked bread, she catches me up on family and village events. "I've been waiting for your visit," she greets me. "We'll talk and talk." While I am there, her daughters and daughter-in-law drop in almost daily to check on her and to visit; grandchildren bearing great-grandchildren to be held and made over stop by for tea; tourists bring copies of the life history to be autographed; and almost always there is some celebratory family event to be attended—a birthday party, an anniversary dinner, a baby shower. My annual pilgrimage to this place of my first

159

fieldwork is not complete without a hike along my favorite portions of North Beach, where I retrace in its hard-packed sands the beginning of my professional career as an anthropologist.

In addition to the personal renewal that my Masset trips afford, they have also allowed me to follow informally the trajectory of *During My Time* and the continuing story of Florence Davidson's long and rich life. In concert with the changes in my own life, these journeys have nourished my reflections on the many-faceted life history process.

My copy of the book was delivered to me in December 1982 at Strong Memorial Hospital in Rochester, New York, where I rested following the birth of my daughter Meryn. As I commented in the first edition of the book, my apparent childlessness made me somewhat more of an anomaly in this community of large families than I already was. My first time motherhood at age thirty-eight both amused and astonished Florence. "When you going to have another?" she demanded of me as my daughter approached the end of her first year of life. This turning point in my own life had a considerable impact on my understanding of the life history process. In the summer of 1982, six-months pregnant, I interviewed Florence regarding Haida perspectives on pregnancy. The immediacy of my own experience led me to ask numerous questions that had not occurred to me during our earlier life history interviews. As my focus turned to my young daughter in the months and years ahead, I thought often of the questions I might have asked, but had not, on Haida views of child development and child rearing. Aside from the opportunities not taken, the changes in my own life were a powerful lesson in how life experiences of the interviewer can affect the course of life history interviewing, a point to which I shall return.

Shortly after she received her hardcover copy of *During My Time*, Florence was flown to Vancouver by CBC to be interviewed on a national radio program during which the interviewer suggested that a film of Florence's life was surely in order. On that same trip she was photographed and featured in the book-review section of the Sunday *Vancouver Sun*. Not long after followed a full-page review of her life history in the Canadian news magazine, *Macleans*. Florence reported to me that she received letters "from all over the world" in response to the book, and by the summer of 1983 a small but steady stream of visitors had begun to trickle to her doorstep. Their presence has been abetted by the local sale of the book at Claude and Sarah's Haida Arts and Jewellery, owned by Florence's son and daughter-in-law. Many tourists to the Queen Charlotte Islands buy the book there, then walk down the hill to meet Claude Davidson's mother. Despite her deafness, Florence, with consummate Haida hospitality, welcomes them all, frequently serving tea while she autographs their books.

Biographies, autobiographies, and life histories—especially best sellers—hold the potential for having a major impact on their subjects as world attention focuses on the intimate revelations of often heretofore unknown individuals. By contrast, the impact of *During My Time* on Florence has been relatively minor and her life has not been substantially altered. CBC crews did not arrive to commit her story to celluloid or videotape, the visitors and letters have all easily been taken in stride, and the royalties which accrue exclusively to her have been very modest by best-seller standards. Florence was a high-ranking, prominent woman in her community long before the life history project was conceived; she is accustomed to being important. She has served often as an ambassador for her people, has dined with former Prime Minister Pierre Elliot Trudeau, and has welcomed Queen Elizabeth II to the Queen Charlotte Islands. Certainly her stature was a factor in her selection as a life history subject, and she explains her involvement in the project accordingly. She once told another woman in the community (in reference to the research contract I received from the National Museums of Canada to fund the work): "They ask for my story from Ottawa; that's why I'm doing it."

Yet the book is not without its impact on her life. I think it fair to say that its publication has further extended her importance beyond her own community and society to the outside world. For Florence, that is measured in the letters, the visitors, the local purchases of books by outsiders. She laughingly expresses this extension of self in a kinship metaphor: "I must be the world's Nani," she says. "The whole world calls me Nani, Nani Florence. That's what I like." Though, as I noted in the first edition, such statements bespeak her universal "grandmother-ness," they also testify to her perceived significance beyond the Queen Charlotte Islands.

More subtly, perhaps, the book has now become incorporated into Florence's life story. Known simply as "the book," it is a perennial topic of conversation between Florence and me. She often begins our telephone conversations with news of the latest autograph seeker, or she recounts the book's local sales to me upon my return in the summer. She remembers and relates, with amusement and delight, the personal responses: the lady who, patting her on the cheek, kept remarking, "You're wonderful! You're wonderful!"; the man who came to her with twelve copies to autograph; the teasing comment from a white friend, "The whole world knows you, just like the

Queen!" The book is a tangible link between us. As it has become incorporated into Florence's continuing life story, so also, professionally and personally, it has become part of mine, leading me to additional life history research and drawing me back to the Queen Charlottes each year.[1]

In 1989 I had visited Florence just six weeks before I returned again to join in the celebration of her 95th birthday party.[2] Celebrations are important in this community where even a small gathering of "just the family" can bring together more than 100 people. Birthdays, anniversaries, holiday feasts, funerals and memorials for the deceased all accentuate the rhythm of Masset life. Increasingly there are "new" rituals—reworkings and adaptations of old forms to contemporary times, like Robert Davidson's 1989 first salmon ceremony held at the Yakoun River, where the people go each year to subsistence fish for salmon. Or his 1980 Celebration of the Living Haida, a counterpoint to the Haida's apparent ceremonial focus on death. Claude and Sarah Davidson have also done much to rekindle Haida ceremonial forms, serving as instructors for a large and eager dance group of Masset Haida youth.

The organization of Nani's birthday celebration was in the hands of her daughters, particularly Aggie Davis, who in the months preceding the party carried around a large red notebook labeled "Nani's 95th birthday party," and consulted with her sisters on details ranging from the menu, the guest list, the speakers, to the color of family members' dress (purple, Nani's favorite). Her prominent role indicates how much women's ceremonial roles have changed in the twentieth century for, as Florence recounted, Florence and her husband were the first to invite couples instead of just men to Haida feasts. The celebration planned and executed by Aggie and her sisters in September 1989 included many more than "just the family" and was much more than just a birthday celebration.

For the first time in my nineteen years of journeys to the Queen Charlotte Islands it took me just one day to get to Masset. At 8:40

1. See, for example, Blackman (1989).

2. Florence calculates her birth date as 1895, citing a genealogy her uncle Henry Edenshaw kept of the family (see p. 159). This made her 94 at the time of her party. A community-wide celebration was held five years earlier in honor of her 90th birthday (when she was 89), because, according to Florence, she had been ill and there was some concern that she might not survive to 90. Her 95th celebration was held five years following her 90th.

Florence Davidson and Margaret Blackman, 1989
(photograph by Ulli Steltzer)

A.M. EDT on September 13, 1989, I helped my daughter cross the street to walk to school, and by 11:00 P.M. PDT I had dropped my bags at Nani's front room and was sitting beside her on the couch. Despite my delight in traveling so quickly, Masset—"the field"—is mentally more than a day removed from upstate New York—"home."

The plane from Vancouver included several birthday party guests—Robert Davidson, his wife Dorothy, his brother Reg, and their children. We whiled away the flight admiring Reggie's art work and Dorothy's album of "Feastwear," the couture collection of clothing she has created incorporating Robert's Haida designs. On the Charlottes, I caught a ride with Robert, Dorothy, and Reg alongside the mountains of gear brought for their Rainbow Creek Dancers performance at the party. The sun was just setting as we piled the gear in the car, and by the time we boarded the 9:00 P.M. ferry for Graham Island, a nearly full moon played its light across Alliford Bay. We stood on the ferry deck in the cool night air, watching a falling star, and we noted that the moon would be full in honor of Nani's day.

It was after midnight New York time when we drove off the ferry. I had thought I might sleep during the remainder of the trip to Nani's, but instead we talked while Robert and Reg sang Haida songs in practice for the birthday party. I listened to their strong, sonorous voices, watched the silhouettes of the trees in the waxing moon, glimpsed the occasional deer frozen by the car's headlights, smelled the heady smell of the cedar forest, and anticipated seeing Nani. It was a magical night. . . .

At 11:00 P.M. the lights still burned in Nani's front room and kitchen. Dozens of round layer cakes on three long tables were being decorated by seven women professionally wielding pastry bags. On the dining table in the red parlor were trays of purple sugar flowers to ornament the cakes (with enough left over for a future celebration). Nani was on her couch on the far side of the room, watching over the proceedings. She looked small and almost overwhelmed by the activity that swirled about her. At midnight when the cake preparers left Nani's, I settled into my bed on one of the couches in the parlor. That first night I had the parlor to myself, but I was later to be joined by photographer Ulli Steltzer and ethnobotanist Nancy Turner.

Soon after breakfast the next morning the house filled with a small army of helpers—relatives, friends, out-of-town visitors. First there were turkeys to stuff. Aggie placed a bathtub-sized metal basin on the kitchen table and began breaking up bread cubes. She then

doled out knives and some of the strongest onions imaginable;
within minutes all the onion cutters were crying. During the next
hour we stuffed eight enormous turkeys. I paused periodically to
document the preparations with my camera. Meanwhile, up at
Claude's, a group of people were peeling potatoes and cutting up
hard-boiled eggs. In all, 150 pounds of potatoes and 18 dozen eggs
were processed that morning, and an additional 50 pounds of
potatoes were added the next day.

By early afternoon the eight turkeys and eleven hams had been
distributed to various homes to cook, in accord with the master list
in Aggie's red notebook. Aggie continued to oversee the operations
at Nani's, and all day long the phone rang with requests to talk to
"the boss." Up at Claude's another group spent the afternoon
wrapping purple foil around 500 chocolate frogs and moons
(Robert's "Chocolate Arts," cast from his handcarved molds).

Robert, charged with the speakers' list, told me Nani wanted me
to give a speech. I was tremendously honored and spent much of
the next day (September 15) considering what I might say. A few
words in Haida seemed essential, I thought, remembering Nani's
advice about speechmaking at Haida feasts. I would have to use
virtually all the Haida I knew, for I was not Nani's most ambitious or
dedicated language student. I wanted to share my view of her in her
mid-nineties: still strong in spirit, sharp-witted, in control of her
own life, an inspiration to anyone facing advancing age. I recalled
her oft-repeated remark—"I always try all my best for my
children"—and I mused on how now they were trying all their best
for her. The world could learn much from this extended family in
caring for its elderly. Finally, there was her gift of self. "You don't
have to call me Mrs. Davidson. Call me Nani," she had instructed
me in 1970. Her invitation was far more than a simple change of title;
it was an invitation to learn her life, to form a new relationship with
her, to enter in the large circle of her family and her world.

On the night of September 14th, a community-hall decorating
party for Nani's birthday feast was combined with a birthday party
for a one-year-old great-granddaughter of Nani's. During the
evening, sixty pies that Aggie had put together in one morning came
back to Nani's, baked and ready, and several batches of peanut
butter cookies were delivered by Virginia and Dave Hunter, Nani's
daughter and son-in-law.

I had remained behind with Nani in lieu of decorating the hall, but
feast preparations continued unabated at her house. Nani emerged
from a back room bearing a pile of tablecloths. She gave these to her
granddaughter Arlene Nelson with instructions to ready the white

ones for the head table. Seeing Arlene laden with eight tablecloths to iron, I volunteered to help. An extra iron was fetched and, under Nani's exacting guidance, I set up operations on the end of one of the big tables. Never mind that at age forty-five I had more than thirty years of ironing experience to my credit. It is Nani's habit to take control over proceedings within her household, so I listened dutifully to her instructions. While the tablecloths were being ironed, the butter dishes, creamers, paper plates, and the china and silverware for the head table were collected and taken to the hall to be put in place. Dorothy came home early, exhausted. They had set more than 450 places in the hall.

I went to bed before eleven, inhaling the fragrance of nine boxes of MacIntosh apples that had been polished that afternoon. Luckily I couldn't smell the many heads of cabbage, destined for cole slaw, that were wrapped in plastic and piled against the wall by the door.

The morning of September 15th dawned with birthday greetings to Nani. "Happy Birthday!" she called out again and again, laughing, beating each bearer of natal-day greetings to the punch. "*Wha haaa!*" she intoned reprehensively when son-in-law Brian Hugo wished her "many happy returns." "You crazy!" she retorted. "You think I want to live forever?" She opened presents at the breakfast table, taking an infuriatingly long time to undo the paper and bows. The paper was all saved as per her instructions, to be recycled at some future celebration. Nani continued to open presents all the following day, relishing each gift, trying on her scarves, holding up her nightgowns, passing around her crystal and china presents for everyone to see, reading every card and likely committing it all to memory. Nevertheless, all gifts and givers were entered in a guest book purchased expressly for that purpose. Opened gifts were still piled high on the tables when I left for home on Sunday morning. I laughed then, envisioning Nani trying on all at once her riches of many-colored scarves.

There was still much to be done for the party. Aggie dumped a huge jar of sweet pickles in a wash basin, demonstrating how finely they should be cut. It took three people well over an hour to chop them. During a respite in pickle chopping, I photographed the cakes (89 in all) and the pies being taken from the house to the hall. In the kitchen, others were cutting banana bread for the paper *qawqEɬ* plates of sweets and fruits that would sit atop each dinner plate to be emptied by the dinner guests into paper bags and taken home.[3]

3. See p. 135.

Finally, the eggs, onions, and potatoes were added to the chopped pickles, and helpers working at the big tables in Nani's front room dug down into the mountains of potato salad to mix in the mayonnaise.

At 3:00 P.M. there was a church service. Bishop Hannen of the Anglican diocese, who had come for the party, and Father Ian MacKenzie, a former Anglican minister from Masset here for the party, baptized six people, all of them from Nani's family. The baptism/communion service seemed particularly appropriate in its commemoration of new and renewed life on Nani's special day.

By 5:00 P.M. people had begun to make their way to the hall, which was resplendent with hundreds of purple and white balloons and streamers, the purple theme reiterated in the napkins and the sugar flowers on the birthday cakes. The long head table, covered with the freshly ironed white linens, was set with bone china and fine silver. The colorful, elegant cakes and the pies had been distributed among the tables, and at each place the *qawqEł* plates brimmed with MacIntosh apples, purple foil-wrapped chocolates, buns, homemade cookies and dessert bars. Grandsons, great-grandsons, and great-nephews, looking smart in dark suits and purple bow ties, ushered guests to their seats, taking instructions from Reg Davidson. The hall slowly filled. People chatted and greeted one another; children took their places in the bleachers until it was ascertained if there were free space at the tables; and the Anglican Church Army singer played his electric guitar.

More family helped with the serving of the meal. The older generation had prepared the food; the younger generation served it. Great-grandchildren efficiently carried plates of turkey, ham, potato salad, and cole slaw, two at a time, to the hundreds of guests at the long tables. Most of my "dinner time" was spent forking my meal—untasted—into my mouth while I nervously composed and recomposed the speech I had been asked to give.

Ernie Yeltatzie, eldest male of Florence's Y'akwə'lanas Raven lineage and a sister's son, inaugurated the after-dinner speeches, as is the custom when one of his lineage hosts a feast. He was followed by another sister's son, Sylvester Peele, representing the sizeable Alaskan Haida contingent from Hydaburg and Ketchikan. Victor Adams, a son-in-law and representative of the Git?əns Eagle lineage, to which the town chieftainship now belongs, spoke next. Other speakers included representatives of Haida and non-native organizations on the Queen Charlottes—the Canadian Forces base at Masset, the Masset and Skidegate Band councils, the Council of the

Haida Nation,[4] the Anglican church. In the middle of this group of speakers, I was introduced simply as a friend of the family. Given the presence of many important "friends of the family," I suppose, as Nani's biographer, I was in a sense her spokesperson. Through the words of Father MacKenzie, the evening's final speaker, I saw, for the first time, how Nani's role in the church was perceived by the clergy. He concluded, "She has ministered far more to this community than we have." Had she been able to hear, she would certainly have warmed to his words.

From the moment I sat down after my speech, I began to enjoy the evening. And there was much to enjoy. Claude and Sarah's *Q'ad nas* (dogfish shark house), a large group of serious young dancers, gave a long and versatile performance.[5] The competition dance was fun to watch as males from the audience strutted their stuff to the drums. I had a secret desire to see the bishop, in his flowing purple (how appropriate!) robes, cut loose in ecstatic dance, but he remained seated throughout the competition.

Between performances by the two dance groups, Nani's "official" cake—a large rectangular fruitcake iced in white and lavender—was brought out on a rolling table cart; Nani stood by it for pictures and then posed again with her eight surviving children as guests came forward with their cameras to take snapshots. The cake was cut and distributed to guests at the head table.

In introducing the Rainbow Creek Dancers, Robert Davidson credited his grandmother's role in their performance, speaking of her link to the past and to the dancers, as carriers of that past. She was their source of information on the dances, the details of certain masks, and some of the songs themselves. He spoke, too, of her contribution to growth. "The thread becomes a rope," he explained. A story evokes the creation of a mask, of a dance, even of a song. Today's singer of old songs becomes, in turn, the composer. And Nani, inspirational, instigational, somehow in it all.

Citing his uncle Alfred Davidson, Robert noted that it is okay to "make it up," to create new dances, new rituals. And so the Rainbow Creek Dancers come each time to Masset with something new. This time it was Reg as a seven-foot-tall *gagid* wearing dry

4. The Council of the Haida Nation, comprising the Masset and Skidegate Bands, was founded in 1983 to pursue their joint interests; namely, comprehensive land claims and management of island forestry and fish resources.

5. In the orthography developed by linguist John Enrico, and now used locally, the group is called the Kaa.aads nee Dancers.

Robert Davidson in the men's competition dance, 15 September 1989
(photograph by Ulli Steltzer)

waller's stilts hidden behind fur leggings, an arresting and imposing figure.[6] Robert's magnificent oversized salmon mask, with which the Rainbow Creek Dancers had first performed upriver that spring was also brought out. The concluding dance was an invitational honoring Nani. Reg dubbed it "the purple dance" and invited all women in purple to dance, including by name certain others lacking purple attire. We danced the circumference of the long, long head table, smiling and bowing to the drum as we passed before Nani.

The birthday party ended about 10:00 P.M. and was, by any reckoning, a grand and impressive feast. A tired Nani was escorted home to bed. The tables were cleared, silverware and plates were gathered up to be washed and brought home later, and grandsons and sons-in-law put away the tables and ferried home the gifts, dishes, and dirty tablecloths.

Nani in her quiet way seemed to have enjoyed the five hours of festivities immensely. She smiled and stood for photos, received those who came to pay homage, and wore her new ermine stole royally.[7] Though the Haida songs and the speeches may have fallen literally on deaf ears, she knew the performances and had personally chosen the evening's speakers. Much of the meaning for her lay in the process: the mobilization of family and village in preparation for the feast, the parade of arriving guests, the cards and presents, all testimony to who she is. From it all she seemed to derive energy. On September 13th, two days before the party, she was weak, but as Aggie said, she'd be better once her "babies" (Robert and Reg) arrived. Indeed she was, and with each new wave of visitors she seemed to grow stronger. On the morning following her party, she was up early as usual bustling about her kitchen making biscuits, a favorite "departure" breakfast, to feed Brian and Clara Hugo (son-in-law and daughter) and the bishop, who were all leaving that morning.

All day September 16th Nani continued to open her presents and receive visitors. For the rest of us, there were dishes and partyware

6. The *gagid* is a person narrowly escaped from drowning, transformed into a veritable monster whose deformed face bristles with sea-urchin spines. The cold, wet, unsuspecting victim of a canoe accident is lured to shore by a brightly burning fire lighted by the Land-Otter people. Going in search of the elusive fire, he becomes possessed and turns into a *gagid* (see Swanton 1909:26–27; also Boelscher 1988:186–90).

7. A birthday present from Bill and Martine Reid, presented to her at the feast.

to put away. Finally there was time for reflection, the beach, those other parts of the Charlottes that I love. I took a long walk with Ulli Steltzer, the warm September angled sun slanting through the wet hemlock boughs on the path to North Beach; we scoured the pebbly beach for agates, compared our perceptions of the party, remarked on Nani's different relationships with her, me, and Nancy Turner, and shared some of our personal histories and current research. I thought as we walked of how Nani has provided each of us with connections to people we otherwise might not have known. To be brought together under Nani's roof with interesting and companionable people is indeed one of the privileges of knowing her.

In the days following the party I thought often of its greater significance. I talked with Woody Morrison over a beer in the Vancouver Airport as we waited for our planes home. Woody, originally from Hydaburg, had served, along with Reg Davidson, as Master of Ceremonies for the party. He believed that the birthday itself was ultimately irrelevant to the relationships that were drawn upon and activated there. Most of all, he asserted, Nani's 95th birthday celebration was an event of relationships, a celebration of who the Haida are; each time there is such a celebration, those bonds, those relationships, that identity, are strengthened. In the end it was the larger "event" or process that was the more significant. This was a celebration of community and of unity as the Haida Nation. Nani was crucial in the drawing together of those forces and in her endurance—as Frank Collison noted in his speech—of nearly one-half of the history of Haida contact with the outside world. She is emblematic of quiet perseverance in the face of dramatic change, of today's Haida's connection with the past and of the potential of that past to give meaning to the future. She was the hinge, the fulcrum for this celebration of modern Haida-ness.

During the year prior to her 95th birthday fête, when Florence was relating to me some event which I have now forgotten, she queried, "Did I talk about that in the book?" When I noted that it had happened after the book was published, Emily Goertzen, one of her daughters, laughingly suggested that it was "time to write volume two." Emily's comment remained with me, and in the summer of 1990 I set out to "update" Florence's life story in some manner short of writing a second volume. I wanted to include not just Florence's reflections on life after publication, but the heretofore unexplored views of family members on "the world's Nani," their reactions to the text, and their assessment of its impact in the local community. An "update" would also allow me reflection on *During My Time* in light of recent developments in ethnographic writing.

So my visit in July of 1990 was in part a working visit. For the first time since 1982, I pulled out my tape recorder and, over the course of several days, conducted informal interviews with Nani, four of her daughters, her son, her daughter-in-law, and two grandsons.

In the knowledge that I had come to update Florence's story, I scrutinized the village as I drove in, conscious of its many changes since I had described it in the introductory pages of *During My Time* ten years before. The 40-kmh speed limit along its three-kilometer length invited such observation and reflection, and I was most struck by the apparent greater prosperity of the village and by its manifest "Haida-ness." At the reserve boundary a "Welcome to Haida" sign now greets visitors. The uprooted stumps once piled up at the south end of the reserve had been removed to make way for a new, prosperous-looking subdivision, its large houses reminiscent of those built by Nani's generation of home builders, unlike the boxy, look-alike houses built by the Department of Indian Affairs during the 1960s and 1970s. Two village residents have built massive cedar-plank homes closely resembling the old-style longhouses. Bright red-orange flags silkscreened in white with Robert Davidson's 1981 Eagle/Raven design fly from several homes and from the community hall, built in the 1980s. A simple totem pole with a carved Eagle at its apex stands before the home of Reno Russ, who was installed as town chief in 1984. On the hill behind Nani's are two more longhouse structures—Victor Adams's "House of Silver" art shop and Claude Davidson's nearly completed longhouse, constructed with his expanding dance group in mind. An Eagle/Raven painting adorns the weathered cedar-plank façade of Claude and Sarah's home/art shop, and a totem pole, carved by Reg and raised in 1987 to mark Claude's assumption of the chieftaincy of the old Haida village of Dadens, stands at the edge of their property. Across from Nani's home, Robert's silvered totem pole, carved twenty-one years ago, is a respected reminder of the beginning of the renaissance in Haida art. Behind it, though, the old white clapboard Anglican church, the victim of a 1984 fire, has been replaced by a modern cedar structure.

Nani's house, too, is not without its changes. A gently inclined ramp from her front door allows her easier egress to the road. The front yard brims with neat potato plants and summer flowers, and a church group from the town of Williams Lake on the mainland is busy building a fence around her property.

Nani and I sat across the kitchen table from each other that first night, falling into our familiar ritual of tea and talk. She looked wonderful, I thought, smart in her purple cotton shirtdress and black sweater, grandmotherly in her checked apron. Her wispy hair was braided and twisted into its usual bun. "I'm not getting another perm," she asserted, explaining her nearly straight hair in front: "I want to be ready to go, anytime." She made a sleeping gesture, then laughed at her casual reference to death. Seated in the comfortable, pillow-padded captain's chair that has been hers for nearly sixty years, she split cedar bark for the hat she was weaving while I bundled the narrow strips for her, listening to the events she elected to share with me. She had been greatly saddened by the recent death of her husband's niece, Dora Brooks, and she talked at length about Dora's illness, sudden death, and the funeral. Funerals often fill our first conversations, but we talk of life, too, "the book" being one of our topics. "Tomorrow," she said, we would talk about the book: "I'll weave while you ask me questions," she explained. At 12:30, responding to my yawns, she suggested we go to bed. I gave her a good-night hug; "I see you one more time!" she grinned.

When I awoke to bright sunshine at 7:00 A.M., Nani had already been in the kitchen for two hours. She wore a sweater over her long flannel nightgown, and the door of her electric range was propped open to supplement the heat from her furnace. She had been weaving in the early morning hours but was now cutting up fresh strawberries from daughter Emily's garden. Emily always brings her strawberries, she said (with the idea that she will eat them fresh), but Nani was doing with them what she almost always does with berries, making jam. Those were not the only berries that were destined for her jam jars during my short visit. Someone had picked the gooseberries from her side yard for her, and after a trip to the meadowland at Rose Spit we returned home with half a bucket of wild strawberries. Though Nani is no longer able to enjoy the rhythmic solitude of "picking" and the respite it offers women from the demands of family life, she remains an active part of the process, cleaning and preserving the offerings that are brought to her by her daughters and granddaughters.

I slid into my chair at the kitchen table across from Nani to drink my morning tea while she "jammed" her berries. When I first wrote *During My Time*, I commented on the presence of this kitchen in our life history interviews, of its dominance in Florence's life. It is where, then and now, she spends most of her day, and it is the favorite site of our interviewing. The kitchen not only occupies a prominent place in Florence Davidson's life but is an arena for

significant family and community activity. A well-known visitor to
the house will be entertained at the kitchen table instead of in the
more formal front room. Here the women of the family gather to
pick over buckets of fresh berries and talk, to prepare and bake food
for feasts; great- and great-great-grandbabies are brought here to be
held by Nani. The kitchen is also the very active backstage for
doings held in the house. Family helpers gather to pile the food on
plates which are taken to the long guest tables in the front room,
and at the dinner's end they return here to do the dishes and,
always, to talk. As increasing age has limited her mobility and Nani
has become more a fixture in her kitchen, so it has become a more
important arena for action. Through it flows virtually every
important activity concerning her household.

The kitchen cabinets, flooring, and paint are all new since first I
wrote of this room, but its contents are in the same place, down to
the African violets atop the washing machine and the two plastic
buckets of fresh rainwater for making tea. New technology—a
microwave oven and, thankfully, a dishwasher—stands beside old
familiar fixtures. Always the kitchen reflects Nani's current activities.
In July of 1990 her weaving and jam-making paraphernalia told of
how she spent her days: little strips of cedar bark spattered across
the table and floor, her bowl of water for wetting her weaving to
keep it pliable, the small knife with "FD" carved in its handle for
splitting the strands of bark, the hat stand bearing a partially
completed hat, jars of newly made jam stacked in the center of the
table, a bucket of cleaned berries ready for the stove, and on the
table, Nani's seven-day pill dispenser containing her arthritis and
iron pills and her vitamins.

Watching Nani in her environs, I contrast the rhythm of her days
with the daily routine of Hannah, a 98-year-old woman described by
Dorothy Gallagher in *Hannah's Daughters . . .* (1976:14–15). Writes
Gallagher of Hannah's days:

> All through the afternoon Hannah sits in her chair. She daydreams,
> sometimes she sleeps; the distinction between the two is no longer
> important to her. At six o'clock she eats white bread again; sometimes
> she fries potatoes in Crisco and makes a potato sandwich. She washes
> the dishes, and then she calls her daughter-in-law. She makes this call
> night and morning, to let someone know that she is still alive.
> Sometime during the evening she moves from the vinyl chair to the
> rocking chair, covers herself with a blanket and goes to sleep.

That morning Nani worked on her berry and hat projects until
about 10:00 A.M., when she retired to a comfortable couch in the

living room where she fell asleep before the TV set. Just after eleven
the government nurse came by as she does every weekday to check
on Nani and to apply hot packs to ease the arthritis in her legs.
Daughter-in-law Sarah usually stops in sometime before lunch to
have tea with Nani, but today she was held up by a stream of
tourists at her shop. I fixed lunch for us, stopping Meryn from
digging into a salmon sandwich just in time for Nani to say the grace
in Haida. Lunch over, Nani turned again to her weaving, then lay
down on the couch about 1:30 for a nap. It wasn't long, however,
before she was back at her chair in the kitchen. Just after 4:00 she
walked into the front room, lamenting, "I hate to leave my weaving,
but I really want to watch this TV show." The minute the program
ended she picked up the cedar bark strands to her hat and resumed
weaving. "I don't worry about anything when I'm weaving," she
confessed a couple of years ago. On Mondays and Thursdays a
young woman from the Reserve comes and cleans house for Nani, a
service provided by the Masset Band to members who need
assistance. When Nani doesn't have guests, Aggie brings dinner
down to her about 5:00 P.M.—except on Sundays when Merle and
her husband Knud bring dinner and share the meal with Nani.
Whenever I'm visiting, Nani takes full advantage of my love of
cooking. And I take full advantage of the largesse of fresh and
frozen seafood in her freezer when planning my menus. "You're real
Akaaná" [from a chief's family, high class], Nani exclaims of outsiders
who sample and relish such Haida delicacies as dried fish, herring
eggs, and eulachon grease. I, in turn, test her willingness to eat
what is placed before her, subjecting her to curries, pastas,
Southwestern cuisine, and preparing her native halibut and salmon
in ways foreign to her palate. She eats them all and requests that I
write her favorites in a recipe book I began for her in 1974.

Always there are visitors in the evening. On the dining table
Aggie has spread a button blanket she is making for Nani to give as
a gift to a friend. Other women in the family who come by in the
evening sometimes join her in appliquéing the red wool grizzly bear.
It is not unusual for some sewing project to be laid out in the front
room. Three summers ago when the daughters were making
coverlets to be given out at a memorial potlatch, they came here
every night to work on them. As they sew, the women talk—of their
sons and daughters and grandchildren, of work, vacation time, of
upcoming community/family events. There is much laughter too;
good-natured sibling jousting and sarcasm abound, into which
unsuspecting visitors are often pulled. The conversation swirls about
Nani, engrossed in her weaving and deaf to most of it. Amusing

stories are occasionally related about her in her presence, and when caught by circumstance, she readily laughs at herself. One evening, her daughters mentioned the visiting Anglican minister from Terrace, Peter Zimmer. Nani asked what his last name was but had difficulty hearing it. "Himmer?" "Skipper?" "Zipper!" she shouted in exasperation. Her audience howled, and tears ran down her cheeks as she joined in the fray. When she got it right, they all applauded, and she retold in Haida the joke on herself.

Through all my visiting, Meryn plays happily with Christine, Aggie's granddaughter who is two years younger than she. When they were outside this afternoon catching ladybugs, Nani dispatched me to them with a warning. "Old people believe that you shouldn't touch ladybugs. If you touch them all the little bugs will come out, and if you touch your eyes with your hands, you'll go blind." Too late, Meryn and Christine tell me; they've already handled the bugs. Undaunted, they collect more. Later the two girls play house in Nani's red parlor, pretend to have boyfriends, and travel to Prince Rupert to a dance. Christine at five and a half is exactly the age her mother Helen was when first I came here in 1970. The grandchildren are all parents now, and Nani has become great Nani.

Nani still lives alone but in close proximity to five daughters, one son,[8] and numerous grandchildren and their families. It would not be unusual for a grandchild to live with her, and from time to time, a few have done so for short periods. She can be very exacting, however, unhesitatingly offering strong advice on everything from dress to mate selection, which may deter live-in relations. Too, she has definite opinions on whom she will and will not live with. Nonetheless, Florence's family seem both unusual and exemplary in their attentiveness. Their offerings are obvious even to the casual visitor: a case of grapefruit and a case of oranges from a grandson, fresh crabs from another grandson, dinners, peanut butter cookies, grocery shopping by a daughter, the trash emptied, the rainwater buckets refilled, and more. Relatives at farther remove also routinely provision Florence, sending fresh fruit from the Okanagan, money, and other gifts. She acknowledges their gifts: "Some people think it's not nice to have a big family, but when you're old, you find out how nice they are." Indeed, it is then you finally reap the benefits from all those years of trying all your best for them.

It was the third day of my visit before we began our interview about the book. We sat in the front room, Nani on the couch, I in the

8. Claude died of cancer in November 1990.

rocking chair next to her, the tape recorder and microphone resting on the coffee table in front of us. Because of her hearing problem and because she complains that I talk too fast, I wrote out my questions for her on a yellow pad of paper while speaking them into the tape recorder. I began by noting that it had been ten years since the book had been written, and I asked what had occurred in her life since then that she would like included.

> After you got the book ready, after you quit with me the longhouse burned.[9] I think Sunday, Saturday night, they burn the house. Dorothy and Robert was in here, and Robert opened the kitchen door and I'm all alone in there. He looked real sad and Dorothy was with him. "Nani, we heard the bad news what happened." He couldn't say it for a while; it was hard on him. "The long house burned down. Three men did it.". . . We cry just like someone dead. Dorothy and I and Robert. It was so pretty. Just before they burn it, Ulli [Steltzer] took me down and she took picture of it. It's real pretty; it's in here somewhere. In the album. Nothing left; just the ground was there.

Florence talked of the spate of arson attempts in the village which followed the burning of the longhouse: on Robert Davidson's totem pole by the church (which was salvaged), on the Anglican church (burned to the ground in 1984), on the community hall and the kindergarten, both burned in 1981. "My, that was real bad," she said of the church, "just like the longhouse."[10]

A long pause. "What else," I asked.

> I was real sick several years ago. I start puking; I use too much aspirin for my arthritis pains. My stomach start bleeding." She laughs: "I was 135 lbs. I put two face towels under my brassieres; I looked too funny. That's when I have birthday party, when I almost died. They celebrate 90 one year before [when I was 89].

She provides a few more details of her life-threatening illness of five years ago then queries: "You want me to talk about Alfred and them?" "Yes, please," I respond. Alfred Davidson, her eldest son and a lay minister in the community, together with his wife Rose,

9. The longhouse with its four carved interior house posts and its carved and painted façade was constructed in 1979 as a memorial to Charles Edenshaw under the direction of Robert Davidson and apprentice artists Reg Davidson, Jim Hart, Don Yeomans, and Gerry Marks. It was burned in 1981.

10. The arsonist, an emotionally disturbed young man from the village, was finally caught.

Florence Davidson and her daughters, 15 September 1989. *Left to right:* Emily Goertzen, Merle Andersen, Aggie Davis, Myrtle Kerrigan, Florence, Primrose Adams, Virginia Hunter, Clara Hugo (photograph by Ulli Steltzer)

died tragically in 1986 from fish-egg poisoning.[11] She describes the events leading to their death, and the funeral.

Talk turned to a more felicitous event, her 95th birthday party.

> When my family is going to do something they always have meeting together, and they tell how much they are going to donate towards the doing. They keep on having meeting. And they don't want me to do anything; they don't want me to spend things. The ones coming from Alaska, I bought them things, what to eat. I gave money to some people. My family thought it was all right what I did. They didn't say anything.
>
> All the Skidegate people come to the dinner. They all gave me present—$50 bill in card. I bought bone china set—cost over $1000. I make myself happy. I got it so Aggie will have it. She always take me to hospital, spends a lot of time on me. Sam [her husband] don't ever kick about it. Knud and Sam, they real nice to me. All my sons-in-law, they all nice to me. It's still hard on me; two of my son-in-law left their family; they die young. I miss them very bad.

Her thoughts continued with the birthday party. "All the ones from states, they give me money, too. I bought big TV with it, too. Lots of food, too. It seems more than anything else all kinds of food. And just like I'm a young woman, they give me all kinds of makeup, too." She laughed at thoughts of being treated like a young woman.

"I always think of how nice people are. They come far away from their homes, spend lots of money. The ones didn't come, they send me nice cards."

"What else about the party," I asked after a while.

"I can't think . . . I'm still happy when I think about it. I thought sometimes I'm getting too old. I thought I'm in people's way. They always surprise me. It's nice to have big family."

The tape rolled on, but nothing else came to her about the party.

She concluded, "I'm still working; I'm weaving away.[12] It costs real lots to live in one big house." With that, Florence decided to lie on the couch and rest, so we quit for the time being.

In updating her life story, Florence chronicled events that occurred subsequent to publication, focusing on the tragedies that have befallen her—the burnings, the sudden deaths, her own illness. She talked about her 95th birthday, a major positive event, but only after

---

11. Botulism, from salmon eggs allowed to ferment in air-tight jars. One family member found the account too painful to read and requested that it be deleted.

12. In 1990 Florence wove sixteen hats.

I asked about it; and, for whatever reasons, she did not choose to talk about other positive celebratory events—the births of new family members, weddings, etc. Perhaps because of the way I began the questioning, she did not reflect on the book itself, nor retell, revise, or amplify any of its stories. I did ask her if there were anything we forgot to put in the book the first time. "I used to think of lots of things," she said, "but I can't remember now." Florence has often made the point that memories cannot be called up on command during interviews. They come unbidden, most often when no one is present to record them (see p. 18).

I interviewed Aggie, Emily, and Merle together one evening at the kitchen table; Claude one morning at his house; Sarah the same afternoon. Reg joined us for part of the last interview. The following afternoon, the day before I was to depart the islands, I visited Virginia in New Masset to talk with her about the book. I covered the same ground with all of the children: their responses to the published work, whether any of their mother's commentary surprised them, their favorite memories/stories of her, advice she gave them while they were growing up. We spent some time, too, adding up the great- and great-great-grandchildren.[13] Later in Vancouver I interviewed Robert Davidson, focusing on the role his grandmother has played in his intellectual development as an artist, performer, and creator of modern Haida rituals.

The memories, the stories flowed easily from Nani's children. Their accounts reinforced some of my views of Nani, but changed others. They provided a portrait of their mother in her late thirties to mid-forties, when they were children, and they added details of their own lives, missing from Florence's brief mention of her children in her story.

Recalling that Florence most often spoke of her earlier years with young children in tow, I was struck by Aggie's image of her mother going off by herself, or at the very least without children, thirty-five miles up the inlet to can salmon.

> I remember when we were young, there used to be a dock down there [by the inlet] and Bipsy [Primrose, a sister] and I used to go down there when Mom's going up to the inlet to can fish. She used to go up on a rowboat. Bipsy used to stand there crying. I don't know how old mom was then. She used to feel so sorry for Bipsy. That's the only

13. With Aggie's help, right before the mauscript went to press in February of 1992, we counted 72 great-grandchildren and 27 great-great-grandchildren. With 8 living children and 33 grandchildren, Florence currently has 139 descendants.

thing I always think about. I don't know how old I was, but I remember she used to go up there and can fish.

From Virginia I learned that Florence even went to Alaska to work in the cannery, leaving her young children behind. "She left me in charge of my sisters," Virginia asserted. "I've been like a mother to them all their lives." She hastened to add that when she returned home from Alert Bay boarding school at fifteen, she also took over sewing the younger girls' clothing.

Though recalling herself as a stand-in for her mother, Virginia also recalled Florence in a larger mothering role.

> One year Mary Parnell passed away and I phoned down and said, "Is Mom home?" Myrtle [a sister] said, "No, she went up to see Patsy 'cause her mother died." And she said, "Do you realize that Mom's the mother to the whole town." And I said, "Yeah, I didn't even think about it, but come to think of it she is." Soon as there was a death, she was right there to comfort them and help them. Didn't matter who it was, she was always there to help, but then she got too old, she couldn't handle it anymore. But she was there when she was able to. She used to have a [church] meeting every Wednesday, and I used to scrub and wax the dining room, sitting room, living room, and kitchen floors every Tuesday afternoon so it'd be ready for the ladies the next night. They enjoyed her refreshments, so they were there all the time; soon as Lent come, there was hardly anybody, because she would quit giving refreshments out during Lent.

Through Florence's own words I associated her with a lifetime of baking and putting up food. So do her children. Remarked Claude: All I know is that she used to do a lot of baking—baking pies, baking bread, baking buns. You name it, she had all the pastries. So I kept pretty fat all my life." Florence speaks of accompanying her husband to North Island to fish, putting up food there and baking goods to sell to fishermen (p. 112); the two older children also recalled these trips with their parents.

> She used to can fruit, and deer meat. Any fruit in season, she used to have bulk loads of it. I think Dad must have made two trips coming out, because she used to can up enough food for us to use all winter. Even during the Depression in the thirties we never went hungry [Virginia Hunter].

The advice their mother proffered over the years was well ingrained, for Florence's children all provided numerous examples of her instruction and discipline:

> "Not to drink water or we'll never get married . . . not to lick bowls or spoons after making a cake 'cause we won't know how to dance."

"Never talk about anybody; don't talk about their faults or anything. It's not nice."

"Sunday's a day of rest; nobody should do any work on Sunday."

"Don't drink too much. That's the only advice I know that she's given me all my life."

The daughters especially remembered their mother chaperoning them at community dances; Virginia shared the following vivid memory of her mother's curfew enforcement.

> She just didn't want me to go around at night. She was really strict with me. If I was going to a dance, she used to take me. She used to stay there and she'd look really ugly at me. Mean. Every time I would dance by her, I would smile at her. And one day I said, "Mom, why is it you look so mean at me when I'm dancing and enjoying myself and Charlotte [Marks] sitting next to you smiles at her daughters and looks happy about everything, but you don't even smile at me?" I remember that New Year's Eve, she sat there until seven in the morning. I can't remember what she said to me, but imagine me being that bold to ask!
>
> And she used to tell me she didn't want me to go out after dark or go anywhere. I went to church one evening in the summertime; I had some friends that went too. I got brave. I walked past our house down along the highway. I was walking along and Ida Jones said to me, "Virginia, your dad's coming." I turned; he was trotting up real fast after me. Mom sent him after me. So I turned around and ran home real fast. I didn't even stop to say anything to Dad. I ran home and I ran up to my room. I jumped into bed and coverered myself with all my clothes. So he came over and he pulled the blanket off my face and he said, "Look, your mom don't want you walking around at night." It was daylight, you know, summertime; it was real light out, so he said, "That's why I had to go after you." See, that's the kind of man he was. And Mom wanted, and Mom got.

This was not the only comment that portrayed Nani as a forceful personality in her younger years. I had often mused whether, in some respects, Florence existed in Robert Davidson, Sr.'s, shadow, really only coming into her own authority after she was widowed. All her children assured me that she had long been practiced in directing others and delegating tasks she wanted done. And, they noted, she continues to do so. "Tell about the Easter dinner she had this last Easter," Aggie urged Merle. "She plans," explained Merle, 'Oh, I think I'll have a dinner sale for the church.' So we all get busy, and she just sits back. She makes a thousand dollars." Emily chimed in: "Remember when we had the memorial dinner for Alfred and Rose?" [Imitating Nani], 'I think I'll sew about ten quilts.' We made more than forty." Emily laughed, "She knows she doesn't have to worry about a thing. Her little elves are here doing everything for her!"

In many respects age has conferred its advantages on Florence. Her position may be even more advantaged because she is the oldest member of the Masset Haida Band. As is customary, she is treated as a senior member of her lineage, referred to by its members in public as "our grandmother," seated in a position of honor at feasts and potlatches, and accordingly called upon to speak. As most senior member of her lineage she has also acted as custodian of its chieftainship.[14] A few years ago she advised Claude to take up the Dadens Y'akwə'lanas chieftainship, and she publicly bestowed the name on him when he did so. Claude explained:

> At first she had Alfred in mind. Just that year he died she was going to ask him to become the chief of Dadens. And then he died, and later on she decided that I should be the chief, so she appointed me. My mother explained [how several people held that particular position]. She's read the Bible so many times, she start thinking: "My golly, there's so many different people that become king someplace, and so many kings in one place, why couldn't there be more chiefs from this one village." And so she decided, well, one of her sons got to become a chief.

Robert commented on his grandmother's selection of Claude for the chieftainship: "When she gave my dad the chief's name, what it created was a challenge for value. Even though another person claimed that chieftainship, my dad took it upon himself to claim the chieftainship also.[15] And what it did was to give the role of a chief more depth; it brought back the fact that there are chiefs and subchiefs. What I got from my dad becoming chief is that it's OK to have more than one chief per clan, like in the old days."

Robert also reflected on Nani's role as ceremonial advisor: "She doesn't give me too much advice now, but I'm always honored by her presence. Like she's become the witness; she's become the authority. It's really important to do your homework before you actually host an event, and if you don't do your homework, then she's the critic." He describes her as a "cultural guru." More than a

---

14. See Boelscher (1988) for a discussion of the role of women in conferring names on their sons.

15. The chieftainship had been claimed by a lineage nephew (and sister's son of Florence) of the preceding holder but had not been validated by a potlatch. That claimant took his case to the larger public, declaring his right to the title in a public notice published in the *Queen Charlotte Islands Observer*, the weekly newspaper.

universal grandmother, she is a *"cultural* Nani," and her role as living link to the past is given added significance by virtue of her longevity.

Florence's advisement role is continuous in more mundane areas of life, as Claude noted about drinking. Emily, who lost her husband in 1989, recalled, "She told me exactly what to do before Dave died. She said, 'Dave's going to go, and it's the hardest thing when your husband dies. And when he does die, you have to respect yourself, not go around visiting. Don't even use the phone. Wear black.' And later she said, 'It's time to quit wearing black.' Then, 'It's time to quit crying.' " Another of Nani's roles emerged from my interviews with family. "A smart businesswoman," asserted Sarah, who sometimes markets Florence's cedar bark hats for her. "The family banker," declared Reg, portraying his grandmother as stingy when it comes to spending money on herself, but storing cash in $100 bills at the ready for relatives in need. Still thinking ahead, in the summer of 1990 she had begun to purchase goods to be given out at the dedication of Claude's new longhouse in November.

Conversations with members of the Davidson family underscored the partiality of Florence's life history, of any life history. Their pictures of her were drawn with love and humor; they reinforced my views of how hard Nani has always worked and of her continued astonishing level of activity. Through their words she seems more dominant than I had come to envision her. In their childhood memories she was not the young submissive wife to a much older husband but a woman who made a number of important decisions within her household, including how the children were to be raised and disciplined. And she apparently had no qualms at sending her husband off to do her bidding. The family's pictures of Robert Davidson, Sr., are affectionate as well. Virginia, in particular, adored her father. If Florence was determined and strong-willed, he was kindly. "Not a mean bone in his body," Virginia insisted. "People just loved him." Florence too, despite her remembered harsh words from younger years, recalled what deep roots her relationship with him had. "I grew up with him," she said simply.

Too soon it was time to head north to Alaska, where my research now takes me. Were I to spend more time with Florence, I would undoubtedly hear more of her story, including elaborations on portions already told. I do, of course, hear more each time I visit—leaving for a picnic at Tow Hill, I hear how she and her husband used to pack up the boat in fine weather after church, "when we were still strong," to spend the afternoon picnicking. There is, as well, the unrecorded "now" that is always part of her life narrative: the discussion of family and their ongoing lives, the "off the record" narrative that is as much her story as those portions told for public consumption. In the end, the written text provides but a glimpse, a hint of the richness of human life experiences and their expression.

With Nani, my leavetakings are as poignant as my arrivals are joyous, for always I wonder if there will be "one more time." There was a period when Nani herself insisted that each visit was likely our last, but now, in her nineties, she exhibits a reserved optimism. "Hope for the best," she called out to me as Meryn and I drove off in the summer of 1990. We do, we do.

Note: Florence Davidson died on December 13, 1993. A memorial potlatch was held for Florence in Masset on October 7, 1994. For an account of the potlatch, see Margaret B. Blackman, "Death Comes to the Anthropologist: Reflections on the Haida Mortuary Potlatch." In Perspectives: Dying and Death, ed. Kathleen Hunter, pp. 93-104. Madison: Coursewise Publications, 1999.

Unedited Life History Narrative

The following passages, presenting a portion of Florence's narrative of her arranged marriage as it was transcribed from the tape, can be compared with the edited version on pages 95–99.

Here, Florence noted that she was fifteen when her marriage was arranged. Her birth certificate and baptismal record show that she was born in 1896, making her fourteen at the time of her marriage. Florence believes a mistake was made and that she was born in 1895. The 1896 date has been used in the edited account.

Tape 5/side 1

MB: So it was *C'at'lanas* and *Stl'əng'lanas*?

FD: Yes. They are all streaming in and I don't know what was going on. I went to my uncle's house.

MB: Henry Edenshaw's house?

FD: Yes. I don't know what's going on so I ran there. I told Josie who all came in and she was just laughing at me. Laughing real hard at me. She didn't tell me. Maybe week after, my cousin Dolly, Henry's daughter, "You smell this, Florence." She got ammonia in one quart bottle and she open it and she make me smell it. "Smell it. You sniff it real hard," she said. I sniff and I almost fell. You know how ammonia smells. I don't see ammonia before. "You know why I make you smell it?" she said. I don't know why she say that to me. I told my mother what Dolly say to me. "Don't say anything when I tell you something," my mother say. "They propose to you who all came in last week." I don't know what to say. Propose, why? I thought. I was just a kid yet. I know I was a kid yet. I don't know what to say and mother advise me not to say anything about they came in to propose because they're high class people.

Next time, Josie . . . week's time, Josie told me, "Florence, you know they propose to you." I don't know anything. I don't know English. She say "propose." "No, I don't know what you're talking about," I said. "They want you to marry Robert Davidson," she said. And she laugh and laugh. I thought she was just teasing me. I told my mother what my cousin say. "They want you to marry that man." "Why did you say yes?" "No, your dad sent them to your uncle. Your dad say he's got nothing to do with you. It has to go through your uncle. So you don't have to say anything. You have more respect for your uncle than us," she said. "That's the only brother I got." "You're going to make me marry," I said. "Yes, you're going to marry him." "I'm not going to marry him." "Why do you say that, Florence; don't say that. *L y'aʔʌEyt iwan geng.*" "He's a real prince," that's what she said. "*L y'aʔʌEyt iwan geng.*" "Don't say anything about it." It bother me so much. I couldn't sleep for long time when I go to bed.

Every day I bother mother. "I'm not going to marry that old man. I'm not going to marry him. If you make me marry him, I'm going to run away summertime. You're not going to see me again," I said. My mother didn't say anything. Every day I used to bother her. My dad didn't say a word to me about it. Finally, my mother say, "Don't say anything, dear. Your uncle thought it's best for you to marry him. He's a prince. He's going to respect himself when you marry him and he's going to respect you all your life, and if you don't want to marry him you're going to feel bad all your life. He belongs to clever people. He's real clever. You're not going to [be] hard up for anything. We need help, young man's help, too. You must remember that. We belong to chiefs, too. You're not supposed to say, talk any old way. You have to [have] respect for yourself more than what you worry about," she said. I don't want to say any more because my mother say I'll be sorry rest of my life if I don't marry him. I'm going to just say nothing. I make my mind up not to as much as I dislike it but I don't want to say a word about it anymore. One time he took me to New Masset to do some shopping. He told me anything I want I could buy it.

MB: Who, Robert?

FD: Yes, my husband going-to-be. It was snowing, lots of snow on the ground. We take the beach to town. I walk real fast so I don't go close to him.

MB: How old were you when they came in to propose?

FD: I was fifteen in September and maybe they came in around Christmas time. We got married in February, twenty-third. They propose for next year, but soon as they agree with it they want to have the big doing right away. It makes me . . . I wish I was dead. You know how you could be. He was married before. I thought he was real old man.

MB: How old was he?

FD: He was married . . . he got married around 1907.

MB: And he married Annie Adams, right?

FD: Yes.

MB: Didn't you say you used to take care of their baby?

FD: No, I didn't. I used to just look at him. He wasn't. . . . That's a boy.
I guess they got about two. His wife wasn't healthy. She got TB.
She died young. I don't know how long they'd been married. We got
married same time Emma Matthews.

MB: Same day?

FD: No. She was going to get married before me, but she got sore throat.

MB: Was this when she married Daniel Stanley?

FD: Yes.

MB: Was her marriage also arranged?

FD: Yes. I guess so. I didn't know. They used to do that.

MB: Even after your time?

FD: No. Just me was the last one.

MB: You said that they had to go and talk to your uncle?

FD: Yes. The next night they all went to my uncle's house. They ask someone to go there first and my uncle say that they could come in and talk
to him. So, next night they went there and my uncle was saying . . .
he agree with it right away. In olden days it's disgrace for get a baby
without husband. That's what they used to be scared of and they let
the girls marry early. It's disgrace for their uncle or their parents. That's
why the whole family . . . that's why they don't want the girls stay
single.

MB: In the old days did they ever arrange marriages when the girls were
really young?

FD: Yes.

MB: Before their *təgwəná*?

FD: No. When they *təgwəná* they supposed to marry. I'm going to let you
. . . if I got little boy and you got girl: "Margaret, I'm raising my boy for
your girl." They just kind of joking.

MB: When they're little kids?

FD: Yes. They really got married later. They the ones supposed to marry
each others. If they haven't got any for the chief's family. If I was chief
and you my wife and we got grownup girl and someone else from
different village, chiefs, they come to ask you if they can get married to
your daughter. They agree with each other and they get married right
there at the girl's home town. The girl not supposed to go to the man's.
They always come for the girl.

MB: When your grandmother was married to Albert Edward Edenshaw, did
they have a doing in Klinkwan or not?

FD: No, they took them home to get married to her. He didn't marry her at
Klinkwan. He took the girls to his home town for his doing in Naden.
They didn't go to bed together unless they get married. They have big
ceremony like nowadays. They would propose to the girl and the day
they set the day and they have the girl. I'm supposed to be princess
now, head of the house. They put the mattress there and the girl with
new clothes on sitting there at the head of the house.

MB: In the old days?

FD: Yes. All the people who came in for the feast they sitting around on the *day cɨndu*. They all sitting around there and they take the boy in.

MB: The girl's in the back of the house in the chief's place in the rear part of the house?

FD: Yes. The longhouse this way and here's the back of the house and there's partition there, just like bedroom. Front of that the chief and his wife used to sit there. When their daughter gets married and when they come in from the other chief's house with the boy just like how they come in to propose. The boy come in, the young boy would come in with his uncle or with his dad. They all relative go in after them. They have the room for them where they're going to sit. They bring the boy in. They make him sit down by the girl.

MB: Is the girl sitting by her parents?

FD: Yes. I guess her parents are there with her. They bring the boy in and they make them sit together and they serve meal then.

BIBLIOGRAPHY

Ames, Michael
  1986   *Museums, The Public and Anthropology: A Study in the Anthropology of Anthropology.* Vancouver: University of British Columbia Press.
Amoss, Pamela
  1981   "Coast Salish Elders." In *Other Ways of Growing Old: Anthropological Perspectives,* edited by Pamela Amoss and Stevan Harrell, pp. 227–477. Stanford: Stanford University Press.
Appleton, F. M.
  1970   "Life and Art of Charlie Edenshaw." *Canadian Geographical Journal* 81:20–25.
Barbeau, Marius
  1944   "How Raven Stole the Sun: Charles Edenshaw's Argillite Carvings." *Transactions of the Royal Society of Canada* (ser. 3) 38:59–69.
  1957   *Haida Carvers in Argillite.* National Museum of Man, Bulletin 139. Ottawa.
Bartlett, John
  1925   "A Narrative of Events in the Life of John Bartlett." In *The Sea, the Ship, the Sailor.* Salem, Mass.: Marine Research Society.
Bataille, Gretchen, and Kathleen M. Sands
  1984   *American Indian Women: Telling Their Lives.* Lincoln: University of Nebraska Press.
Blackman, Margaret
  1973   "Totems to Tombstones: Culture Change as Viewed through the Haida Mortuary Complex, 1877–1971." *Ethnology* 12:47–56.
  1977   "Ethnohistoric Changes in the Haida Potlatch Complex." *Arctic Anthropology* 14:39–53.
  1989   *Sadie Brower Neakok, An Iñupiaq Woman.* Seattle: University of Washington Press; Vancouver, B.C.: Douglas and McIntyre.

Boas, Franz
   1943   "Recent Anthropology." *Science* 98:311–14, 334–37.
The British Colonist
   1862   "The Smallpox," May 13, p. 3.
           "From Bentinek Arm, Fort Rupert and Nanaimo," June 21, p. 3.
Boelscher, Marianne
   1988   *The Curtain Within: Haida Social and Mythical Discourse.* Vancouver:
           University of British Columbia Press.
Brumble, H. David
   1981   *An Annotated Bibliography of American Indian and Eskimo
           Autobiographies.* Lincoln: University of Nebraska Press.
   1988   *American Indian Autobiography.* Berkeley: University of California
           Press.
Bruner, Edward M.
   1986   "Ethnography as Narrative." In *The Anthropology of Experience.*
           Edited by Victor Turner and Edward Bruner. Urbana: University
           of Illinois Press.
Campbell, Maria
   1973   *Halfbreed.* Toronto: McClelland and Stewart, Ltd.
Clifford, James
   1988   "On Ethnographic Authority." In *The Predicament of Culture:
           Twentieth-Century Ethnography, Literature, and Art.* Cambridge:
           Harvard University Press.
Clifford, James, and George Marcus, editors
   1986   *Writing Culture: The Poetics and Politics of Ethnography.* Cambridge:
           Harvard University Press.
Clifton, James
   1989   *Being and Becoming Indian: Biographical Studies of North American
           Frontiers.* Chicago: Dorsey.
Collison, William H.
   1915   *In the Wake of the War Canoe.* London: Seeley, Service and Co., Ltd.
Curtis, Edward S.
   1916   *The Haida. The North American Indian,* vol. 11, pp. 115–75, 186–93.
           Norwood, Illinois.
Dawson, George
   1880   *Report on the Queen Charlotte Islands.* Geographical Survey of
           Canada, Report of Progress for 1878–79.
Deans, James
   1891   "Carved Columns or Totem Poles of the Haidas." *American
           Antiquarian and Oriental Journal* 13:282–87.
Deasy, Thomas
   1913   "How the Haida Indians Celebrate Weddings." *Masset Leader*
           (February 6, 1913), 1(21):4.
   1915   Report of Thomas Deasy, Indian Agent for Queen Charlotte
           Agency, British Columbia. *Annual Report of the Department of Indian
           Affairs,* Canada.

1917   Report of Thomas Deasy, Indian Agent for Queen Charlotte
        Agency, British Columbia. *Annual Report of the Department of Indian
        Affairs*, Canada.

Dixon, George
    1789   *A Voyage Round the World . . .* London.

Dougherty, Molly
    1978   *Becoming a Woman in Rural Black Culture.* New York: Holt, Rinehart
        and Winston.

Du Vernet, ?
    1906   Letter, December 20, 1906. Church Missionary Society Archives,
        London.

Duff, Wilson
    n.d.   Unpublished field notes on the Haida.
    1964   *The Indian History of British Columbia.* Vol. 1: *The Impact of the White
        Man.* Anthropology in British Columbia, Memoir 5. Victoria, B.C.:
        Provincial Museum.

Dunn, J.
    1846   *History of the Oregon Territory.* London.

Ford, Clellan
    1941   *Smoke From Their Fires: The Life of a Kwakiutl Chief.* New Haven:
        Yale University Press

Gallagher, Dorothy
    1976   *Hannah's Daughters: Six Generations of an American Family, 1876–
        1976.* New York: Thomas Crowell Company.

Green, Jonathan
    1915   *Journal of a Tour on the Northwest Coast of America in the year 1829.*
        New York: Charles Heartman.

Harrison, Charles
    1911–   History of the Queen Charlotte Islands: The Haida and Their
    13   Legends. *Queen Charlotte Islander*, vol. 1, no. 11 (November 6,
            1911)—vol. 2. no. 34 (April 28, 1913).
    1925   *Ancient Warriors of the North Pacific.* London.

Holm, Bill
    1981   "Will the Real Charles Edensaw Please Stand Up?: The Problem of
        Attribution in Northwest Coast Indian Art." In *The World Is as
        Sharp as a Knife: An Anthology in Honour of Wilson Duff*, edited by
        Donald N. Abbott, pp. 175–200. Victoria, B.C.: Provincial
        Museum.

Howay, F. W., ed.
    1941   *Voyages of the* Columbia *to the Northwest Coast, 1787–1790 and 1790–
        1793.* Boston: Massachusetts Historical Society.

Ingraham, J.
    1971   *Joseph Ingraham's Journal of the Brigantine* Hope *on a Voyage to the
        Northwest Coast of North America, 1790–92.* Edited, with notes and
        an Introduction by Mark D. Kaplanoff. Barre, Mass.: Imprint
        Society.

Jackson, Marni
   1983   "A Woman Whose Work was Never Done." *Maclean's*. 14
           February 1983:56.
Jackson, Sheldon
   1880   *Alaska and Missions on the North Pacific Coast*. New York: Dodd,
           Mead and Company.
Jamieson, Kathleen
   1978   *Indian Women and the Law in Canada: Citizens Minus*. Canada:
           Advisory Council on the Status of Women, Indian Rights for
           Indian Women.
Jelinek, Estelle
   1980   "Women's Autobiography and the Male Tradition." In *Women
           Autobiography: Essays in Criticism,* edited by Estelle Jelinek, pp. 1–
           20. Bloomington: Indiana University Press.
Jenness, Diamond
   1955   *The Faith of a Coast Salish Indian*. Anthropology in British
           Columbia, Memoir 3, pp. 1–92. Victoria, B.C.: Provincial
           Museum.
Jones, Rex, and Shirley Jones
   1976   *The Himalayan Woman*. Palo Alto: Mayfield Publishing Company.
Keen, J. H.
   1894   Letter, May 28, 1894. Church Missionary Society Archives,
           London.
   1914   "Haida Burial." *North British Columbia News*, vol. 4, no. 17:6.
Keesing, Roger M.
   1983   *'Elota's Story: The Life and Times of a Solomon Islands Big Man*.
           Chicago: Holt, Rinehart and Winston.
Kelley, Jane
   1978   *Yanqui Women: Contemporary Life Histories*. Lincoln: University of
           Nebraska Press.
Kluckhohn, Clyde
   1945   "The Personal Document in Anthropological Science." In *The Use
           of Personal Documents in History, Anthropology, and Sociology,* ed. by
           Louis Gottschalk et al., pp. 79–175. Social Science Research
           Council, Bulletin 53.
Krause A.
   1885   *The Tlingit Indians*. Translated by Erna Gunther. Seattle: University
           of Washington Press.
Kroeber, A. L.
   1908   "War Experiences of Individuals." In *Ethnology of the Gros Ventre*.
           Anthropological Papers of the American Museum of Natural
           History 1(4):196–222.
Krupat, Arnold
   1985   *For Those Who Come After: A Study of American Indian Autobiography*.
           Berkeley: University of California Press.

La Pérouse, J. F. G. de
  1798 *The Voyage of La Pérouse Round the World in the Years 1785, 1786,
        1787, and 1788, with the Nautical Tables.* Arranged by M. L. A. Milet
        Mureau at Paris. Translated from the French in two vols. London:
        John Stockdale.
Langness, L. I.
  1965 *The Life History in Anthropological Science.* New York: Holt, Rinehart
        and Winston.
Langness, L. I., and Gelya Frank
  1981 *Lives: An Anthropological Approach to Biography.* Novato, Calif.:
        Chandler and Sharp.
Lawrence, Erma
  1977 *Haida Dictionary.* Fairbanks: Alaska Native Language Center.
Levine, Robert
  1973 "Notes on a Haida Text." *The Charlottes: A Journal of the Queen
        Charlotte Islands,* vol. 2, pp. 28–32.
Liberty, Margot
  1978 *American Indian Intellectuals.* 1976 Proceedings of the American
        Ethnological Society.
Lurie, Nancy
  1961 *Mountain Wolf Woman, Sister of Crashing Thunder. Autobiography of a
        Winnebago Indian.* Ann Arbor: University of Michigan Press.
Marchand, Etienne
  1801 *A Voyage Round the World Performed during the Years 1790, 1791, and
        1792.* 2 vols. London: T. N. Longman.
Marcus, George, and Michael Fischer
  1986 *Anthropology as Cultural Critique: An Experimental Moment in the
        Human Sciences.* Chicago: University of Chicago Press.
Martin, M. K., and B. Voorhies
  1975 *Female of the Species.* New York: Columbia University Press.
Mead, Margaret
  1972 *Blackberry Winter.* New York: William Morrow.
Mitchell, Marjorie
  1976 "Women, Poverty, and Housing: Some Consequences of
        Hinterland Status for a Coast Salish Indian Reserve in
        Metropolitan Canada." Ph.D. dissertation, Department of
        Anthropology, University of British Columbia.
Morley, Alan Palmer
  1967 *Roar of the Breakers: A Biography of Peter Kelly.* Toronto: Ryerson
        Press.
Murdock, George Peter
  1934a "Kinship and Social Behavior Among the Haida." *American
        Anthropologist* 36:355–85.
  1934b "The Haidas of British Columbia." In *Our Primitive Contemporaries,*
        edited by George Peter Murdock. New York: McGraw-Hill.

1936   *Rank and Potlatch Among the Haida.* Yale University Publications in Anthropology, no. 13.
Neithammer, Carolyn
1977   *Daughters of the Earth: The Lives and Legends of American Indian Women.* New York: Collier.
North British Columbia News
1911   "Holiday Doings at Masset." Vol. 6, p. 71 (April, 1911).
Oates, Stephen B.
1986   *Biography as High Adventure: Life Writers Speak on Their Art.* Amherst: University of Massachusetts Press.
Panday, Trikoli Nath
1978   "Flora Zuni, Zuni, 1897–." In *American Indian Intellectuals,* edited by Margot Liberty, pp. 217–25. 1976 Proceedings of the American Ethnological Society.
Parsons, Elsie Clews, ed.
1922   *American Indian Life.* New York: B. W. Huebsch, Inc.
Phillips, Herbert
1973   Comment on David Mandelbaum's *The Study of Life History: Gandhi. Current Anthropology* 14:200–201.
Poewe, Karla
1981   *Matrilineal Ideology: Male-Female Dynamics in Luapula, Zambia.* New York: Academic Press.
Pomerleau, Cynthia
1980   "The Emergence of Women's Autobiography in England." In *Women's Autobiography: Essays in Criticism,* edited by Estelle Jelinek, pp. 1–20. Bloomington: Indiana University Press.
Poole, Francis
1872   *Queen Charlotte Islands: A Narrative of Discovery and Adventure in the North Pacific.* London: Hurst and Blacklett.
Quinn, Nancy
1977   "Anthropological Studies on Women's Status." *Annual Review of Anthropology* 6:181–225.
Radin, Paul
1913   "Personal Reminiscences of a Winnebago Indian." *Journal of American Folklore* 26:293–318.
Robinson, Michael P.,
1978   *Sea Otter Chiefs.* Vancouver. Friendly Cove Press.
Rohner, Ronald
1966   "Franz Boas: Ethnographer on the Northwest Coast." In *Pioneers of American Anthropology: The Uses of Biography,* edited by June Helm, pp. 149–212. Seattle and London: University of Washington Press.
Rosaldo, Michelle
1974   "Women, Culture, and Society: A Theoretical Overview." In *Women, Culture and Society,* edited by M. Rosaldo and L. Lamphere, pp. 17–42. Stanford: Stanford University Press.

Rosman, Abraham, and Paula Rubel
 1971 *Feasting with Mine Enemy: Rank and Exchange Among Northwest Coast Societies.* New York: Columbia University Press.
Shadbolt, Doris
 1986 *Bill Reid.* Seattle and London: University of Washington Press; Vancouver, B.C.: Douglas and McIntyre.
Shostak, Marjorie
 1981 *Nisa: The Life and Words of a !Kung Woman.* Cambridge: Harvard University Press.
Spradley, James
 1969 *Guests Never Leave Hungry: The Autobiography of James Sewid, a Kwakiutl Indian.* New Haven: Yale University Press.
Stearns, Mary Lee
 1975 "Life Cycle Rituals of the Modern Haida." In *Contributions to Canadian Ethnology,* no. 31, edited by David Carlisle, pp. 129–69. Ottawa: National Museums of Canada.
 1981 *Haida Culture in Custody: The Masset Band.* Seattle and London: University of Washington Press.
Steltzer, Ulli
 1976 *Indian Artists at Work.* Seattle: University of Washington Press; Vancouver, B.C.: Douglas and McIntyre.
Stewart, Hilary
 1979 *Robert Davidson: Haida Printmaker.* Seattle and London: University of Washington Press; Vancouver, B.C.: Douglas and McIntyre.
Strathern, Marilyn
 1972 *Women in Between: Female Roles in a Male World.* New York: Seminar Press.
Swan, James
 1883 Journal of a Trip to Queen Charlotte Islands, B.C. Microfilm. Seattle: University of Washington Library.
Swanton, John R.
 1909 *Contributions to the Ethnology of the Haida.* American Museum of Natural History, Memoir 8.
Turner, Nancy
 1974 "Plant Taxonomic Systems and Ethnobotany of Three Contemporary Indian Groups of the Pacific Northwest (Haida, Bella Coola, and Lillooet)." *Syesis,* vol. 7, supplement 1.
Underhill, Ruth
 1936 *The Autobiography of a Papago Woman.* Memories of the American Anthropological Association, no. 46.
 1978 *Papago Woman.* Revised edition. New York: Holt, Rinehart and Winston.
Vanderburgh, R. M.
 1977 *I Am Nokomis Too: The Biography of Vera Patronella Johnson.* Don Mills, Ontario: General Publishing Company, Ltd.

Wagner, Henry R., and W. A. Newcombe, eds.

1938   "The Journal of Jacinto Caamaño." Translated by Capt. Harold Grenfell, R.N. *British Columbia Historical Quarterly* 2:189–222, 265–301.

Weiner, Annette

1976   *Women of Value, Men of Renown: New Perspectives in Trobriand Exchange.* Austin: University of Texas Press.

Wike, Joyce

1951   "The Effect of the Maritime Fur Trade on the Northwest Coast Indian Societies." Ph.D. dissertation, Department of Anthropology, Columbia University.

Willis, Jane

1973   *Gensen: An Indian Girlhood.* Toronto: New Press.

Zimmerman, William

1979   *How to Tape Instant Oral Biographies.* New York: Guarionex Press.

Index

The page numbers for illustrations are given in boldface type.

Library of Congress Cataloging-in-Publication Data

Blackman, Margaret B.
  During my time : Florence Edenshaw Davidson,
a Haida woman / Margaret B. Blackman
    p. cm.
  Includes bibliographical references and index.
  ISBN-13: 978-0-295-97179-7; ISBN-10: 0-295-97179-7
(pbk.: alk paper)
1. Davidson, Florence Edenshaw, 1896–   2. Haida
Indians—Biography.   3. Haida Indians—Women.
I. Title.
E99.H2D383   1992   91-45973
973′.0497202—dc20   CIP

Library and Archives Canada Cataloguing in Publication

Blackman, Margaret B. (Margaret Berlin), 1944–
  During my time
Includes bibliographical reference and index.
ISBN-13: 978-1-55054-024-6; ISBN-10: 1-55054-024-6
1. Davidson, Florence Edenshaw, 1896–
2. Haida Indians—Biography.   3. Haida
Indians—Women—Biography.   4. Indians of
North America—British Columbia—Queen
Charlotte Islands—Women—Biography.   I. Title.
E99.H2D383   1992   971′1200497′2   C92-091082-3

CPSIA information can be obtained
at www.ICGtesting.com
Printed in the USA
FSHW020059201118
53845FS